JAPAN'S SECURITY STRATEGY IN THE POST-9/11 WORLD

THE WASHINGTON PAPERS

. . . intended to meet the need for an authoritative, yet prompt, public appraisal of the major developments in world affairs.

Series Editor: Walter Laqueur

Managing Editor: Donna R. Spitler

MANUSCRIPT SUBMISSION

The Washington Papers and Praeger Publishers welcome inquiries concerning manuscript submissions. Please include with your inquiry a curriculum vitae, synopsis, table of contents, and estimated manuscript length. Manuscript length must fall between 30,000 and 45,000 words. All submissions will be peer reviewed. Submissions to *The Washington Papers* should be sent to *The Washington Papers*, Center for Strategic and International Studies, 1800 K Street NW, Washington, DC 20006. Book proposals should be sent to Praeger Publishers, 88 Post Road West, P.O. Box 5007, Westport, CT 06881-5007.

THE WASHINGTON PAPERS/183

JAPAN'S SECURITY STRATEGY IN THE POST-9/11 WORLD

Embracing a New Realpolitik

Daniel M. Kliman

Foreword by Michael H. Armacost

Published with the Center for Strategic and International Studies, Washington, D.C.

 PRAEGER

Westport, Connecticut
London

Library of Congress Cataloging-in-Publication Data

Kliman, Daniel M.

Japan's security strategy in the post–9/11 world : embracing a new realpolitik / Daniel M. Kliman ; foreword by Michael H. Armacost.

p. cm. — (Washington papers ; 183)

"Published with the Center for Strategic and International Studies, Washington, D.C."

Includes bibliographical references and index.

ISBN 0–275–99059–1 (cloth : alk. paper) — ISBN 0–275–99060–5 (pbk. : alk. paper)

1. Japan—Military policy. 2. Japan—Defenses. 3. World politics—21st century. 4. East Asia—Strategic aspects. I. Title. II. Series.

UA845.K45 2006

355'.033552—dc22   2005036334

The Washington Papers are written under the auspices of the Center for Strategic and International Studies (CSIS) and published with CSIS by Praeger Publishers. CSIS, as a public policy research institution, does not take specific policy positions. Accordingly, all views, positions, and conclusions expressed in the volumes of this series should be understood to be solely those of the authors.

British Library Cataloguing in Publication Data is available.

Library of Congress Catalog Card Number: 2005036334
ISBN: 0–275–99059–1 (cloth)
       0–275–99060–5 (paper)

First published in 2006

Praeger Publishers, 88 Post Road West, Westport, CT 06881
An imprint of Greenwood Publishing Group, Inc.
www.praeger.com
Printed in the United States of America

The paper used in this book complies with the Permanent Paper Standard issued by the National Information Standards Organization (Z39.48-1984).

10 9 8 7 6 5 4 3 2 1

Contents

Foreword

Michael H. Armacost

I first met Daniel Kliman when he was working on the precursor
to this book at Stanford University under the supervision of my
colleague, Professor Daniel Okimoto. Kliman's initial manuscript
concerned Japanese defense policy and offered an analysis that
was remarkably comprehensive, precise, and nuanced. Following
a summer at the U.S. Department of Defense and a year in Japan,
during which Kliman extended his research to include extensive
interviews with many Japanese defense officials and political figures, he has completed this important and timely book.

This volume addresses a critically important subject that is
too often neglected. The U.S. government is understandably preoccupied with radical Islamist threats to American security—
mainly in the Middle East and Persian Gulf. Yet Asia's importance
to the United States continues to grow. It is, after all, the region in
which our interests intersect most directly with those of the other
Major Powers. It possesses the world's most dynamic economies.
It is home to the world's most impressive emerging powers—
China and India. And it is the locus of two of the most dangerous
legacies of the Cold War—a divided Korea and the unresolved
Taiwan dispute. It presents the most urgent threat of nuclear

Michael H. Armacost is the Shorenstein Distinguished Fellow at the
Walter H. Shorenstein Asia-Pacific Research Center, Stanford University. He
is the former president of the Brookings Institution and served as U.S.
ambassador to Japan from 1989 to 1993.

proliferation—North Korea. It is an area that deserves—indeed demands—more of America's attention.

Although American scholars and commentators devote much analysis to the "rise" of China, they have been less attentive to a development of comparable significance—Japan's progressive movement toward the status of a more "normal" nation. Daniel Kliman's book helps reduce that imbalance by reminding us that recent adjustments in Japan's defense policy have enabled Tokyo to carve out a new and more ambitious international security niche as a provider of offshore, noncombat logistics and other services in support of international peacekeeping ventures.

These adjustments are transforming the U.S.-Japan alliance, lending it greater balance and wider geographic scope. They are enhancing the technological sophistication of Japanese forces without altering the essentially defensive character of its capabilities. They are stretching the scope of Japan's participation in peacekeeping missions and augmenting the potential role of the Self-Defense Forces in responding to regional contingencies. They are modifying old taboos—e.g., past inhibitions against cooperating with the United States on ballistic missile defenses. They are exposing controversial subjects—such as the revision of Article 9 in the Constitution or the exercise of the right to collective self-defense—to open debate. They are extending the "reach" of Japanese naval and air forces. And they are easing other limitations on defense policy that have long been embedded in Japan's postwar political culture.

Yet, these changes, as Kliman observes, are being accomplished incrementally. They have been pursued within the framework of a revivified alliance with the United States, with attentiveness to the sensitivities of its neighbors and without dramatic changes in the size or composition in Japan's defense budget, its long-standing ban on overseas combat activities, or its widely accepted "non-nuclear principles."

Kliman offers not only a finely balanced description of the evolution in Japan's defense policy, but a convincing analysis of the forces that are driving change—above all, a tough neighborhood, U.S. influence, the role of Japanese executive leadership, and the impact of generational change in Japan's society and politics. He asks how significant the policy changes are, what is driving them, and where they may impel Japan in the years ahead.

Equally important, Kliman measures these changes against the dominant expectations generated by existing international relations theories—realism, neorealism, hegemonic stability, comprehensive security, complex interdependence, and alliance theory. And he offers his own variation, which he terms "transitional realism," to explain Japan's move from a norms-based to interests-based security policy.

I strongly commend this volume. It is a valuable contribution to the understanding of an important subject at a timely moment, and I hope that it will be widely read by policy specialists and international relations theorists alike.

Acknowledgments

This book reflects the contributions of many individuals. I am particularly grateful to Daniel Okimoto of Stanford University. Without his guidance and support, this book would not have been possible. I am also indebted to Michael Armacost for sharing his perspective as a policymaker and for writing the foreword.

At Stanford, individuals who read parts of the initial manuscript are Lynn Eden, Yasuko Nishimura, Scott Sagan, Todd Sechser, and Steven Stedman. While in Kyoto, I received feedback from Hiroshi Nakanishi of Kyoto University and Koji Murata of Doshisha University.

The Japanese and U.S. officials, Diet members, SDF officers, academics, and reporters who donated their time through interviews to this project merit a special appreciation. I thank Kazuo Aichi, Masao Akamatsu, Otohiko Endo, Shigeru Ishiba, Yukio Hatoyama, Seiji Maehara, Masaharu Nakagawa, Yoshinori Ohno, and Shunji Yanai. Most interviewees have chosen to remain anonymous. I am equally grateful for their contribution.

These interviews would not have occurred without the support of multiple individuals. In addition to sharing her knowledge of Japanese politics, Kuniko Nakamura directed me to potential interviewees, as did James Delaney, Hiroshi Nakanishi, David Satterwhite, and many of the interviewees themselves.

I am indebted to several Japanese news organizations for providing unpublished poll material. Specifically, Junichi Yamamoto at *Yomiuri Shimbun*, Akio Takahata and Noriaki

Kondoh at *Mainichi Shimbun,* and Mikio Haruna and Hirofumi Iseri at Kyodo News. To ensure correct translation, I relied upon Yuichi Nakai and Yasuko Nishimura.

Two organizations offered funding for this project: The Japan-U.S. Educational Commission (Fulbright Commission) provided a Fulbright grant for a year of study and research at Kyoto University, and Stanford University enabled a weeklong trip to Tokyo in March 2004.

At the CSIS Press, Donna Spitler has worked to prepare this book for publication. I am grateful for her editorial advice.

Several personal words of thanks are in order. The Beniya family has offered warm hospitality during each of my visits to Tokyo. Finally, my parents, Audrey and Wayne Kliman, have supported this book in innumerable ways. This work is dedicated to them.

Abbreviations

ASDF	Air Self-Defense Force
ASEAN	Association of Southeast Asian Nations
BBC	British Broadcasting Corporation
BMD	Ballistic Missile Defense
C4I	Command, Control, Communications, Computers and Intelligence
COMJAN	Commission on Missing Japanese Probably Related to North Korea
CSIS	Center for Strategic and International Studies
DOD	Department of Defense
DPJ	Democratic Party of Japan
DPRK	Democratic People's Republic of Korea
EU	European Union
GDP	Gross Domestic Product
GOJ	Government of Japan
GSDF	Ground Self-Defense Force
IAEA	International Atomic Energy Agency
IPCC	International Peace Cooperation Corps
JDA	Japan Defense Agency
LDP	Liberal Democratic Party
MOFA	Ministry of Foreign Affairs
MSDF	Maritime Self-Defense Force
MTDP	Mid-Term Defense Plan
NATO	North Atlantic Treaty Organization
NDPG	National Defense Program Guidelines

NDPO   National Defense Program Outline
NGO   Nongovernmental Organization
NPT   Nuclear Non-Proliferation Treaty
ODA   Official Development Assistance
PAC-3   Patriot Advanced Capability Missile
PRC   People's Republic of China
PSI   Proliferation Security Initiative
R&D   Research and Development
ROK   Republic of Korea
SCC   Security Consultative Committee
SDF   Self-Defense Force
SDPJ   Socialist Democratic Party of Japan
UN   United Nations
UNHCR   United Nations High Commissioner for Refugees
WMD   Weapons of Mass Destruction

1

Japan's Strategic Evolution

The period following September 11, 2001, marks a turning point in Japan's defense strategy. A sea change has occurred in several elements of Japan's security policy: antiterrorism support, missile defense cooperation, and overseas deployment of the Self-Defense Force (SDF). Constitutional revision, once the "third rail" of Japanese politics, is now an agenda item for all the major political parties. Most scholars and policymakers would agree that these changes are indeed unprecedented. However, the first 50 years of Japan's postwar defense policy were not static: the geographic scope, roles, and capabilities of the SDF increased as constitutional restrictions became less binding.

Comparing recent and past changes in Japan's defense policy leads to three related questions. First, how significant are recent changes in Tokyo's defense posture? Do these developments constitute a major shift in the Japanese government's approach toward national security? Or will they rather conform to the traditional pattern of change in Japan's security policy—that is, incremental expansion of the SDF that lacks strategic consequences? Second, what factors are responsible for Japan's strategic evolution? Are these factors endogenous to Japan or externally imposed? Do they explain Tokyo's behavior across diverse foreign policy crises? Third, can these factors be generalized to describe strategic change in other national settings?

Although significant, new Japanese defense policies fall short of a strategic shift. Japan has yet to complete the transition from a norms-based to an interest-based defense policy. Since September 11, elites and the public have increasingly viewed national security through the framework of realpolitik. However, both groups are still unprepared to completely dismantle the normative structures that constrain Japan's defense posture. Instead, political circles and the general populace favor, or at least accept, the continued weakening of institutionalized norms.

Even so, Tokyo has experienced a distinct turning point in its security strategy, as the erosion of normative restraints has markedly accelerated. Indeed, the years since September 11 have witnessed greater change in Japan's defense policy than the previous 40. In the aftermath of September 11, Tokyo dispatched the Maritime Self-Defense Force (MSDF) to participate in Operation Enduring Freedom. This deployment established a new historical precedent: Japanese troops provided logistics support to U.S. forces conducting out-of-area operations.

On December 19, 2003, the Koizumi administration proclaimed its decision to introduce ballistic missile defense (BMD). The Japanese government's announcement heralded a larger adjustment of SDF roles and capabilities to counter extant threats. Moreover, acquiring BMD ensured the further diminution of two legal constraints on Tokyo's defense policy—arms export restrictions and the prohibition on collective defense. Finally, in the run-up to the Iraq War, Japan constituted one of a handful of major states to endorse U.S. military action. After Saddam Hussein's regime collapsed, Tokyo dispatched SDF personnel to participate in reconstruction. The Iraq deployment signified a major departure from the SDF's previous overseas missions. Japanese forces entered Iraq without the sponsorship of the United Nations and operated in a de facto combat zone. Collectively, September 11, missile defense, and Iraq attest to Japan's growing realism. In all three cases, calculations of national interest motivated Tokyo's security behavior.

Japan's strategic evolution is the product of four factors: foreign threats, U.S. policy, executive leadership, and generational change. The first variable—foreign threats—has catalyzed Tokyo's ever greater realpolitik orientation. In the case of BMD, unfavorable changes in the security environment—North Korea's nuclear weapons program and its deployment of medium-range missiles—compelled Japan to acquire a new defense capability. Foreign threats have also indirectly contributed to Tokyo's strategic transition by increasing the value of the U.S.-Japan alliance. In the wake of September 11, Japan dispatched the MSDF to the Indian Ocean to maintain the alliance as a hedge against an uncertain threat environment. With the advent of the Iraq War, strengthening the bilateral security relationship served a more immediate purpose: enhancing U.S. extended deterrence vis-à-vis a nuclear North Korea. Consequently, Tokyo offered political support for the U.S. invasion and later deployed troops to participate in postconflict reconstruction.

The second factor—U.S. policy—has exerted a profound effect over specific Japanese defense initiatives. Indeed, by altering Japan's strategic calculus, U.S. influence engendered policy outcomes that might not have otherwise occurred. Except for deepening the bilateral alliance, Japan derived few immediate security benefits from the MSDF's involvement in Operation Enduring Freedom and its support of the Iraq War and reconstruction. In fact, dispatching the MSDF after September 11 and, in particular, deploying troops to Iraq entailed potential costs like terrorist retaliation. To a significant degree then, Tokyo's response to September 11 and the Iraq War reflected the impact of U.S. policy. However, Washington's influence cannot be described as mere *gaiatsu*.[1] Rather than employ official requests and direct pressure, the United States set two broad expectations for Japan's global conduct—that Tokyo assume both its international and alliance responsibilities. This approach proved remarkably effective. By the outbreak of the Iraq War, Japanese policymakers had fully internalized both expectations.

The third factor in Tokyo's strategic transition is executive leadership—that of Prime Minister Junichiro Koizumi. Unlike his predecessors, Koizumi enjoyed sustained public support. By leveraging his popularity, the prime minister decisively intervened in security-related policy debates. Following September 11, Koizumi circumvented the Japanese government's standard policymaking procedures when he publicly outlined Tokyo's role in the war on terror. In doing so, the prime minister risked his domestic and international credibility without any assurance of requisite Diet support. To enable timely MSDF dispatch to the Indian Ocean, Koizumi also shepherded legislation through the Diet in record time. Prime ministerial leadership played an even more critical role in the case of Iraq. At the war's outbreak, Koizumi flouted popular opinion to unequivocally endorse the U.S. invasion. And after the end of formal hostilities, the prime minister again defied his electorate by deploying the SDF to Iraq. Koizumi proved a "Teflon" prime minister. His public opinion ratings rapidly recovered in the wake of implementing unpopular defense initiatives.

The fourth factor behind Japan's evolving defense posture is generational change. Politicians born after 1950 increasingly occupy positions of power. In general, young Diet members across the mainstream parties are unburdened by the legacy of World War II and share a common vision of Japan as a nation that possesses balanced capabilities and actively participates in maintaining global security. With respect to specific security initiatives, however, partisanship has thwarted generational cohesion. MSDF participation in Operation Enduring Freedom and Japan's stance on Iraq pitted young lawmakers against one another. Demographic change has widened the scope of acceptable defense policies, but other variables have determined Japan's actual security behavior.

Together, foreign threats, U.S. policy, executive leadership, and generational change underlie Japan's transition from a norms-based to a realpolitik defense policy. Although applicable to other cases of strategic change, these factors are only relevant across a small subset of national actors—those characterized by a security dependence on the United States. Even so, Japan provides broader theoretical insights into strategic evolution. A state's approach to national security reflects its socialization into the international system. Strategic change occurs through resocialization into a transformed world order. Indeed, Japan's historical experience provides the basis for a new theory of strategic evolution—*transitional realism.*

Policy, Pragmatism, and Theory

The evolution of Japan's defense strategy should hold considerable interest for both U.S. policymakers and scholars of international relations. A change in Japan's security strategy would have major ramifications for the United States. Foreign policy elites within the Democratic and Republican parties recognize that, through the U.S.-Japan security alliance, "Japan remains the keystone of the U.S. involvement in Asia."[2] A shift in Japan's defense strategy would alter the character of the alliance and consequently affect U.S. influence within the region. Even if recent Japanese defense policies fall short of strategic change, these policies have real significance. For example, Japan's provision of fuel oil to U.S. ships during Operation Enduring Freedom expanded the sphere of direct security cooperation beyond the alliance's traditional geographic focus—the Far East. In sum, changes in Japan's defense strategy (or individual policies) are inextricably linked to the future presence of the United States in East Asia.

A simple assessment of national capabilities demonstrates that a shift in Japan's defense strategy might profoundly alter the Asian security landscape. Despite more than a decade of economic malaise, Japan remains the world's second largest economy.[3] Tokyo's military capabilities, though not commensurate with its economic resources, are still relatively formidable. In particular, the MSDF constitutes the most powerful navy in the world behind the U.S. Navy. Although quantitatively inferior to most East Asian militaries, the Ground and Air Self-Defense Forces (GSDF and ASDF, respectively) possess a qualitative advantage over their potential adversaries in the region. Finally, Japan's sophisticated technological-industrial base allows for a host of latent military capabilities including the production of nuclear weapons.

Finally, the evolution of Japan's defense strategy provides a rich case study for scholars of world affairs. An extensive body of political science literature has emerged to explain postwar Japan's "unique" approach toward defense. Seminal works within this literature, such as Peter Katzenstein's *Cultural Norms and National Security*, have contributed new theories to the field of international relations. Recent changes in Japan's defense policy offer an opportunity to test existing international relations theories. Moreover, an examination of new Japanese security initiatives offers insights into the larger dynamic of strategic change.

Analytical Approaches

Assessing Strategic Change

What is the significance of recent Japanese defense policies? The categorization of these security initiatives depends largely on the criteria used to define strategic change. To be pertinent to the broader field of international relations, benchmarks for a strategic shift should be articulated in abstract terms: (1) expected versus observed behavior; (2) elite conceptions of security; and (3) public attitudes toward defense. Alone, none of these criteria could definitively categorize new defense initiatives. When combined, however, the three criteria become a rigorous measure for evaluating strategic change.

Expected versus Observed Behavior. A strategic shift should produce multiple, sustained policy changes. These policy changes should establish new precedents and may even violate principles that formerly guided a state's international conduct. Counterfactual analysis premised on this logic serves as a tool to identify cases of strategic change. If strategic change occurs, one might expect to witness the implementation of certain policies. Conversely, certain policies would not be implemented in the absence of a strategic shift. This baseline projection is premised on several dimensions: a state's domestic politics, institutionalized security arrangements, and past defense policies. Determining a baseline is a subjective process. Although no absolute measure exists for calculating the relative influence of each dimension, a true strategic shift should result in policies that cannot be explained as mere variation in the range of plausible baseline projections.

Elite Conceptions of Security. A state's defense strategy is closely linked to the conceptual framework through which government elites approach national security.[4] This ideational lens influences perceptions of national interest, threat evaluations, the ranking of policy choices, and, consequently, strategy. Two measures are used to gauge elite conceptions of security—loaded terms and convergence of opinion. *Loaded terms*—words or phrases that encapsulate a conceptual framework of security, such as the "war on terror"—appear in various contexts like high-level speeches, policy documents, and personal interviews.

Changes in elite usage of loaded terms should foreshadow or indicate a strategic shift. Growing elite consensus on a once controversial defense issue may also signify new conceptions of security. Both qualitative and quantitative sources—public statements, personal interviews, and opinion surveys—may reveal the convergence of elite opinion.

Public Attitudes toward Defense. Elite conceptions of security do not automatically translate into tangible policies. Public views on national defense constrain decisionmakers. In a democracy, implementing defense policies that run contrary to popular opinion may engender a political backlash and subsequently electoral defeat. Members of a "soft" authoritarian regime, though not publicly accountable through elections, are nevertheless subject to similar constraints. Therefore, new elite conceptions of security are most significant when accompanied by parallel shifts in public opinion. Over an extended time period, opinion surveys should reveal changes in public attitudes toward national security.

On "Reluctant Realism"

What factors triggered recent changes in Japan's security posture? Do the same factors account for Japan's behavior across multiple foreign policy crises? International relations theory provides one framework for addressing these questions. I am not a proponent of any mainstream theoretical school, but instead favor an eclectic approach that incorporates elements of realism and cultural norms. This approach is similar to Michael Green's idea of "reluctant realism"—that "Japanese strategic culture is increasingly sensitive to relative power relations" and that the "powerful idealism of Japanese pacifism . . . is losing ground to a sharper-edged and somewhat narrower definition of national interest."[5] However, my evaluation of Japan's defense policy is more expressly theoretical. Although Green raises the concept of "reluctant realism," he does not develop the idea into a coherent theory. I expand "reluctant realism" into a theoretical framework capable of explaining Japan's recent security behavior.

International Relations Theory and Japan's Defense Policy

Mainstream international relations theory fails to explain recent changes in Japan's defense policy. Predicting global crises naturally lies beyond the scope of theory. But theory should predict Japan's *reaction* to these exogenous foreign policy shocks. The utility of current theories can be assessed through a counterfactual analysis of three world crises—September 11, the Iraq War, and North Korea's nuclear and missile programs. In almost all cases, expectations of Japan's behavior that are derived from theory deviate significantly from actual policy responses.

The Realist Paradigm

Long dominant among students of international relations, realism encompasses multiple philosophies of state behavior. Variants of realism include neorealism, hegemonic stability, and alliance theory. Although additional distinctions exist, assessing the three main variants should suffice to highlight the inadequacies of the realist approach. An examination of realist expectations and Japan's actual response to recent foreign policy shocks demonstrates two flaws commonly associated with structural arguments—oversimplification and indeterminancy.

Neorealism. Neorealism is premised on five assumptions. Foremost is the belief that states exist in an anarchic world. Neorealists also maintain that great powers inevitably possess some offensive military capabilities. No state can be certain of another state's true intentions. Survival represents the ultimate goal of every great power: as unitary, rational actors, states strategically pursue national preservation.[6] Under the neorealist paradigm, shifts in the relative balance of economic and military power dictate state behavior. States may form coalitions to preserve a favorable balance of power against a stronger rival (balancing). Or, in the absence of viable allies, a state may align with the dominant power (bandwagoning).[7] Alternatively, a state may directly challenge the dominant power by increasing its own military capabilities.

When broadly applied to Japan's defense policy, neorealism provides several insights.[8] This paradigm suggests that, in the short term, Tokyo will maintain its security alliance with the United States. The U.S. presence in Asia serves many of Japan's vital interests—freedom of navigation, extended nuclear deterrence, and prevention of regional conflicts. At the same time, neorealism suggests that Japanese military capabilities should steadily increase as structural constraints on rearmament weaken.[9] A long-term assessment of Japan's defense policy using neorealism yields very different predictions. If "there are no status quo powers in the international system,"[10] changes in the relative balance of world power might cause Japan to balance or challenge the United States.

How should a neorealist Japan have responded to September 11? It would have used September 11 to become a "normal" nation. In the aftermath of September 11, Japan possessed an ideal opportunity to expand its security activities. The international community, fixated on Al Qaeda and the U.S. campaign in Afghanistan, would have, and did, largely overlook changes in Japan's defense policy. Domestically, public opinion overwhelmingly backed military support for U.S. forces.[11] Even the liberal *Asahi Shimbun* found that 48 percent of Japanese approved of the SDF's transporting supplies, including weapons and ammunition.[12] Tokyo's actual response to September 11—dispatching tankers and escort destroyers—falls far short of neorealist expectations. Clearly, because Japan could have done more, particularly in terms of on-the-ground logistics support, neorealism fails to accurately predict Japan's actual response to September 11.

By similar logic, the Iraq War provided a further occasion for Japan to overcome remaining constraints on its defense policy. However, although Tokyo promised to participate in reconstruction, the SDF did not provide rear-area support to U.S. forces during the conflict. Instead, Japan once again refrained from utilizing a window of opportunity to rearm. Japan's responses to September 11 and the Iraq War highlight a key weakness in the neorealist argument—oversimplification. In failing to account for domestic factors, neorealism cannot explain or accurately predict state behavior in specific crises.

Japan's response to North Korea's missile and nuclear programs demonstrates the second major flaw in realist arguments: indeterminancy. When assessing the North Korean threat, a neorealist would anticipate two modes of Japanese behavior. If the U.S. nuclear umbrella remained credible, Tokyo should respond indifferently to the Democratic People's Republic of Korea (DPRK). Conversely, if U.S. extended deterrence was no longer convincing, Japan should develop its own defenses vis-à-vis Pyongyang. In reality, Japan's reaction has resembled neither of these predictions. The Japanese government's decision to procure BMD is a direct response to the North Korean threat. This decision is significant, particularly because U.S. forces in Japan's vicinity will independently deploy a missile defense system.[13] Yet, BMD alone does not indicate that Tokyo has lost faith in U.S. extended deterrence. If this were the case, new power projection capabilities like cruise missiles and ICBMs—the tools of preemption and deterrence—should have accompanied missile defense. They have not. Moreover, the Japanese government has not seriously considered developing nuclear weapons. By providing contradictory and incorrect predictions, neorealism doubly fails to explain Japan's response to North Korea.

Hegemonic Stability. Although based upon many of the same assumptions that underpin neorealism, hegemonic stability emphasizes the role of a dominant state in shaping the international system. The theory of hegemonic stability contains two central propositions: "order in world politics is typically created by a single dominant power," and "maintenance of order requires continued hegemony." A hegemonic state is defined by a preponderance of economic power and sufficient military capabilities to deter or roll back aggression against the international economy.[14] Legitimacy is also a prerequisite if hegemony is to be long-lived. According to this theory, the hegemon provides free trade regimes, an open market for imports, a stable currency, and security—the essential ingredients for a liberal international economy. Because these ingredients constitute collective goods—any state can partake of them without providing for their upkeep—hegemonic stability is vulnerable to "free rider" problems. A state may cease to be a hegemon if the "free rider" problem becomes prevalent and the costs of hegemony exceed the associated benefits.[15]

What general suggestions does the theory of hegemonic stability provide for Japan's security behavior? Given the "free rider" incentives inherent to hegemonic stability, the theory implies a calculated defense policy: Tokyo should extract maximum economic benefits from the U.S. security umbrella while offering the minimum upkeep needed to preserve the bilateral alliance. In specific terms, Japan should develop indigenous military capabilities and deploy forces overseas only when not doing so might jeopardize the U.S. security guarantee.

Would Japan's refusal to deploy the SDF in the wake of September 11 have seriously jeopardized the bilateral alliance? Any prediction based on the theory of hegemonic stability hinges on this question. If the fate of the bilateral alliance depended on Japan's response to September 11, hegemonic theory would suggest some form of active SDF support for U.S. forces. Conversely, if the continuance of U.S. security guarantees did not require SDF deployment, Tokyo's contribution to Operation Enduring Freedom should have been limited to financial assistance. In reality, the survival of the bilateral alliance was never contingent upon Japanese military support for the war on terror. Yet, Tokyo dispatched MSDF ships to the Indian Ocean. Consequently, Japan's actual response to September 11 does not conform to hegemonic stability's expectations.

Japan's reaction to the Iraq War partially supports the logic of hegemonic stability. The SDF's absence from the Iraq conflict, even in a rear-area logistics capacity, corresponds to this theory. U.S. officials never articulated on-the-ground wartime responsibilities for Japan.[16] Nor did they exert significant pressure for Tokyo to provide rear-area naval support during the conflict.[17] Clearly, the bilateral alliance was not at stake, and as hegemonic stability suggests, Japan followed a course of military inaction. However, the SDF's role in Iraq reconstruction defies hegemonic stability's predictions. In this case, U.S. officials set clear expectations for Japan's participation in postwar rebuilding. Yet, failure to meet these requests would not have imperiled the alliance. Thus, although hegemonic stability would suggest "free riding," Japan instead opted to support reconstruction through contributing troops.

Tokyo's response to the North Korean threat further demonstrates the gap between hegemonic stability's expectations and actual policies. How should Japan have reacted to North Korea if hegemonic stability holds true? Although the United States pressured Japan to develop new capabilities vis-à-vis the DPRK, failure to do so would not have jeopardized the bilateral alliance.[18] Consequently, the logic of hegemonic stability suggests that Japan should be indifferent to the DPRK threat. Acquiring new indigenous capabilities like BMD or power projection would be redundant because the U.S. security umbrella already contains (or will contain) similar systems. In short, Tokyo should "free ride" on the United States for protection against North Korea. Japan's actual response to the North Korean threat differs radically from this prediction. Instead of "free riding," Japan opted to deploy an expensive BMD system and to purchase limited power projection capabilities in the form of in-flight refueling aircraft. Clearly, hegemonic stability alone cannot adequately explain Japan's security behavior.

Alliance Theory. Alliance theory, a third variant of realism, focuses on the link between alliance relationships and a state's overall defense strategy. According to alliance theory, the "abandonment" versus "entrapment" dilemma—a problem inherent to every alliance—influences a state's security behavior. Abandonment constitutes a continuum of actions that undermine or fragment an alliance. These behaviors can include realigning with an opponent, de-aligning into a neutral position, or failing to meet alliance commitments. Entrapment, on the other hand, occurs when a state is dragged into an unwanted conflict by its ally. The risks of abandonment and entrapment vary inversely. For example, a state might reduce the possibility of abandonment by demonstrating commitment to its ally. This policy, however, might lead the ally to engage in reckless behavior toward a third state, increasing the likelihood of entrapment.[19] The abandonment versus entrapment dilemma is not static. Shared interests and threat perceptions can decrease abandonment and entrapment anxieties. Mutual dependence, or the existence of viable alternatives to the alliance, can also mitigate these concerns.[20]

How do abandonment and entrapment influence Japan's overall defense policy? Tokyo depends on the United States for fundamental types of security—extended deterrence and power projection. Moreover, no credible alternatives exist to the bilateral alliance. Therefore, alliance theory would suggest severe abandonment and entrapment fears that are partly alleviated by shared interests and threat perceptions. When applied to Japan, the logic of alliance theory predicts a gradual strengthening of indigenous capabilities. A more robust SDF would decrease the possibility of abandonment by raising the utility of the alliance to the

United States. At the same time, enhanced indigenous capabilities would reduce the likelihood of entrapment by providing Japan with a more credible exit option.

September 11 and other foreign policy shocks discussed in this section do not fit comfortably into the abandonment versus entrapment dynamic. One of alliance theory's main weaknesses is predicting a state's response to a particular crisis. Most crises are neither unambiguously cases of entrapment nor abandonment. Moreover, the defense strategy suggested by alliance theory—minimizing both these concerns—provides little guidance for predicting specific policy choices.

Tokyo's fears of abandonment overshadowed those of entrapment in the aftermath of September 11. Although not grounds for alliance termination, Japanese inaction might have increased the possibility of limited forms of abandonment.[21] Thus, the theory suggests that Japan's response to September 11 would signal the minimum commitment required by alliance considerations. However, the theory provides no guidance as to what a minimum commitment would constitute in policy terms. Whether dispatch of the MSDF fell short, met, or exceeded this minimum requirement is largely a subjective determination.

Unlike September 11, the Iraq War can be classified as a case of entrapment. The future vitality of the bilateral alliance did not hinge upon Japanese participation in the Iraq War. Moreover, U.S.-Japan threat perceptions of Iraq diverged; initially, only the United States advocated a hard-line policy. In this case, alliance theory would suggest that to avoid entrapment, Tokyo should have distanced itself from Washington's position on Iraq. Instead, as the likelihood of war increased, Japan became one of the few major nations to publicly support the United States. Japan's approach toward Iraq reconstruction further demonstrates the gap between expectations based on alliance theory and actual state behavior. Deploying the SDF to postwar Iraq represented a literal form of entrapment. Yet Tokyo contributed troops, even though the abandonment costs of doing otherwise would have been relatively low.

The North Korean crisis, in particular, demonstrates the limitations of alliance theory. Clearly, the DPRK threat heightened Japan's dependence on the bilateral alliance; given the SDF's lack of power projection, only U.S. forces can preempt or deter a North

Korean attack. However, both alliance partners share similar perceptions of the danger posed by North Korea. Together, these two factors simultaneously exacerbate and alleviate the abandonment/entrapment dilemma. Thus, the severity of abandonment and entrapment anxieties is ambiguous. In the case of North Korea, entrapment concerns—a U.S. preemptive attack—should outweigh fear of abandonment. Is Tokyo's decision to deploy BMD a means of avoiding entrapment? Not necessarily. Missile defense minimizes the damage associated with entrapment—North Korean retaliation—rather than lowering the risk of a U.S. preemptive strike altogether. Once deployed, BMD might even encourage the United States to use force because Japan would (arguably) be invulnerable from North Korean retribution. Again, alliance theory fails to explain Japan's recent security behavior.

Normative Explanations

Unlike realist approaches, normative theories do not view states as unitary actors. Instead, states are a set of relationships "within the state, between the state and society (or polity), and between the polity and some features of the international environment."[22] Two types of norms determine the behavior of political actors. Regulatory norms establish appropriate standards of political conduct, while constitutive norms define an actor's identity and interests. Norms neither arise nor change directly in response to traumatic historic experiences. Instead, norms emerge slowly through protracted, intense, political debate. Once institutionalized—often through law, policy, or precedent—norms dictate and constrain an actor's behavior.

Two related schools of thought address the impact of norms on Japan's defense policy—cultural norms and comprehensive security. The *cultural norms* approach, which focuses on broad links between norms and Japan's security strategy, predicts that social and institutionalized norms will limit the size of Japan's defense budget, inhibit SDF dispatch overseas, frustrate efforts to amend Article 9, and preclude Japanese acquisition of nuclear weapons.[23] Policies that run contrary to these norms should generate heated controversy. If successfully implemented, these policies should require substantial time and political resources.

The second school of thought, *comprehensive security*, emphasizes the economic dimensions of Japan's defense policy. This approach claims that economic security is equal to or more important than military security in Tokyo's strategic calculus.[24] As a result, Japan's defense policy should stress nonmilitary priorities including energy security, trade relationships, and technology acquisition.[25] Although both cultural norms and comprehensive security rely on normative theories, these schools of thought emphasize different aspects of Japan's defense policy, and thus merit separate treatment.

Cultural Norms. How should Japan have responded to September 11? According to this school of thought, historical events have no immediate impact upon the norms that govern defense activities. Consequently, cultural norms would suggest that Japan's reaction to September 11 should have conformed to previous defense policies. Yet, in reality, dispatch of the MSDF to the Indian Ocean broke with existing policy precedents. Past overseas deployment of the SDF had been confined to multilateral peacekeeping and disaster relief.[26] MSDF participation in Operation Enduring Freedom constituted a new type of out-of-area mission—rear-area support for U.S. forces. Thus, theoretical expectations and Tokyo's actual response diverge. Furthermore, cultural norms would predict that political controversy should accompany precedent-breaking policies. However, MSDF dispatch generated little debate and was overwhelmingly supported by the Japanese public. In the case of September 11, norms provide an inadequate framework for understanding Japan's defense policy.

By similar logic, Japan's reaction to the Iraq War reveals the limitations of cultural norms. Dispatching the SDF to support Iraq reconstruction clearly violated two existing precedents. First, Tokyo promised to participate in an occupation that not only lacked a formal international mandate, but was regarded as illegitimate by much of the world community. Second, dispatch of the SDF to Iraq entailed a much greater risk of casualties than previous overseas deployments. According to the logic of cultural norms, the decision to dispatch the SDF should therefore have generated significant public debate. In fact, the controversy surrounding SDF participation in Iraq reconstruction was relatively minor, particularly given that a majority of the Japanese public opposed both the war and postconflict troop contributions. Once again, expectations based upon cultural norms and Japan's actual policy responses diverge.

Only Japan's approach toward the North Korean threat is somewhat consistent with cultural norms. Tokyo's response to the DPRK threat has not diverted significantly from norms related to the defense budget and nuclear weapons. Although the Japanese government decided to introduce missile defense, funds for BMD have been taken from existing budgets, not new appropriations.[27] Thus, purchasing BMD has not caused the defense budget to exceed 1 percent of gross domestic product (GDP).[28] Moreover, one potential defense against North Korea—a nuclear deterrent—has not received the government of Japan's (GOJ) serious attention. However, the introduction of missile defense has led to the weakening of another institutionalized norm: the Three Principles on Arms Exports. Notably, relaxing the ban on arms exports to facilitate BMD cooperation aroused virtually no public outcry. Even in the case of the DPRK threat, cultural norms serves as an imperfect predictor of Tokyo's strategic behavior.

Comprehensive Security. Other scholars, Eric Heginbotham and Richard Samuels, have applied comprehensive security to Japan's defense policy. They argue that post-September 11 security initiatives reflect a national strategy that equally emphasizes economic and military interests. According to Heginbotham and Samuels, the Japanese government faced a dilemma when responding to September 11. On the one hand, demonstrating commitment to the bilateral alliance entailed more than financial contributions to Operation Enduring Freedom. Yet, the economic side of Japan's security equation required maintaining cordial relations with Arab states—Japan's primary source of oil. These military and economic priorities directly conflicted because highly visible support for U.S. operations would anger the Muslim world. Heginbotham and Samuels assert that dispatching the MSDF to refuel U.S. ships constituted a means of squaring this circle: Tokyo's contribution exceeded "checkbook diplomacy," yet would not be perceived as true participation in the conflict. The historical analysis provided by Heginbotham and Samuels is convincing. In particular, they link strategic trade concerns with the discrepancy between Japan's actual contribution to Operation Enduring Freedom and Prime Minister Koizumi's original pledge of support.[29] Thus, comprehensive security appears to provide a viable framework for understanding Japan's response to September 11.

When applied to the Iraq War, however, comprehensive security fails to predict Japan's defense behavior. Heginbotham and Samuels's essay, written before the conflict, allows for a strong critique of comprehensive security. The two assert that Japan's concern for its image in the Arab world would be a key determinant of support for U.S. actions against Iraq. They forecast that "regional support for U.S. efforts against Iraq would be necessary for Tokyo to undertake anything more than issuing vague and conditional statements of approval."[30] Arab regimes did not welcome the U.S.-led removal of Saddam. In fact, even traditional U.S. allies like Saudi Arabia and Egypt opposed the invasion. Despite widespread Arab opposition toward the war, Japan became one of the few major states to support U.S. actions against Iraq. Moreover, dispatching the SDF to participate in post-conflict reconstruction threatened to further undermine Tokyo's image in the Arab world. Clearly, Japan's response to the Iraq War indicates that this theoretical approach assigns too much weight to economic considerations.

Tokyo's reaction to recent North Korean provocations further demonstrates that comprehensive security overemphasizes economic interests. The Japanese government's decision to purchase missile defense stemmed directly from concerns regarding the DPRK. Comprehensive security suggests that Japan's evaluation of BMD would focus on the acquisition and indigenization of new technologies.[31] In reality, technology-related issues were strikingly absent from the Japanese government's debate on BMD. Moreover, Tokyo agreed to purchase off-the-shelf missile defense from the United States. The Japanese government's decision to forgo indigenous production and technology transfer opportunities reflects a defense policy that gives primacy to military security, not economic interests.

Complex Interdependence

Another mainstream theoretical approach to international relations—complex interdependence—is characterized by three prop-
erties. First, societies are connected through multiple channels of
communication, including government-to-government contacts,
informal elite networks, and transnational organizations. Second,
the agenda of interstate relationships lacks a distinct hierarchy of
issues; domestic politics, not merely security considerations, influence a state's foreign policy. Third, the use of military force is absent where complex interdependence prevails. In relationships of
complex interdependence, the "distribution of power within each
issue," not overall national capabilities, determines the outcome of
interstate bargaining.[32] Moreover, national initiatives are not ex-
ecuted by unitary state actors; bureaucracies with distinct organi-
zational interests implement policy. Consequently, complex interdependence predicts that transgovernmental bureaucratic alliances may exist on certain issues. Finally, the networks, norms,
and institutions that exist under complex interdependence exert
inertia on new policies; established regimes are difficult to abolish
or reform.[33]

Complex interdependence offers several broad insights into
Japan's defense policy. During the last 50 years, the U.S.-Japan
security alliance has become embedded in a host of institutions
such as the Defense Guidelines and the Security Consultative
Committee. Given the proliferation of supporting institutions,
complex interdependence would suggest that the bilateral alliance should remain central to Japan's security strategy in the in-
definite future. Path dependency constitutes the flip side of heavy
institutionalization. The distribution of roles and missions within
the alliance may reflect the interests and operating procedures of
long-established bureaucracies. Complex interdependence would
therefore predict that path dependency should inhibit Japan from
adopting new roles within the bilateral alliance. U.S. military capabilities dwarf those of Japan. According to complex interdependence, this asymmetry should provide the United States with significant leverage over bilateral security issues. U.S.-Japan complex
interdependence may also generate transgovernmental coalitions
on issues pertaining to defense.

To an even greater extent than alliance theory, complex interdependence cannot offer sound predictions when applied to specific foreign policy crises. Indeed, predictions stemming from this paradigm are so general as to match most policy outcomes. In all three crises, complex interdependence suggests that alliance considerations and differential capabilities should render Japan responsive to U.S. pressure. Yet, the theory provides no mechanism for translating these factors into a measurable degree of U.S. influence. Whether U.S. requests have a deciding or secondary impact on Japanese defense policies remains uncertain. Likewise, complex interdependence cannot predict the significance of path dependency in a particular crisis. Will path dependency overcome U.S. pressure? Or will the formation of transgovernmental alliances permit new bureaucratic innovations? Complex interdependence cannot provide guidance to these critical questions.

The Way Ahead

A new approach is in order given the failure of international relations theory to explain Japan's recent security behavior. The remaining seven chapters will develop and then apply this approach. Chapter 2 assesses the significance of Japanese defense policies using hypothetical scenarios of strategic change. Chapter 3 examines the evolution of elite and public attitudes toward national defense. Chapters 4 through 6 consecutively evaluate Japan's reaction to September 11, the GOJ's decision to introduce missile defense, and Tokyo's response to the Iraq War and postconflict reconstruction. Each case study traces the impact (and interplay) of foreign threats, U.S. policy, executive leadership, and generational change on Tokyo's security initiatives. Chapter 7 identifies fundamental patterns in Japan's evolving defense policy and sets forth transitional realism, a new theory of strategic change. The epilogue applies transitional realism to defense initiatives that have followed the SDF's Iraq deployment—namely, the Araki Report, the new National Defense Program Guidelines, and the February 2005 Security Consultative Committee's joint statement. With an eye toward the next frontier in Japan's security policy—amending Article 9—the epilogue closes with a look at the strategic implications of constitutional reform.

Notes

[1] *Gaiatsu* is a Japanese term for external pressure.

[2] Richard L. Armitage, Joseph S. Nye et al., "The United States and Japan: Advancing toward a Mature Partnership," Institute for National Strategic Studies Special Report (Washington, D.C.: National Defense University, October 11, 2000), 2.

[3] World Bank, "Total GDP 2004," World Development Indicators database, July 2005, http://www.worldbank.org/data/databytopic/GDP.pdf.

[4] This conceptual framework consists of beliefs about the nature of security, a state's international role, and the moral legitimacy of force.

[5] Michael J. Green, *Japan's Reluctant Realism: Foreign Policy Challenges in an Era of Uncertain Power* (New York: Palgrave, 2001), 33.

[6] John J. Mearsheimer, *The Tragedy of Great Power Politics* (New York: W.W. Norton and Company, 2001), 30–31.

[7] Neorealists argue that states generally prefer balancing to bandwagoning. Kenneth N. Waltz, "Anarchic Orders and Balances of Power," in *Neorealism and Its Critics*, ed. Robert O. Keohane (New York: Columbia University Press, 1986), 127.

[8] This paragraph draws from Daniel I. Okimoto, "The Japan-America Security Alliance: Prospects for the Twenty-First Century," occasional paper (Stanford, Calif.: Stanford University, Asia-Pacific Research Center, 1998), 11–12.

[9] Michael J. Green, "State of the Field Report: Research on Japanese Security Policy," *AccessAsia Review* 2, no. 1 (1998): 7.

[10] Mearsheimer, *Tragedy of Great Power Politics*, 2.

[11] Realism usually ignores domestic factors. I include this poll data to emphasize my point.

[12] The *Asahi Shimbun* survey was conducted on September 24, 2001. A *Yomiuri Shimbun* poll on September 26, 2001, found that 87 percent of Japanese favored military cooperation with the United States. Eric Heginbotham and Richard J. Samuels, "Japan," in *Asian Aftershocks: Strategic Asia 2002-2003*, ed. Richard J. Ellings and Aaron L. Friedberg (Seattle: National Bureau of Asian Research, 2003), 126.

[13] The United States will deploy a BMD-equipped Aegis destroyer to the Sea of Japan by the end of 2005. The footprint of this BMD system would provide limited national coverage. Author's interview with MSDF officer, Tokyo, March 2004.

[14] Robert O. Keohane, *After Hegemony: Cooperation and Discord in the World Political Economy* (Princeton: Princeton University Press, 1984), 31–32, 40.

[15] Robert Gilpin, *The Political Economy of International Relations* (Princeton: Princeton University Press, 1987), 73–75.

[16] Author's interviews with U.S. officials, Tokyo, March 2004.

[17] Author's interview with MSDF officer, Tokyo, March 2004.

[18] Here I refer to U.S. efforts on behalf of missile defense cooperation.

[19] Glenn Snyder, "The Security Dilemma in Alliance Politics," *World Politics* 36, no. 4 (July 1984): 466–467.

[20] Victor D. Cha, *Alignment despite Antagonism: The United States–Korea–Japan Security Triangle* (Stanford, Calif.: Stanford University Press, 1999), 39–41.

[21] Limited abandonment could include U.S. refusal to back Japan's position on regional issues such as the return of the abductees and the Kurile Islands.

[22] Peter J. Katzenstein, *Cultural Norms and National Security: Police and Military in Postwar Japan* (Ithaca: Cornell University Press, 1996), 4.

[23] Ibid., 2–3, 18, 118–121, 125, 138.

[24] Heginbotham and Samuels, "Japan," 98.

[25] Ibid., 98–100.

[26] Katzenstein, *Cultural Norms and National Security*, 127.

[27] "Japan to Cut Defense Buildup Target to Fund Missile System," *Jiji Press Service*, September 1, 2003.

[28] Successive Japanese prime ministers pledged to cap defense spending at 1 percent of GDP. This political commitment gradually evolved into a cultural norm. Katzenstein, *Cultural Norms and National Security*, 124–125.

[29] Heginbotham and Samuels, "Japan," 101–105.

[30] Ibid., 117–118.

[31] Here I allude to the "technonationalism" component of comprehensive security. Richard J. Samuels, *"Rich Nation, Strong Army": National Security and the Technological Transformation of Japan* (Ithaca: Cornell University Press, 1994), X.

[32] Robert O. Keohane and Joseph S. Nye, *Power and Interdependence*, 3rd ed. (New York: Longman, 2001), 27.

[33] Ibid., 22–29, 48.

2

What If:
Scenarios of Strategic Change

Comparing observed and expected security behavior provides one criterion for assessing the strategic significance of recent Japanese defense policies. A shift in national strategy should result in new, distinct security initiatives. Counterfactual analysis serves as a mechanism to determine whether policies associated with a strategic-level shift resemble the historical record, which in this case is Japan's actual security policy from 2001 to 2005.

Framing expected behavior necessitates scenarios of strategic change. These scenarios depict an unambiguous shift in Japan's national strategy. Three scenarios include a "normal" Japan that remains allied with the United States; a Japan strongly oriented toward East Asia; and termination of the U.S.-Japan alliance accompanied by a buildup of Japanese military capabilities. A status quo projection provides a baseline for this counterfactual analysis. The baseline is premised upon Japan's domestic politics, institutionalized security arrangements, and defense policies in the year 2000. Comparing observed Japanese security behavior with the behavior of each scenario reveals that recent defense initiatives fall midway between the baseline and strategic-level change. Neither "normal" nor fully constrained by norms, Japan now dwells in a sort of strategic "halfway house."[1]

Observed Behavior: 2001–2005

Defense Capabilities

To what extent have Japan's hard defense capabilities changed in the period following September 11? Japan's total defense budget has declined since fiscal year 2003. In fact, the 1 percent funding reductions in fiscal years 2004 and 2005 are consecutive record budget cuts.[2] This decline reflects a trend in Japan's defense spending—reduced mainline procurements and the early retirement of conventional systems—that will be accelerated by the new National Defense Program Guidelines (NDPG). At the same time, military research and development (R&D), on the decline from 1997 to 2000, has risen from 2.4 percent of Japan's defense budget in 2001 to 3.6 percent in 2005 or, in absolute terms, a 43 percent funding increase.[3] However, military R&D still occupies a paltry share of Japan's defense spending compared with U.S. military R&D, which was 15.5 percent of total U.S. military expenditures in 2005.[4] On the whole, the size and composition of Japan's defense budget has not changed markedly from 2001 to 2005.

Recent procurement decisions augur a modest future expansion of Japan's power projection capabilities. In March 2003, the Japanese government signed a contract with Boeing to purchase four tanker aircraft. When delivery begins in 2006, these aircraft will enable the ASDF to conduct continuous missions over the Asian mainland.[5] Together with Japan's introduction of precision-guided munitions, in-flight refueling will provide Tokyo with a latent preemptive capability.[6] The MSDF will also possess greater power projection capabilities in the coming years. Japan's fleet of Aegis destroyers will expand from four ships to six ships by 2008. Furthermore, the Japan Defense Agency (JDA) will introduce two new 13,500-ton helicopter destroyers. The vessels would be the largest ships in the Japanese navy. However, the impact of future MSDF procurements on Japan's power projection capabilities should not be exaggerated. Although capable of supporting offensive operations, Aegis destroyers are best suited to air defense. And Japan's new helicopter destroyers, ideal for noncombatant evacuations, would not be an effective tool of aggression.

Hard defense capabilities have changed most dramatically with respect to advanced systems. In December 2003, the Japanese government formally endorsed deploying missile defense. The decision came after four years of joint U.S.-Japan research on components of the Standard Missile—a type of interceptor designed for the Aegis destroyer. When deployed, Japanese missile defense will consist of a multilayered system that incorporates PAC-3 (Patriot Advanced Missile Capability) and Aegis-based BMD. As Tokyo embarked on missile defense, another advanced system came to completion—surveillance satellites. Although four satellites were built following North Korea's 1998 testing of a Taepo-dong missile, only the first pair successfully reached orbit. Launched in March 2003, these satellites alternatively contain an early warning radar and an optical sensor. Together, the satellites will allow Japan to monitor developments on the Korean peninsula without fully relying upon U.S. intelligence assets.

SDF Roles and Missions

During the years 2001 to 2005, the distinction has blurred between general SDF roles and activities stemming from the U.S.-Japan security alliance. Indeed, missions typically separate from Japan's alliance commitments—peacekeeping, for example—have become politically and operationally linked to the bilateral security relationship. Furthermore, new SDF missions, particularly counterterrorism, emerged in the context of the U.S.-Japan alliance, but gradually evolved into part of Tokyo's global security role.

Historically, the SDF's raison d'etre has been to protect Japan from an amphibious invasion. Although the possibility of invasion greatly decreased after the collapse of the Soviet Union, Japan's defense posture retained a counterinvasion focus throughout the 1990s. However, the new National Defense Program Guidelines have discounted the likelihood of a foreign power invading Japan. More important, the NDPG articulated major cutbacks in equipment dedicated solely to counterinvasion operations.[7] When fully implemented, the NDPG will lead to a diminution of the SDF's traditional role in favor of other security responsibilities—peacekeeping and more broadly, contributing to the maintenance of global order.

By quietly altering the definition of self-defense, the Japanese government has achieved a de facto expansion of the SDF's ability to participate in regional contingencies. The legal framework governing the SDF's response to regional conflicts dates back to 1999 when the Diet passed the law on situations in areas surrounding Japan. By enabling the SDF to provide rear-area support for U.S. forces during a regional contingency, this legislation maximized Japan's role under the then-prevailing interpretation of Article 9.[8] However, since 1999, the GOJ's interpretation of Article 9 has changed subtly. In the context of the 2003 national emergency bills, the Koizumi administration broadened the right of self-defense to include an armed response to any attack on U.S. forces defending Japan. The SDF could even use force to support U.S. military assets stationed outside the home islands, provided that the ensuing conflict appeared likely to endanger Japanese territory.[9] Most conceivable regional contingencies would threaten to spill over onto Japanese soil, airspace, or waters. Therefore, under the GOJ's modified definition of self-defense, the SDF could, in a limited way, participate in regional conflicts as a belligerent.

Of all SDF roles that existed before 2001, peacekeeping has undergone the most dramatic evolution. The SDF first took part in peacekeeping operations following the enactment of the International Peace Cooperation Law in 1992. However, the legislation precluded Japanese participation in many standard peacekeeping activities: separating combatants, monitoring disarmament, and patrolling buffer zones. Moreover, throughout the 1990s, the SDF viewed peacekeeping as a secondary responsibility. Since 2001, however, the scope of SDF peacekeeping has evolved rapidly. In December 2001, the Diet revised the International Peace Cooperation Law to permit new peacekeeping activities. As part of this revision, the Diet gave SDF peacekeepers greater freedom to use small arms in self-defense.[10] More notably, SDF participation in Iraq reconstruction violated several historical precedents surrounding Japanese peacekeeping. For the first time in its history, the SDF deployed to a country that, in effect, remained a combat zone. And further, the SDF operated under the auspices of a U.S.-led occupation force rather than as part of a UN mission.

The deployment of the SDF to Iraq has facilitated additional changes in Japan's approach toward peacekeeping. In October

2004, the Araki Report advocated that the Japanese government redefine peacekeeping as a primary SDF mission. The report also called for the GOJ to consider new peacekeeping roles such as policing.[11] Reiterating many of the Araki Report's proposals, the NDPG framed "international peace cooperation" as a core objective of Japan's security policy. In addition, the NDPG announced the JDA's intention to establish "necessary infrastructure to quickly dispatch defense force units overseas . . . ."[12] Although not specified, such infrastructure would almost certainly include a permanent dispatch law. Finally, the NDPG outlined a new force structure underpinning the SDF's enhanced peacekeeping role. "Highly ready, mobile, adaptable and multipurpose,"[13] future SDF units will be configured to play an active part in shaping the international security environment.

Until September 11, SDF roles and missions did not include counterterrorism. Japan's National Police Agency held responsibility for thwarting domestic terrorists. The only link between the SDF and terrorism, either foreign or domestic, was consequence management.[14] In the aftermath of the September 11 attacks, counterterrorism emerged as one of the SDF's major roles. Passed by the Diet in October 2001, the Anti-Terrorism Special Measures Law permitted the SDF to provide rear-area support for the United States and other nations in the war on terror. The geographic scope of this legislation included the high seas and the territory of consenting foreign countries.[15]

The legal framework established in the wake of September 11 rapidly translated into a new counterterrorism role for the SDF. On November 9, 2001, Japan dispatched the destroyers *Kurama* and *Kirisame* and the *Hamana*, a supply ship, to the Indian Ocean to provide rear-area support for Operation Enduring Freedom. The following year, the Aegis destroyer *Kirishima* embarked for the Indian Ocean. By May 2005, the MSDF had supplied approximately 400,000 kiloliters of fuel to coalition vessels in the Arabian Sea.[16] Although initially limited to U.S. forces, the MSDF's refueling efforts ultimately grew to include ships from the British, Canadian, German, and Italian navies.

Within Japan, the SDF is assuming a new counterterrorism role. The "Central Readiness Group" envisaged by the NDPG will play a role in combating terrorist and commando attacks on Japan.[17] Both at home and abroad, counterterrorism increasingly represents a major SDF responsibility.

Domestic Political Constraints

In the language often employed by Diet members, Japan is not a "normal" nation. To a unique degree, institutionalized norms shape and sometimes frustrate Tokyo's pursuit of national security.

Japan's Peace Clause. Article 9 underpins the set of legal norms that constrain Japan's defense policy. The peace clause "outlaws war and denies the state the right to belligerency."[18] Throughout the postwar period, cultural norms have frustrated all attempts to amend Japan's constitution; multiple prime ministers—from Nobusuke Kishi through Yasuhiro Nakasone—have tried to revise Article 9 without success. However, the government's interpretation of Article 9 has been less than immutable. Originally, Japan could not possess a fighting force. After 1954, the government decided that Article 9 would permit the maintenance of purely defensive units.[19]

Yet, reinterpretation has not sufficed to overcome the most intractable problems stemming from Article 9: Japan's inability to use armed force overseas and the prohibition on collective defense. The GOJ has interpreted Article 9 as barring the overseas use of armed force. This determination restricts the scope of Japanese peacekeeping operations and limits the SDF's participation in UN-sanctioned multinational coalitions. The prohibition on collective defense, a "semiconstitutional" structure, imposes further constraints on Japan's security activities.[20] In its current form, the prohibition would circumscribe Japanese involvement in a regional contingency. Moreover, without exercising the right of collective defense, the SDF cannot provide full spectrum support to U.S. forces conducting out-of-area missions.

During the years 2001–2005, the Diet laid the groundwork for amending Japan's constitution. In January 2000, the Lower and Upper House Constitutional Research Commissions first convened to discuss revising Japan's supreme law. Five years later, after conducting open hearings and receiving expert testimony, each panel issued a final report. A majority of the Lower House panel favored amending Article 9, but the Upper House commission failed to reach a similar consensus. Japan's major political parties—the Liberal Democratic Party (LDP) and the Democratic Party of Japan (DPJ)—have also conducted research on constitutional reform. While both the LDP and DPJ advocate amending Article 9, inter-party (and intra-party) differences exist as to the nature of specific changes. Although both parties recognize the need to stipulate the right of self-defense, the overseas use of armed force and the prohibition on collective defense remain items of contention. Thus, actual revisions to Article 9 will await Prime Minister Koizumi's successor.

Lacking an amendment to Article 9, the ban on the overseas use of armed force has stayed firmly in place. This cannot be said for the prohibition on collective defense. Indeed, the prohibition has eroded despite the absence of constitutional revision. First, the GOJ deployed an Aegis destroyer, the *Kirishima*, to the Indian Ocean without fully addressing the legal ramifications raised by the ship's sophisticated radar system. The *Kirishima's* air defense umbrella inevitably extended to non-Japanese vessels.[21] Furthermore, critics feared that information sharing between the *Kirishima* and U.S. vessels might violate the prohibition on collective defense. When the *Kirishima* embarked for the Arabian Sea in December 2002, the legality of the dispatch had yet to be resolved. Japan's rush to field BMD has further weakened the prohibition on collective defense. By ruling that "if it's judged to have a significant probability of targeting Japan, it will be considered to have justified our right to self-defense," the Cabinet Legislation Bureau condoned the inadvertent use of Japanese BMD to defend U.S. territory.[22] In short, although the official interpretation of Article 9 remains largely unchanged, the Japanese government has in practice relaxed the prohibition on collective defense.

The Three Nonnuclear Principles. The Three Nonnuclear Principles constitute another institutional constraint on Japan's defense strategy. As articulated by Prime Minister Eisaku Sato in 1967, the principles were "not to make such [nuclear] weapons, not to possess them, and not to bring them into Japan."[23] The three principles were institutionalized by a Diet resolution that accompanied the reversion of Okinawa. Japan later reaffirmed the principles when ratifying the Nuclear Non-Proliferation Treaty in 1976 and agreeing to extend the treaty indefinitely in 1995. But perhaps the strongest embodiment of the Three Nonnuclear Principles has been the Japanese people. Historically, an overwhelming majority of Japanese—both elites and the public—have opposed acquiring nuclear weapons. On the whole, from 2001 to 2005 Japan's nonnuclear principles have remained inviolate. Japanese politicians can now openly debate the nuclear option without risking public disgrace, but the public remains opposed to nuclear armament. Furthermore, most elites continue to view nuclear weapons as antithetical to Japan's national interest.

Military Export Restrictions. The Three Principles on Arms Exports prevent Japanese firms from selling military hardware and technology on the international market. Like the Three Nonnuclear Principles, these export restrictions were established by Prime Minister Sato in 1967. Since then, the GOJ has institutionalized the export restrictions through successive Diet interpretations. In addition to stunting the growth of Japan's defense industry, military export restrictions have obviated Japanese participation in multinational defense projects. The transfer of Japanese military technology to the United States, though exempted from the Three Principles on Arms Exports, is still greatly circumscribed. With the exception of BMD, Japanese firms can transfer technology design papers but not hardware to the United States.[24] And U.S. firms cannot export military systems containing Japanese technology.

The GOJ's decision to introduce missile defense led to a limited relaxation of the Three Principles on Arms Exports. If strictly enforced, these principles would have prevented the United States and Japan from exchanging BMD hardware, raising the cost of missile defense and possibly hindering interoperability.[25] As a result, the Japanese government exempted missile defense from the nonexport principles in a statement by Chief Cabinet Secretary Hiroyuki Hosoda at the end of 2004. Notably, this exclusion only applied to BMD technology rather than all forms of U.S.-Japan defense-industrial cooperation. But Hosoda's statement did signal that future exemptions to the nonexport principles are at least possible.[26] Still, even in weakened form, the Three Principles on Arms Exports remain one of the three institutionalized constraints on Japan's defense policy.

Expected Behavior

Britain of the East: A "Normal" Japan

Suppose that in 2001 the Japanese government had embraced a new strategic vision: Japan as the UK of East Asia. What policies would result from such a decision? How would Japan respond to recent foreign policy shocks? In short, how would a "normal" Japan carry itself on the international stage? This scenario rests upon one fundamental assumption: in becoming a "normal" nation, Japan will find strengthening the bilateral alliance desirable, if not indeed necessary. Of course, legal and normative constraints might be cast aside without a concurrent deepening of the U.S.-Japan alliance, a scenario explored in the latter part of this section.

By 2006, what capabilities might Japan possess under this scenario? Despite becoming a "normal" nation, Japan would probably continue to spend only 1 percent of GDP on defense. Tokyo's ongoing fiscal crisis rather than societal norms would preclude higher defense budgets. At the same time, the composition of Japan's defense budget would shift. As a proportion of defense spending, allocations for military R&D would approach that of major European countries, if not U.S. levels. In addition, procurement budgets would emphasize light expeditionary forces at the expense of traditional heavy units. Concerned by the North Korean threat, Japan would deploy or be developing preemptive capabilities: cruise missiles and long-range bombers. However, the reaction of neighboring states and the strength of U.S. security guarantees would lead Japan to eschew nuclear weapons. Other forms of power projection—heavy sealift or heavy airlift capacity—would undergo a modest increase to allow for greater SDF involvement in peacekeeping. And finally, the missile threat posed by the DPRK would propel U.S.-Japan BMD cooperation beyond joint research. After North Korea announced its withdrawal from the Nuclear Non-Proliferation Treaty in early 2003, the Japanese government would immediately decide to introduce missile defense.

As the UK of East Asia, Japan would possess a palette of options for dealing with regional contingencies. In addition to economic sanctions and rear-area support, a new legal framework would enable Japan to deploy the SDF alongside U.S. forces at any stage of a conflict. Peacekeeping would constitute a primary SDF role. The Diet would enact a permanent dispatch law. SDF personnel would be allowed to participate in peace enforcement missions and to use armed force to protect peacekeepers of foreign nationalities. In the wake of September 11, counterterrorism would become an SDF priority. Like other U.S. allies and friends, Japan would provide some form of on-the-ground support for Operation Enduring Freedom. Furthermore, the MSDF would fully participate in the Proliferation Security Initiative (PSI).[27] In fact, the United States and Japan would achieve new levels of maritime cooperation under the "Britain of the East" scenario. The U.S. 7th Fleet and the MSDF would fully integrate command and control structures, and elements of both navies would jointly patrol the sea-lanes between the Persian Gulf and Japan.

The aforementioned capabilities and roles hinge on the weakening or outright elimination of normative constraints on Japan's defense policy. To transform Japan into the UK of East Asia, the Diet would amend Article 9 to allow the overseas use of armed force and the unfettered exercise of collective defense. At the same time, the Diet would cease to interpret Article 9 as requiring an "exclusively defense-oriented defense policy," thus clarifying the legality of preemptive capabilities. A commensurate shift in public norms would accompany constitutional reform: the Japanese people would support SDF participation in combat-like peacekeeping operations and regional contingencies. Like Article 9, the Three Principles on Arms Exports would undergo major revision. To facilitate missile defense cooperation, the Japanese government would relax the nonexport principles to permit the transfer of hardware to the United States. In fact, a desire to take part in other multinational defense projects would lead Japan to roll back military export restrictions across the board. The only unmodified restraint on Japan's defense policy would be the Three Nonnuclear Principles. But these principles would reflect calculations of national interest rather than a deeply held nuclear taboo.

Japan in Asia: Regionalism to the Fore

Suppose that in 2001 Tokyo had adopted a new, regionally focused defense strategy. Under this scenario, political leaders would perceive Japan's interests and responsibilities as regional rather than global. Japanese policymakers would avoid deepening the U.S.-Japan security relationship. But Tokyo would expend the minimum material and political resources necessary to sustain the alliance. Moreover, the Japanese government would seek to enhance multilateral security organizations in East Asia. Japan would also cultivate closer bilateral relationships with South Korea, members of ASEAN (Association of Southeast Asia Nations), and possibly China. In response to regional threats, Japan would seek an East Asian solution rather than look to the United States.

What would be the impact of regionalism on Japan's defense capabilities? Absolute levels of defense spending would probably remain constant. Japan's fiscal state of affairs would prevent higher defense budgets. Like absolute spending, the composition of Japan's defense budget would be unchanged. Unconvinced of the need to achieve greater alliance interoperability, Japan would not invest substantially in military R&D. Procurements would continue to emphasize counterinvasion units. Conversely, Tokyo would possess no imperative to produce light expeditionary forces that could be deployed outside of East Asia. Given Japan's legacy of imperialism, power projection capabilities would only frustrate a defense strategy premised on regional integration. Thus, Japan would forgo cruise missiles and in-flight refueling. For similar reasons, Japan would eschew missile defense; BMD would antagonize both China and North Korea while strengthening the U.S.-Japan alliance. Indeed, when responding to the North Korean threat, Japan would pursue a regional solution—something a la Kim Dae-jung's "sunshine" policy—rather than follow a hard-line U.S. approach.

Within this scenario, the scope of SDF missions in 2006 would be smaller than in 2001. Tokyo would downplay the rear-area support role enabled by the 1999 law on situations in areas surrounding Japan. Instead, the Japanese government would emphasize regional efforts to defuse future conflicts in East Asia, which would lead Japan to advocate strengthening regional security institutions, particularly the ASEAN Regional Forum.

SDF participation in peacekeeping would decline after Japan adopted a regional focus. Japanese peacekeepers would operate primarily in East Asia; the SDF would not take part in the reconstruction of Iraq. Rather than legislate a permanent SDF dispatch law, the Diet might attempt to place Japanese peacekeeping activities under the auspices of a regional security institution. Finally, counterterrorism would not constitute a new, major SDF role. Japan would decide against deploying the MSDF to the Indian Ocean in the wake of September 11.

A regional shift in Japan's defense strategy could occur without the revision or abandonment of institutionalized domestic constraints. In the case of Article 9, regionalism would discourage possible amendments because neighboring countries would perceive changes to the peace clause as portending a resurgence of Japanese militarism. On the same grounds, priority on regional integration would compel the GOJ to retain an "exclusively defense-oriented defense policy." Thus, Article 9 would remain intact in 2006. A regional focus would reinforce other institutional constraints on Japan's defense policy. Tokyo's acquisition of nuclear weapons would alienate most countries in East Asia. Therefore, the Three Nonnuclear Principles would continue as a fundamental tenet of Japan's security strategy. And finally, given Tokyo's lack of interest in missile defense under this scenario, political leaders would have no incentive to review or relax the Three Principles on Arms Exports.

Past as Future: Autarky and Remilitarization

Suppose that in 2001 Japan unilaterally terminated the bilateral security alliance. In place of a U.S.-centric defense policy, the Japanese government adopted a new national strategy—autarky. Whatever the cost—financial and diplomatic—Tokyo would provide for its own defense. Delinked from the U.S. security umbrella, Japan would remilitarize, normative constraints notwithstanding. Additionally, political leaders would calculate Japan's national interest in the narrowest sense.

Under this scenario, Japan's military capabilities would expand rapidly to fill the vacuum left by departing U.S. forces. Placing national security above fiscal restraint, Japan's leadership would boost defense spending above 1 percent of GDP. Procurements would rise as a proportion of the defense budget. Military R&D would also receive a greater share of defense spending as Japan sought to upgrade its technology-industrial base. Both procurements and R&D would attempt to indigenize Japan's defense production. In the quest for national autarky, Tokyo would develop extensive power projection capabilities. Bereft of the U.S. "sword," Japan would deploy cruise missiles, long-range bombers, aircraft carriers, and heavy cruisers. To compensate for the loss of U.S. extended deterrence, Japan would develop nuclear weapons. However, a nuclear arsenal might prove insufficient with respect to North Korea. To hedge against the DPRK, Tokyo would also introduce missile defense.

Narrow definitions of national interest would contribute to a retrenchment of certain SDF missions. After terminating the bilateral alliance, Japan would no longer offer rear-area support for U.S. forces in a regional contingency. Except when Tokyo's vital interests were threatened, the SDF would wholly refrain from intervening in East Asian crises. If intervention became necessary, potential SDF responses would range from blockade to active combat. The leadership of an autarkic Japan would discontinue SDF peacekeeping missions. In the eyes of Japanese defense planners, peacekeeping would have little relation to national interest and divert resources from more useful capabilities. Deterrence, rather than peacekeeping, would come to represent one of the SDF's primary roles. In the absence of the U.S. security umbrella, the SDF would be charged with deterring nuclear attacks on Japan. To fulfill this mission, the SDF might maintain a nuclear arsenal commensurate to that of Britain or France. Yet, even a Japan armed with nuclear weapons would possess an Achilles heel—dependence on foreign oil. To achieve energy security, an expanded MSDF would patrol the sea-lanes from the Persian Gulf to the Sea of Japan.

A strategy of national autarky would entail the outright elimination of institutionalized constraints on Japan's defense policy. Article 9 would be repealed under this scenario to permit the use of armed force overseas. An accompanying surge in nationalist sentiment would be necessary for rapid rearmament. Other domestic constraints would not survive a strategy of autarky. By definition, the Three Nonnuclear Principles could not exist alongside a burgeoning nuclear arsenal. Export restrictions would also be abolished, as military exports would serve to increase the size of Japan's defense industry. Clearly, becoming a "normal" nation would constitute the first step toward autarky.

A Baseline Projection

Assessing strategic change, real or counterfactual, requires a point of reference. The year 2000 serves as an ideal baseline scenario. Why the year 2000? First, MSDF deployment to the Indian Ocean and subsequent changes in Tokyo's defense posture occurred afterward. Second and more important, 2000 marked the final year of Japan's "traditional" style of political leadership. After Nakasone resigned in 1987, Japan suffered from a series of weak prime ministers. Yoshiro Mori, whose tenure spanned most of 2000, was no exception. By mid-2001 however, the advent of the Koizumi administration signaled a new, dynamic form of executive leadership. Because recent changes in Japan's defense policy are due in part to political leadership, a baseline projection should exclude Koizumi's time in office. Third, Japan did not experience a major foreign policy shock during the year 2000. Thus, defense policies that prevailed in 2000 reflect stable variables.

2000: A Dull Year. What was Japan's national strategy in 2000? The answer lies in the domestic politics, institutionalized security arrangements, and defense policies of the time. In 2000, normative constraints infused political discourse on security issues. One anecdote provides a vivid example of the degree to which norms influenced domestic politics. In an October 1999 interview with *Playboy Weekly Japan*, newly appointed cabinet member Shingo Nishimura called for the Diet to consider nuclear weapons. The ensuing political furor forced Nishimura to resign.[28] Like the nonnuclear principles, Article 9 continued to limit Japan's security options in 2000. However, the founding of the Lower and Upper House Constitutional Research Commissions signaled that norms surrounding Article 9 had weakened. Events in 2000 demonstrated the feebleness of Japanese political leadership. Prime Minister Mori's disapproval rating topped 70 percent, and rival LDP faction leader Koichi Kato threatened to join the opposition party in a vote of no confidence.[29] Not surprisingly, Mori's poor standing undermined his ability to pass key security-related bills. Emergency legislation languished during his tenure. Mori also failed to ease restrictions on Japanese peace-keepers.[30] In short, domestic politics impeded the evolution of Japan's defense strategy.

During the year 2000, most changes in Japan's security arrangements stemmed from the revised Defense Guidelines. Earlier in 1999, the Diet established a legal basis for the guidelines by passing the law on situations in areas surrounding Japan and approving a modified acquisition and cross-servicing agreement. However, several incomplete items remained on Japan's security agenda. Thus, the year 2000 witnessed the creation of a Bilateral Coordination Mechanism to link the U.S. and Japanese governments in time of war and to facilitate joint contingency planning.[31] Likewise, to ensure the effectiveness of the revised Defense Guidelines, the Diet passed a bill permitting the SDF to conduct maritime interdiction operations. The bill, however, required the MSDF to receive UN authorization or consent of the boarded ship before commencing inspections.[32] In addition to these changes, the institutional arrangements that compose the U.S.-Japan alliance continued to function smoothly. Policymakers from both governments consulted on defense issues through a variety of bilateral forums. The continued presence of the 47,000 U.S. troops stationed in Japan appeared certain.

From the perspective of new defense initiatives, the year 2000 was quite unremarkable. Peacekeeping remained a secondary SDF mission. Indeed, the Japanese government decided against dispatching the SDF to East Timor despite encouragement from then-U.S. ambassador Thomas Foley.[33] Joint research on missile defense progressed slowly; in 2000, the Japanese government insisted that fielding a BMD system would require separate decisions at both the development and deployment stages.[34] The Cabinet Office endorsed a new Mid-Term Defense Plan (MTDP) in December 2000. Although emphasizing cyber terrorism and C4I (Command, Control, Communications, Computers, and Intelligence), the document also included traditional programs like an indigenously produced maritime aircraft. The new MTDP planned for a modest expansion of Japan's power projection capabilities: new procurements included tanker aircraft and two helicopter destroyers. In addition, the MTDP called for a small increase in Japan's defense budget.[35] Finally, the report issued by the Prime Minister's Commission on Japanese Goals in the 21st

Century hinted at Japan's future security strategy. The report noted that "after seeing Chinese and North Korean missile tests . . . there is recently a strengthening of opinion that Japan itself should overcome its post-war taboos and consider capabilities and policies for the security of our own country . . . ."[36] Moreover, the report advocated a foreign policy of "enlightened self-interest." Thus, even in a "dull" year, a degree of latent change characterized Japan's defense policy.

Relative Stasis: A Projection for 2006. What if Japan's strategic evolution had continued along similar lines until 2006? Under this scenario, Japan's defense capabilities would undergo an uneven, halting expansion. Absolute defense spending would perhaps rise, or more likely stagnate, as Japan's fiscal crisis rendered the MTDP's budget request untenable. Given the JDA's new emphasis on information technology, military R&D would receive a greater share of the defense budget. But procurements would focus on traditional items—heavy units and indigenous weapon development programs. The power projection capabilities advocated in the new MTDP would prove contentious. In particular, tanker aircraft might require more political capital than Japan's weak leadership could muster. Diet members would continue to harbor deep reservations about BMD's technical feasibility, cost, and regional impact. As a consequence, U.S.-Japan missile defense cooperation would remain in the research phase. Alternatively, North Korea's nuclear program might provide sufficient impetus for the Japanese government to move forward on joint development. In either case, Japan's timid leadership would prove incapable of rapidly introducing BMD.

SDF roles and missions in 2006 would largely resemble those of 2000. Japan's participation in a regional contingency would be strictly limited to rear-area support for U.S. forces. In 2006, resisting a large-scale invasion would still constitute the SDF's raison d'etre. Lacking a popular mandate, Japan's leadership would fail to amend the International Peace Cooperation Law. Thus SDF peacekeepers would remain subject to numerous operational restrictions. Indeed, the continuation of these legal constraints would relegate peacekeeping to a minor SDF role. The Iraq War would pose a quandary for Japan's prime minister. Despite U.S. expectations, unfavorable public opinion combined with the absence of political leadership would preclude SDF dispatch to Iraq.

On the other hand, public opinion would facilitate a new SDF role—counterterrorism. In the wake of September 11, Japan's prime minister would possess the popular backing needed to deploy MSDF ships to the Indian Ocean. However, fear of violating the prohibition on collective defense would prevent Japan's leadership from dispatching an Aegis destroyer.

How would institutional constraints on Japan's defense policy evolve under this scenario? The normative strength of Article 9 would gradually decline. Both policymakers and the public would increasingly favor constitutional revision. But in 2005, *both* the Lower and Upper House Constitutional Research Commissions would issue reports equivocating on Article 9. To avoid controversy, government leaders would preserve the prohibition on collective defense both in form and practice. By 2006, Japan's nuclear "allergy" would diminish as the public became acutely aware of the threat posed by North Korea. Nevertheless, politicians would approach the nuclear option circumspectly; openly advocating nuclear weapons would still engender a political backlash. Finally, the GOJ's decision to jointly develop missile defense would challenge the Three Principles on Arms Exports. By 2006 if not earlier, export restrictions would be under review in order to permit the exchange of BMD development prototypes.

Halfway to Strategic Change: Or Japan as Germany

No scenario of strategic change closely describes observed Japanese security behavior. "Britain of the East" is an extrapolation of current trends rather than an accurate depiction of Japan's current national strategy. The complete rollback of normative constraints, a prerequisite for this scenario, has yet to occur. "Regionalism to the Fore," the second scenario, is disconnected from a world where U.S.-Japan security cooperation has reached an unprecedented level. Moreover, Japan's defense strategy is increasingly global in scope. Like the previous two scenarios, "Autarky and Remilitarization" bears little resemblance to reality. Japanese leaders push for greater independence within, not outside the bilateral alliance. And institutionalized norms, though in many cases weakened, continue to limit Tokyo's strategic options.

At the same time, observed Japanese defense policies clearly differ from the baseline scenario. First, the Japanese government decided to purchase BMD off the shelf rather than wait for joint development. Second, peacekeeping became a major SDF role, a development that observers in 2000 would not have predicted. In particular, the baseline projection does not include the amalgamation of peacekeeping and Japan's alliance obligations represented by SDF dispatch to Iraq. Third, the baseline scenario fails to describe the erosion of institutionalized constraints that occurred between 2001 and 2005. Projections based on the year 2000 do not anticipate the Lower House Constitutional Research Commission endorsing the revision of Article 9. Nor does the baseline scenario predict the deployment of Aegis destroyers to the Indian Ocean.

Counterfactual analysis therefore reveals that recent Japanese defense policies fall somewhere between the status quo and strategic-level change. To borrow a metaphor coined by Ralph Cossa of Pacific Forum CSIS, Japan is now the Germany of a decade ago. Like Germany of the early 1990s, Japan is unable to deploy troops for combat missions overseas. But by contributing rear-area support, Japan, like Germany during the Persian Gulf War, can free U.S. troops to participate in combat. Indeed, as the next chapter illustrates, elite and public opinion appear to favor the German path: steady progress toward becoming a "normal" state.[37]

Notes

[1] Michael H. Armacost suggested this term.

[2] "Japan Cuts FY 2004 Defense Budget by Record 1 Percent," *Japan Economic Newswire*, December 23, 2003; and "Defense Budget Slips 1% to 4.86 Trillion Yen," *Japan Times*, December 21, 2004.

[3] Japan Defense Agency, *Defense of Japan 2003* (Tokyo: Intergroup, August 2003), 437; and *Heisei 17 nendo: boeiryoku seibi to yosan no gaiyou* (Fiscal Year Heisei 17: Defense Capability Adjustment and Budget Outline), http://www.jda.go.jp/j/library/archives/yosan/2005/yosan.pdf.

[4] Office of Management and Budget, *Budget of the United States Government, Fiscal Year 2006*, "Department of Defense," 2005, http://www.whitehouse.gov/omb/budget/fy2006/defense.html.

[5] Author's interview with SDF officer, Tokyo, March 2004.

[6] "ASDF to Introduce Precision-Guided Bombs Receiving Signals from U.S. Military Satellites," *Yomiuri Shimbun*, September 18, 2003.

[7] Japan Defense Agency, "National Defense Program Guidelines, FY 2005–," December 2004, 3, 9, http://www.jda.go.jp/e/policy/f_work/taikou05/fy20050101.pdf.

[8] Noboru Yamaguchi, "Japanese Adjustments of Security Alliance with the United States: Evolution of Policy on Roles of the Self-Defense Forces" (paper presented at conference of the Asia-Pacific Research Center, Stanford University, California, January 14, 2004), 7–8.

[9] "Government Outlines New View on Self-Defense," *Yomiuri Shimbun*, January 26, 2004.

[10] Yamaguchi, "Japanese Adjustments of Security Alliance with the United States," 8.

[11] The Araki Report, cited in full as the Prime Minister's Council on Security and Defense Capabilities (the Araki Commission), "Japan's Visions for Future Security and Defense Capabilities" (Tokyo, October 2004): 20, http://kantei.go.jp/jp/singi/ampobouei/dai13/13siryou.pdf.

[12] Japan Defense Agency, "National Defense Program Guidelines," 9.

[13] Ibid.

[14] Author's interview with SDF officer, Tokyo, March 2004.

[15] Cabinet Office, "The Anti-Terrorism Special Measures Law," October 2001, http://www.kantei.go.jp/foreign/policy/2001/anti-terrorism/1029terohougaiyou_e.html.

[16] "Antiterror Law May Be Extended, but MSDF Flotilla Could Be Reduced," *Japan Times*, May 13, 2005.

[17] Japan Defense Agency, "Mid-Term Defense Program (FY 2005–2009)," December 2004, 2–3, http://www.jda.go.jp/e/policy/f_work/taikou05/fy20050301.pdf.

[18] Katzenstein, *Cultural Norms and National Security*, 118.

[19] Ibid., 116–120.

[20] The Cabinet Legislation Bureau defines the right of collective defense as "the right to use actual force to stop an armed attack on a foreign country . . . even when the state itself is not under direct attack." Japan Defense Agency, *Defense of Japan 2001* (Tokyo: Urban Connections, July 2001), 78.

[21] Brad Glosserman, "Vindication!" *Comparative Connections* 4, no. 4, (October–December 2002): 15–23.

[22] Cabinet Legislation Bureau Director General Osamu Akiyama quoted in "Ishiba: Japan to 'Counterattack' if North Korea Prepares to Attack," *Yomiuri Shimbun*, January 25, 2003. In reality, the trajectory of a missile aimed

at the United States could be easily differentiated from that of a missile targeted at Japan.

[23] Katzenstein, *Cultural Norms and National Security*, 128–129.

[24] Author's interview with Japanese defense specialist, Tokyo, August 2002.

[25] Daniel M. Kliman, "U.S.-Japan Missile Defense Cooperation: Future Challenges and Recommendations" (paper presented at the Harvard Project for Asian and International Relations, Seoul, South Korea, August 21–24, 2003), 21–24.

[26] Cabinet Office, "Statement by the Chief Cabinet Secretary," December 10, 2004.

[27] Inadequate legal authorities and lingering regional concerns have prevented the MSDF from playing a major role in PSI.

[28] Barbara Wanner, "Obuchi under Pressure from JDA Official's Gaffe," *Japan Economic Institute Report*, no. 41B (October 29, 1999): 4–7.

[29] Michael J. Green, "Preparing for New Teams in Tokyo and Washington . . . and a Muddy Field in Both Capitals," *Comparative Connections* 2, no. 4 (October–December 2000): 13–18.

[30] In April 2000, Mori stated he would like to pass the emergency legislation and ease restrictions on SDF peacekeepers. Michael J. Green, "Security and Economic Ties Stabilize before the Okinawa Summit," *Comparative Connections* 2, no. 2 (April–June 2000): 20–25.

[31] Michael J. Green, "Small but Important Steps," *Comparative Connections* 2, no. 3 (July–September 2000): 23–29.

[32] Green, "Preparing for New Teams in Tokyo and Washington."

[33] SDF peacekeepers were ultimately dispatched to East Timor in February 2002. Michael J. Green, "The Security Treaty at 40—Strong but with Complaints about Back Pain," *Comparative Connections* 2, no. 1 (January–March 2000): 17–23.

[34] Japan Defense Agency, *Defense of Japan 2001*, 336.

[35] Ibid., 293–299.

[36] Green, *Japan's Reluctant Realism*, 33.

[37] Ralph A. Cossa, "U.S.-Japan Defense Cooperation: Can/Should Japan Become the Britain of Asia," (paper presented at conference of the Asia-Pacific Research Center, Stanford University, California, January 14, 2004).

3

Elite and Public Opinion:
Creeping Realism

Counterfactual analysis revealed that Tokyo's post–September 11 defense policy falls somewhere short of strategic change. Examining elite and public opinion provides a more nuanced understanding of Japan's strategic evolution. The larger populace and the political class exhibit creeping realism: both groups are gradually adopting realpolitik attitudes toward national security. Not surprisingly, this pragmatism has made greater inroads among elites than the public. In both cases, creeping realism has weakened the pacifist norms that traditionally constrained Japan's defense policy. However, elite and public opinion have not surpassed key benchmarks of strategic change. Insufficient support exists within the Diet to amend Article 9. Likewise, a minority of the public favor revising Japan's constitution for this purpose. Most elites continue to view nuclear weapons unfavorably. And a growing, but small percentage of Japan's population want to strengthen the SDF.

Creeping realism is the product of two factors—foreign policy shocks and generational change. International crises, particularly the North Korean nuclear program, have heightened the public's sense of insecurity. Elite references to preemption indicate that Japanese politicians are similarly concerned by foreign threats. Generational change operates differently at the elite and mass levels of Japanese society. The conventional understanding of generational change applies only to elites: young politicians are more supportive of a "normal" defense policy than their elders. Among the general public, young Japanese are neither as left-wing nor as nationalistic as is commonly assumed. More important, in the past decade the older generation has become considerably more pragmatic on multiple security issues.

Elite Conceptions of Security

To what degree have elite conceptions of security actually changed? Have new loaded terms entered high-level discourse on national defense? Have Article 9 and acquiring nuclear weapons—once contentious security issues—become items of elite consensus? In reality, the evolution of elite views has been incremental. Japanese elites do approach national security more pragmatically than ever before. Indeed, the loaded terms featured in contemporary political dialogue—national interest and preemption—might have sprung from a realist primer on international relations. However, the use of these terms has not coincided with sudden consensus on key defense issues. Less than two-thirds of Diet members support revising Article 9. Moreover, despite rhetoric by prominent Japanese politicians, elites as a whole strongly oppose acquiring nuclear weapons. Finally, conceptions of security have evolved along generational lines: pragmatic views on national defense largely characterize younger elites while older politicians remain more pacifist.

A New Language of Security

Articulating a defense strategy requires a language of security. Loaded terms constitute this language's vocabulary. Since the late 1990s, several loaded terms have entered Japan's strategic lexicon. These phrases—national interest and preemption—provide a new framework for elite discussion of national defense.

National Interest. References to national interest constitute a new development in Japanese discourse on security.[1] As an academic loaded term, *national interest* implies a host of realist assumptions concerning state-to-state relations and the international system. However, the term *national interest* bears a special meaning in the Japanese context. Diet members began referring to national interest in the wake of the 1998 Taepo-dong flyover. The term was, and still is, used in contrast to *taibei tsuizui gaikou*, a diplomatic policy of blindly following Washington's lead. In effect, the concept of national interest connotes a policy of pursuing Japan's self-interest even if, at times, Japan's national interest should deviate from that of the United States.

And yet, except for the notion that Japan's national interest is sometimes separate from that of other countries, the term lacks a uniform definition.[2] No common agreement exists among elites as to what Japan's national interest entails. In fact, national interest is simultaneously a loaded term and a buzzword. When used by policy-oriented Diet members—often young lawmakers in the LDP and DPJ—the term loosely corresponds to the academic definition of national interest. In the case of the LDP, however, the term may also contain nationalist overtones.[3] On the other hand, Japanese politicians also employ national interest as a form of rhetoric. For example, when justifying the SDF's dispatch to southern Iraq, Prime Minister Koizumi told the Japanese press that the "reconstruction and stability of Iraq will be directly related to Japan's national interest."[4] Alternatively, during speeches and interviews, politicians may refer to national interest out of a desire to appear intellectual.

Politicians who refrain from using the term national interest may actually provide more valuable insights into elite conceptions of security. Tellingly, government officials seldom refer to national interest in public. Even young, policy-oriented lawmakers, after obtaining senior government positions, become more discreet in their usage of national interest. If they publicly refer to national interest, the term is usually a buzzword. Furthermore, Diet members from the older generation rarely speak of Japan's national interest. Reluctance to use the term stems from Japan's prewar legacy, when *kokutai*—a word associated with national interest—was employed to mobilize the population to support imperialist policies.[5] The emergence of national interest as part of Japan's strategic lexicon thus signals a gradual rather than abrupt change in elite conceptions of security.

Preemption. Since September 11, *preemption* has appeared with increasing frequency in elite discourse. By encapsulating a military doctrine and specific capabilities, *preemption* represents a loaded term. Before North Korea's nuclear confession in late 2002, usage of the term preemption was limited to ultranationalists.[6] However, the dual threat posed by North Korea's nuclear weapons program and No-dong arsenal has catapulted preemption into the political mainstream. Shigeru Ishiba, then JDA director general, introduced the concept of preemption into respectable political circles while testifying before the Lower House Budget Committee in February 2003. Ishiba framed preemption as a form of self-defense, arguing that in an impending attack, Japan's constitution would permit a strike on North Korean missile sites.[7] Young lawmakers have been less cautious advocates of preemption. On June 23, 2003, a group of 103 junior Diet members issued a statement calling for a reexamination of Japan's "defense-only principle [in order] to adopt the option of empowering Japan to attack enemy bases . . . ."[8] Clearly, the idea of preemption has penetrated mainstream political discourse.

Preemption constitutes more than a catchphrase. First, Japanese elites understand the connotations of the term. According to Diet member Keizo Takemi, "preemptive attacks are an effective deterrent [against North Korea]."[9] Pragmatic Japanese politicians also recognize that preemption will require new capabilities such as cruise missiles.[10] Some elites in the foreign policy and defense bureaucracies hold similar views, though not publicly.[11] Second, advocating preemption is not politically profitable. Vigorously supporting preemption and the acquisition of cruise missiles might alienate constituents.[12] Consequently, Diet members who publicly refer to preemption do so out of a sincere desire to strengthen Japan's security, not for electoral advantage.

The Absence of Elite Consensus

According to some observers of Japan, "rising nationalism . . . has taken hold in one of America's closest allies."[13] Typically, this assertion is based on two trends: growing support for revising Article 9 and the emergence of an open debate on nuclear armament. Although both trends exist at the elite level, at present, neither constitutes a newfound consensus. In reality, Japanese politicians remain divided on the specifics of revising Article 9, and an overwhelming majority of Diet members oppose arming Japan with nuclear weapons.

Amending Article 9. Is constitutional revision imminent? That a supermajority of Diet members now favors constitutional reform is indisputable. Elite support for amending Japan's constitution has substantially increased over the past five years. According to a 2000 *Asahi Shimbun* poll, 29 percent of DPJ and New Komeito candidates backed a constitutional amendment. The corresponding figure for LDP candidates was 75 percent.[14] A survey conducted by *Mainichi Shimbun* in mid-2004 highlighted a dramatic shift in elite attitudes toward the constitution. Within the DPJ, New Komeito, and the LDP, support for amending the constitution stood at 73 percent, 80 percent, and 96 percent respectively. Altogether, the pro-revision camp encompassed 78 percent of legislators, well over the two-thirds majority required to modify Japan's supreme law.[15]

The emergence of a Diet consensus favorable to constitutional reform does not qualify per se as evidence for strategic change. Although elite opinion has clearly converged in favor of revising Japan's constitution, politicians are still divided over whether and how to amend Article 9. Altering the first paragraph of Article 9, the "war renunciation" clause, remains strictly taboo. According to a *Mainichi Shimbun* poll, in 2004 a mere 23 percent of Japanese lawmakers approved of rewording it. Support for revising Article 9's second paragraph also fell short of a supermajority, albeit by a narrow margin. In mid-2004, 57 percent of Diet members favored amending the second paragraph to clarify the SDF's status; 64 percent wanted to stipulate the SDF's international contribution in Article 9; and 55 percent advocated that Japan exercise the right of collective defense, presumably through constitutional reform rather than reinterpretation.[16]

The reports unveiled by the Lower and Upper House Constitutional Research Commissions in April 2005 testify to the difficulties that will attend any effort to amend Article 9. Maintaining the "war renunciation" clause constituted the only majority opinion to bridge the Lower and Upper House panels. The Upper House commission failed to achieve a consensus on embedding the SDF in Article 9, whereas two-thirds of the Lower House panel endorsed revising the second paragraph for this purpose. Even then, the Lower House panel offered a rather halfhearted opinion. It did "not deny taking some sort of constitutional means regarding the right to self-defense and the Self-Defense Forces."[17] Although acknowledging that Japan should participate in international activities, members of the Upper House panel were split over using Article 9 to emphasize the SDF's global security contribution. On the other hand, two-thirds of the Lower House panel called for an amendment to stipulate Japan's participation in UN collective security activities. Finally, both panels failed to arrive at a common understanding regarding the prohibition on collective defense.[18]

The number of lawmakers who favor amending Article 9 will likely surpass the two-thirds threshold in the coming years. Still, it is unclear whether revising Article 9 will result in a strategic-level change, particularly if New Komeito continues to wield disproportionate influence as guarantor of the LDP's legislative majority. On the specifics of amending Article 9, New Komeito remains deeply out of step with the LDP. In mid-2004, 56 percent of New Komeito legislators opposed stipulating the SDF's existence in Article 9; 72 percent were against exercising the right of collective defense.[19] So long as the current political alignment endures, revisions to the text of Article 9, though symbolic, may have little real impact on Japan's defense policy.[20]

The Nuclear Option. An elite consensus favoring the acquisition of nuclear weapons would clearly presage a strategic change in Japan's defense policy. Yet, proof of such a consensus is generally lacking. Outside predictions of a nuclear-armed Japan have cited then Chief Cabinet Secretary Yasuo Fukuda's public assertion that Article 9 does not preclude the possession of nuclear weapons.[21] Ichiro Ozawa, head of the Liberal Party before its merger with the DPJ, has further fueled the rising chorus of Japan watchers who foresee Tokyo's eventual acquisition of nuclear arms. At a speaking engagement in April 2002, Ozawa stated that, to counter China's superpower ambitions, "it would be so easy for us to produce nuclear warheads . . . ."[22] Finally, some right-wing intellectuals have begun to call for exercising the nuclear option. Most notably, in "A Nuclear Declaration for Japan," Kyoto University professor Terumasa Nakanishi and literary critic Kazuya Fukuda asserted that "the best way for Japan to avoid being the target of North Korean nuclear missiles is for the prime minister to declare without delay that Japan will arm itself with nuclear weapons."[23]

The level of domestic debate surrounding Japan's nuclear option is historically unprecedented. Japan's "nuclear allergy," the taboo that once forestalled mere discussion of nuclear weapons, has largely evaporated in the face of growing external threats. As a result, government elites who advocate nuclear

weapons need no longer fear public disgrace and forced resigna-
tion.[24] Still, discussing the nuclear option does not inherently foreshadow acquisition. Despite increased public debate on nuclear
weapons, most Diet members view exercising the nuclear option
unfavorably. According to a 2004 Kyodo News survey, 78.5 percent of lawmakers believed that Japan should not revise the Three
Nonnuclear Principles.[25]

Ultimately, Japan's national interest will foreclose the nuclear
option. A decision by Tokyo to develop a nuclear arsenal would
generate alarm throughout East Asia. The security costs of acquiring nuclear weapons might be extreme. At a minimum, China
would likely respond by deploying larger numbers of ICBMs, initiating a nuclear arms race with Japan. South Korea, as the remaining nonnuclear power in Northeast Asia, might be compelled to
embark on a crash nuclear weapons program.[26] More immediately, a Japanese decision to acquire nuclear weapons would dash
any hope of peacefully eliminating North Korea's nuclear arsenal.

That considerations of national interest justify forgoing
nuclear armaments represents a significant aspect of Japan's
emerging nuclear debate. Japanese defense planners have traditionally opposed nuclear weapons on the grounds that such arms
would undermine rather than increase Tokyo's security.[27] Likewise, politicians have long eschewed nuclear weapons, but for a
different reason. External and internalized norms rendered the
nuclear option unsupportable. External norms, the public's
"nuclear allergy," have weakened in recent years. Equally important is that internalized norms may no longer shape elite views on
the nuclear issue. To a degree, pragmatic considerations of national interest now dictate elite perceptions of nuclear arms. In
short, elite attitudes toward nuclear weapons exhibit the same
creeping realism that characterizes most other aspects of Japan's
defense policy.

Generational Change and Elite Opinion

Generational change at the elite level of Japanese society is well
documented. The most definitive work on this subject—*Generational Change in Japan: Its Implications for U.S.-Japan Relations*, a
2002 report by the Center for Strategic and International Studies
(CSIS)—modifies the previously accepted generational hypothesis:

that young elites were significantly more nationalistic than their elders and less inclined to support U.S. interests and policies. Arguing that "generational differences of opinion in Japan are subtle and represent a gradual evolution rather than a sharp change," the report correctly characterizes nationalism on the part of young elites as an assertion of Japanese identity rather than a form of xenophobic sentiment. The report also notes that young elites, though supportive of the U.S.-Japan security structure, are more aggressive than the older generation in pursuing an equal alliance partnership.[28] Finally, the report claims that young elites lack a sense of historical shame over Japan's wartime conduct and thus view defense issues with fewer inhibitions.

Building upon the findings of this report, to what extent is generational change manifested in elite usage of loaded terms? References to national interest and preemption are indeed a generational phenomenon. When not in government, Shigeru Ishiba, Seiji Maehara, and Yasukazu Hamada represent Japan's foremost proponents of national interest.[29] All three of these Diet members belong to the "Young Turks," the generation of elites born after 1952. Indeed, usage of the term *national interest* extends to the Young Turks as a whole. Still, the relationship between generational change and national interest deserves one caveat. Elites from the older generation generally refrain from using the term national interest. Yet internally, older elites may view national security from an increasingly realist perspective.

Like national interest, *preemption* constitutes a loaded term primarily used by young elites. Public advocates of preemption—Shigeru Ishiba and Keizo Takemi—belong to Japan's Young Turks generation.[30] Most strikingly, in the Diet the largest base of support for preemption is a nonpartisan defense study group conducted by young lawmakers. The group's formation testifies to the younger generation's growing interest in national security. Founded in November 2001 as a forum to discuss the prohibition on collective defense, the group's membership totaled 103 lawmakers by July 2003—at the time a majority of Diet members under age 60. Clearly, the study group's flourishing membership reflects generational change. At the same time, the group's rapid expansion has been facilitated by external threats, chiefly North Korea.[31] The growing realism of elites thus results from *both* generational change and foreign policy shocks.

However, on Article 9 and nuclear weapons, a generational dynamic is less evident at the elite level. Historically, lawmakers from the younger generation have been marginally more support-ive of revising Article 9. In 2003, attitudes toward amending the peace clause exhibited a modest generational gap. Approximately 56 percent of the Diet's membership favored revising the constitu-tion to define the SDF.[32] The figure for lawmakers in their twenties and thirties was 60 percent.[33] Furthermore, young elites are no more likely than their elders to advocate the nuclear option. When queried by *Asahi Shimbun* in mid-2003, some 80 percent of law-makers under age 30 opposed acquiring nuclear weapons.[34] This figure closely matched the level of opposition among Diet mem-bers as a whole. Although the younger generation conceives na-tional defense in a more realist light, these elites do not signifi-cantly deviate from their elders on the issues that fundamentally determine Japan's national strategy.

Public Attitudes toward Defense

A major shift in public attitudes toward defense should character-ize strategic change. Does Japan meet this criterion? Not as mea-sured by popular opinion surveys. The public's view of the SDF has remained largely constant: most Japanese continue to favor the SDF's present capabilities and budget. Beginning in 2004, public support for constitutional revision repeatedly surpassed the 50 percent threshold needed to realize an amendment. How-ever, according to most opinion surveys, those who advocate re-vising Article 9 are still in the minority. Indeed, threat perceptions constitute the one area where public attitudes have undergone a major shift.

The impact of generational change on public conceptions of security is more complex than many Japan watchers have previ-ously assumed. Though still relatively pacifist, Japan's youth are sensitive to foreign threats, and a growing percentage hold prag-matic views on national defense. The elderly, a group regularly excluded from generational hypotheses, have, to a considerable extent, joined the burgeoning ranks of Japanese adherents to realpolitik.

The Self-Defense Force

At first glance, Japanese popular opinion appears to defy realist expectations. Although the public has experienced high levels of insecurity during the past four years, a large majority of the population still supports maintaining the SDF at its current force level and budget. According to triennial surveys conducted by the Cabinet Office, since 1988 more than 60 percent of Japanese poll respondents have favored "the SDF's current force size" (see figure 3.1). This majority actually increased to 66 percent in the years following the 1998 Taepo-dong flyover. Despite North Korea's announced departure from the NPT five months earlier, in mid-2003 public support for the status quo defense posture was only five points below public support in 2000.[35] Yet, a shift in popular attitudes has occurred at the margins of the majority opinion. Although still a small percentage of the general public, proponents of strengthening the SDF more than doubled from 7.5 percent in 1997 to 16 percent in 2003. Over the same time period, the number of Japanese who support downgrading the SDF's capabilities halved to 8.4 percent of the population.

These developments, characterizing only a small fraction of the populace, do not exceed any reasonable threshold of strategic change. However, when viewed in a historical context, changes in public opinion toward the SDF are nonetheless significant. Throughout the mid-1980s and the first half of the 1990s, a sizeable minority of Japanese favored a smaller defense capability. This minority peaked in 1991 at 20 percent of the population. The number of poll respondents who supported enhancing SDF capabilities declined over the same 10 years. Notably, the 1994 North Korean nuclear crisis constituted an inflection point in popular views of the SDF. From then on, public opinion underwent a decisive reversal: support for strengthening the SDF gradually increased, and fewer poll respondents found a smaller defense capability desirable.

Poll data on the SDF illustrate a nascent shift in Japanese attitudes toward national security: the public's view of defense increasingly tends toward pragmatism. To borrow a phrase from international relations theory, a small but growing percentage of the public are realists. The emergence of realists among the population is particularly remarkable given Japan's economic difficulties.

Figure 3.1. Poll: The Correct SDF Force Level

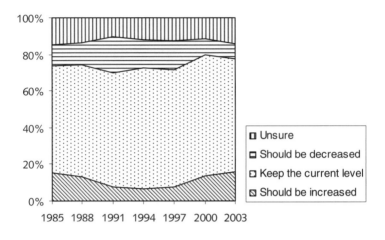

Source: Cabinet Office, "Jieitai-bouei mondai ni kan suru seronchousa," 1985–2003.

Despite an imploding pension system and huge government deficits, an increasing number of Japanese believe that their government should devote greater resources to national defense.

Constitutional Revision

Of all public opinion measures, poll data on constitutional revision are potentially most related to strategic change. Even if reflected in government policies, public support for strengthening the SDF does not automatically entail a strategic-level shift. Indeed, Japan's defense capabilities expanded throughout the 1980s without a change in national strategy. On the other hand, heightened popular sentiment for revising Article 9 could lead to a broadening of Japan's strategic options.

During the last two years, public support for constitutional reform has consistently exceeded the 50 percent threshold needed for a successful national referendum (see figure 3.2).[36] Still, popular backing for revising Japan's supreme law does not necessarily translate into approval for amending Article 9. Compared with constitutional reform, evaluating public opinion toward Japan's peace clause is a complex, often frustrating endeavor. Newspaper polls typically ask respondents a simple "yes or no" question to

Figure 3.2. Poll: Support for Constitutional Revision

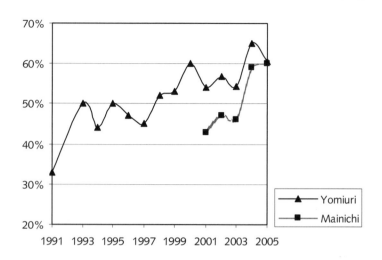

Sources: "Poll on Japan's Constitution," *Yomiuri Shimbun*, 1991–2005; poll questions on constitutional revision from *Mainichi Shimbun*, 2001–2005.

determine public support for constitutional revision, while more than three types of survey questions permit respondents to express an opinion on Article 9.

The first and most widely used question asks survey participants to pick multiple reasons for amending the constitution. Usually, the set of responses includes a variation of the statement, "the Self-Defense Forces' status should be defined."[37] In all newspapers, this query applies only to the subset of respondents who support constitutional reform. Since 2002, *Yomiuri Shimbun* polls have incorporated a separate question on Article 9 that directs respondents to choose among three options: continued reinterpretation of Article 9, amending Article 9, and strictly abiding by Japan's constitution. More recently, *Mainichi Shimbun* and *Asahi Shimbun* began directly querying poll recipients on the peace clause.

The third type of question, also pioneered by *Yomiuri Shimbun*, relates to the prohibition on collective defense. Unfortunately, *Yomiuri Shimbun* allows respondents to equivocate on amending Article 9: "The Constitution should be amended *or* [italics mine] reinterpreted so that Japan can use the right of collective self-defense."[38] The ambiguity of this question is indicative of the larger problem Japan watchers encounter when analyzing public attitudes on the constitution. A significant number of Japanese may oppose constitutional revision but support reinterpreting Article 9. Conversely, some Japanese may object to reinterpretation but welcome future amendments.

Nonetheless, available poll data do provide insight, albeit limited, on public attitudes toward amending Article 9. According to *Yomiuri Shimbun*, the number of respondents who identified "stipulating Japan's right of self-defense and the SDF" as a rationale for revision grew from 19 percent in 2001 to 27 percent in 2005. However, these percentages are based on the subset of respondents who favored amending the constitution. When normalized as a percentage of all survey participants, the *Yomiuri Shimbun* data suggest that only a small minority of Japanese support constitutional revision out of a desire to amend Article 9. This proportion grew a mere five points between 2001 and 2005—from 10 percent to 16 percent of all poll recipients.[39]

When asked directly about Article 9, a much higher proportion of Japanese appear to favor an amendment. In 2005, 43.6 percent of *Yomiuri Shimbun* survey participants answered: "The government's conventional way of responding to problems with its interpretation and operation has now reached its limit, so Article 9 should be amended."[40] Yet, whether the proportion of poll respondents in favor of revising Article 9 has surpassed a simple majority remains uncertain. In the case of Article 9, the phrasing of a particular question significantly influences poll results. Although 43.6 percent of *Yomiuri Shimbun* respondents supported amending Article 9, a 2005 *Mainichi Shimbun* poll cited a substantially lower figure. Unlike *Yomiuri Shimbun*, *Mainichi Shimbun* employed separate questions regarding each clause of Article 9. Some 22.2 percent of poll recipients supported revisions to the "war renunciation" clause, while 34.8 percent backed amending the second paragraph to clarify the SDF's status.[41]

Even within the same survey, word choice can yield divergent results for similar questions. In a 2005 *Asahi Shimbun* poll, 36 percent of participants approved of an amendment when asked, "Do you think it would be better to change Article 9?" But in response to an earlier question, "Which is closest to your opinion about Article 9 and the SDF?" 58 percent of survey recipients selected, "It's all right to retain the SDF, but its existence should be expressly stipulated in a revised constitution."[42] Except for this one instance, all other polls suggest that Japanese who favor revising Article 9 still constitute a minority.

Does popular support for modifying Article 9 at least correlate to recent foreign policy shocks? No. In the four years *Yomiuri Shimbun* has devoted questions directly to Article 9 and collective defense, public attitudes have displayed surprisingly little variation. From 2002 onward, popular support for revising Article 9 has fluctuated between 40 percent and 45 percent. The number of poll recipients who favor exercising the right of collective defense has actually declined by five points, from a high of 35.2 percent in 2002 to 30.5 percent in 2005.[43] Interestingly, popular support for ending the ban on collective defense began to decline following the Iraq War.

Public Insecurity and Foreign Threats

Among measures of popular opinion, only the public's perception of foreign threats has undergone a definitive change. In 1997, the number of poll respondents who believed "the danger of becoming embroiled in war exists" stood at 21.1 percent. By 2003, this number reached 43 percent (see figure 3.3). When combined with individuals who expressed milder concern regarding foreign threats, this number becomes 80 percent of poll respondents. At the same time, survey participants who believed "no danger of war exists" declined precipitously from 30 percent in 1997 to 10 percent in 2003. This level of public anxiety is historically unprecedented. From 1969 to the end of the Cold War, no more than 30 percent of Japan's population ever acknowledged that "the danger of becoming embroiled in war exists."[44]

Heightened public anxiety, however, does not constitute evidence for a strategic shift. Threat perceptions must first influence other popular attitudes that relate more closely to national strategy. As yet, these attitudes—support for strengthening the SDF and revising Article 9—characterize a minority of Japan's population, a far cry from the 80 percent who at some level fear involvement in armed conflict. Why such an asymmetry? Public anxiety derives largely from the North Korean threat. To most poll respondents, neither building up the SDF nor altering Article 9 will clearly mitigate this danger. If directly queried on BMD and

Figure 3.3. Poll: Japan's Risk of Becoming Involved in a War

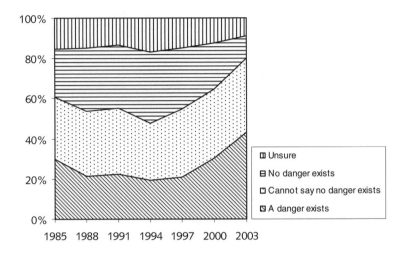

Source: Cabinet Office, "Jieitai-bouei mondai ni kan suru seronchousa," 1997–2003.

preemption, the public might increasingly support these and other policies that unambiguously target Pyongyang.

Generational Change and Public Opinion: A New Hypothesis

To what extent will generational change contribute to new public conceptions of security? In the case of Japan's defense policy, the relationship between generational turnover and public opinion is the subject of contending arguments. Some Japanese elites believe that generational change will lead to more pragmatic views of national security.[45] They argue that unlike individuals born before and immediately after World War II, Japan's youth feel no responsibility for their nation's wartime conduct. Hence, Japanese under age 30 support a "normal" defense policy and, according to some observers, are increasingly nationalistic. The alternative hypothesis, advocated by scholars and elites alike, argues the reverse. This hypothesis claims that younger generations lack a sense of patriotism and exhibit scant interest in issues pertaining to national security.[46]

In reality, neither of these contending hypotheses accurately depicts the complexity of generational change. By all tangible measures, Japan's youth are less nationalistic than their parents and grandparents. In 2003, 22.6 percent of poll respondents under age 30 identified their "feeling to protect the country" as strong, while 26.8 percent professed weak national sentiment. Among the general population, these numbers were 48 percent and 11.4 percent respectively. Lack of patriotic feeling may be particularly ingrained in young Japanese. Between 1997 and 2003—a period of growing foreign threats—the will to defend Japan actually declined by 10 points among 20 to 30 year olds.[47] Clearly, generational change will not lead to an upsurge of Japanese nationalism.

Yet, in the case of Japan, patriotism is not a prerequisite for growing pragmatism on most defense issues. During the last six years, Japan's youth have adopted more conservative views of national security. In fact, young Japanese perceive foreign threats more acutely than their elders. Even before the 1998 Taepo-dong launch, 29.5 percent of Japanese in their twenties believed "the danger of becoming embroiled in war exists." By comparison, the 1997 average for all other age cohorts was 20 percent. Moreover, the youngest generation has shared in the general public's heightened sense of insecurity. As of 2003, 45.1 percent of Japan's youth expressed concern over foreign threats, two points above the national average. In contrast to common assumptions, Japanese in their twenties are keenly aware of foreign threats.

With respect to strengthening the SDF, Japan's youth remain more left-wing than other segments of the population. In 2003, 9.8 percent of respondents below age 30 favored expanding the SDF's capabilities. Average popular support stood at 15.8 percent.[48] Yet, the youngest generation's view of the SDF has become more pragmatic since 1997 (see figure 3.4). The last six years witnessed a doubling in the number of young respondents who favored strengthening the SDF. At the same time, among Japanese in their twenties, support for downgrading the SDF's capabilities declined from 16.8 percent to 8.5 percent. When analyzed as growth rates, these changes match similar shifts in the total population.[49] Young Japanese, though still relatively liberal, are no less receptive to the trend of creeping realism than the general population.

Observers of Japan often cite constitutional revision as an issue that highlights the younger generation's emergent nationalism.

Figure 3.4. Poll: Support for Strengthening the SDF

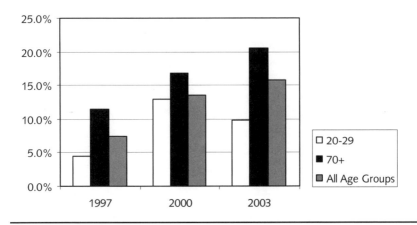

Source: Cabinet Office, "Jieitai-bouei mondai ni kan suru seronchousa," 1997–2003.

They argue that the younger generation, unburdened by war guilt, possesses fewer misgivings about revising Article 9. Poll data demonstrate the fallacy of this claim. Young *and* middle-aged Japanese are more inclined to amend the peace clause than other age cohorts. By 2005, 50.9 percent, 45.5 percent, and 48.6 percent of poll respondents in their thirties, forties, and fifties favored revising Article 9. The corresponding figure for 20 to 29 year olds was 47.2 percent.[50] If support for amending Article 9 signifies resurgent nationalism, the youngest generation is no more prone to such sentiment than other Japanese born after World War II.

Ironically, current hypotheses of generational change usually ignore the fastest growing segment of Japanese society—individuals over age 65.[51] This age cohort has been overlooked because most generational arguments focus on elites. Unofficial age limits guarantee that the political influence of older lawmakers must inevitably decline. Therefore, articulations of generational change at the elite level generally center on politicians under age 50. However, this model of generational change cannot be applied to the population at large. In fact, Japan's demographic trends mean precisely the opposite. In the future, the old rather than the young will exert growing political clout. First, the ranks of the elderly will continue to expand rapidly; by 2025, more than 28 percent of Japan's population is projected to be above age 65.[52] Second, older individuals vote with greater frequency than the youth. Although more than 70 percent of Japanese above age 60 participated in the 1996 Lower House elections, less than 40 percent of individuals in their twenties actually voted.[53] Clearly, the oldest segment of Japan's population will increasingly shape public opinion on defense issues.

How will the graying of Japan affect public conceptions of security? Those who are elderly and in late middle age have progressively embraced realpolitik attitudes toward national defense. On some security issues, individuals above age 50 actually hold more conservative opinions than the rest of the population. As of 2003, 20.5 percent of Japanese above age 70 supported expanding the SDF. Individuals in their sixties and fifties favored strengthening the SDF at rates of 17.2 percent and 18.5 percent respectively. In contrast, younger respondents averaged only 12 percent. Generational differences on strengthening the SDF have existed since at least 1997.[54] Although deepening public insecurity has not widened this divide, neither has it led to a convergence of popular opinion. Such generational variation may result from unique historical experiences—World War II and the aftermath of defeat—or instead reflect the structure of Japanese society. If generational differences arise from structural factors, then public opinion—elderly opinion—will increasingly support a more "normal" defense policy regardless of foreign threats.

Overlooking the elderly risks missing another significant trend. It is widely recognized that Japanese perceptions of China have hardened over the last 15 years. However, the most extreme shift in public attitudes toward the People's Republic of China (PRC) has occurred among the elderly. In the early 1990s, the elderly constituted the most pro-China segment of Japanese society. A Cabinet Office poll conducted in 1992 found that 64.5 percent of respondents over age 70 felt a "sense of closeness with China." Only 27.1 percent reported no positive attachment to the PRC. On the other hand, Japanese in their twenties viewed China with greater skepticism. In 1992, 46.4 percent attested to a "sense of closeness," whereas 50.4 percent regarded the PRC with ambivalence or ill feeling. Thus, at the beginning of the 1990s, a double-digit generation gap characterized popular perceptions of China.

Over little more than a decade, cross-generational attitudes toward China have partly converged (see figure 3.5). In December

Figure 3.5. Poll: No Feeling of Closeness with China

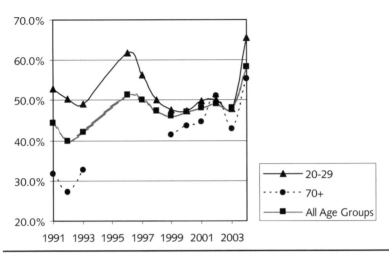

Source: Cabinet Office, "Gaikou ni kan suru seronchousa," 1992–2004.
Note: Cabinet Office polls between 1996 and 1998 do not contain an age 70+ category.

2004, 34.7 percent of Japanese in their seventies and 31.3 percent of 20 to 29 year olds viewed China favorably. At the same time, 55.3 percent of the oldest age bracket professed "no sense of closeness with China." The corresponding figure for Japanese in their twenties was 65.4 percent.[55] Although incomplete, this attitudinal convergence is striking. From 1992 onward, anti-Chinese sentiment within the 30-and-under age bracket grew by 30 percent. Yet, over the same time period, the number of elderly poll recipients expressing "no sense of closeness with China" increased by 104 percent.[56] Anti-Chinese sentiment has expanded among the elderly at a pace dwarfing that of any other age cohort.

To a degree, exogenous factors are responsible for the dramatic shift in the 70-and-above age bracket. Such factors include events like the 1995–1996 Taiwan Strait crisis, and, at a structural level, Beijing's relative gains in economic and military power. However, exogenous factors alone cannot explicate the rate—double that of the population average—at which anti-Chinese sentiment has taken root among the elderly.[57] Generational turnover within the oldest age bracket constitutes the missing, endogenous mechanism. In 1992, Japanese in their seventies and above shared a defining characteristic: all experienced World War II *as adults*. Residual war guilt translated into goodwill toward China.

By 2005, the war generation's share of the uppermost age bracket had declined to approximately 50 percent.[58] The remainder—individuals between ages 70 and 75—were children or teenagers in 1945, too young to bear direct responsibility for Japan's wartime conduct. Although sympathetic toward the PRC when compared with younger age cohorts, this demographic group is less subject to historical guilt than the preceding generation. Thus, as the children of World War II increasingly dominate the ranks of the elderly, anti-Chinese sentiment at the apex of Japan's demographic pyramid will become further entrenched.

What about the elderly and constitutional revision? Most hypotheses of generational change argue that the elderly are more resistant to amending Article 9 than other age groups. This assertion is correct. Indeed, polls on Article 9 highlight a seemingly unbridgeable divide between the elderly and Japanese under age 60. In 2005, respectively 30 percent and 38.5 percent of the uppermost age brackets favored revising the peace clause. The average for all other age cohorts—Japanese between ages 20 and 59—was 48 percent. Since *Yomiuri Shimbun* began directly questioning poll recipients on Article 9 in 2002, this generational gap has shown no sign of converging (see figure 3.6). In fact, the differential between Japanese in their sixties and fifties has actually grown from 3 points in 2002 to 10 points in 2005. Moreover, a generational divide exists even within the ranks of the elderly. Over the last four years, support for revising Article 9 among 60 year olds has, on average, exceeded support in the 70-and-above bracket by 8 points. Clearly, the older generation's growing realism has yet to affect attitudes toward Article 9.[59]

To conclude, how will generational change impact public conceptions of security and, by extension, Japan's defense strategy? With respect to Japan's youth, the effect will be minimal. Although still relatively liberal, young Japanese exhibit the creeping realism that characterizes popular opinion as a whole. Certainly, Japan's youth will not provide the vanguard for a new nationalist movement. For those in their sixties and seventies, generational variation may have a greater impact on future defense policies. Except for Article 9, Japanese above age 60 exert a conservative influence on public views of defense, an influence that will expand as the ranks of the elderly swell throughout the first half of this century.

Figure 3.6. Poll: Support for Amending Article 9

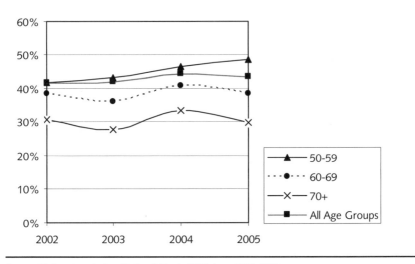

Source: "Poll on Japan's Constitution," *Yomiuri Shimbun*, 2002–2005.

Toward a "Normal" Nation: The End of Creeping Realism

Will creeping realism characterize Japan's defense policy in the future? Yes, in the short term. But most trends examined in this chapter indicate that in the mid to long term, scholars will no longer employ moderating adjectives to describe Japan's national strategy. If current patterns of generational change continue, creeping realism will accelerate as the decade progresses. Indeed, the older generation's departure from politics renders the acceleration of creeping realism all but inevitable. Likewise, the aging of Japan's society cannot be reversed short of massive immigration. Moreover, from Japan's perspective, the security environment in Northeast Asia is unlikely to improve. A solution to the North Korean nuclear crisis appears distant. Ultimately, many of Japan's neighbors might be willing to live with a nuclear North Korea rather than risk war on the peninsula. Such a scenario would greatly magnify the public's sense of insecurity.

Regardless of the North Korean endgame, the rise of China will prove a constant concern to both elites and the public. As Japan declines in relative military, political, and economic power, its citizens and leaders will increasingly favor a pragmatic defense strategy. In short, the momentum provided by demographics and external threats will accelerate Japan's becoming a "normal" nation.

Notes

[1] E-mail correspondence with former foreign service national at U.S. Embassy Tokyo, January 4, 2004.

[2] Author's interview with Japanese academic, Tokyo, July 2003.

[3] E-mail correspondence with Japanese academic, January 6, 2004.

[4] Koizumi quoted in "It's Official: Ishiba Orders Ground Troops to Iraq," *Asahi Shimbun*, January 10, 2004.

[5] *Kokutai* is usually translated as "national polity." The phrase connotes that the well-being of the state comes before that of the individual.

[6] Eugene A. Matthews, "Japan's New Nationalism," *Foreign Affairs* 82, no. 6 (November/December 2003): 75.

[7] Richard Beeston, "Nervous Japan Tells North Korea It Will Strike First," *Financial Times*, February 14, 2003.

[8] "Non-partisan Lawmakers' Statement Calling for a Review of Exclusively Defense-Oriented Defense Policy and of Right to Collective Self-Defense Causes a Stir," *Asahi Shimbun*, July 3, 2003.

[9] Ibid.

[10] Author's interview with LDP Upper House member, Tokyo, July 2003.

[11] Author's interviews with MOFA official, Tokyo, August 2003, and with SDF officer, Tokyo, March 2004.

[12] Author's interviews with DPJ Upper House member, Tokyo, July 2003, and with LDP Upper House member, Tokyo, August 2003.

[13] Matthews, "Japan's New Nationalism," 75.

[14] Poll described in "Support for New Constitution," *Asahi Shimbun*, November 4, 2003.

[15] Untitled poll, *Mainichi Shimbun*, May 3, 2004, http://www.k3.dion.ne.jp/~keporin/sinbun/yoron/mainichi160503.htm.

[16] Ibid.

[17] Tetsushi Kajimoto, "Change Constitution: Lower House Report," *Japan Times*, April 16, 2005.

[18] "Upper House Panel Split on Putting SDF Clause in Constitution," *Kyodo News*, April 20, 2005.

[19] Untitled poll, *Mainichi Shimbun*, May 3, 2004.

[20] Ibid.

[21] Robyn Lim, "So Much for Japan's Nuclear Taboo; Worried by China and North Korea," *International Herald Tribune*, June 13, 2002.

[22] Brendan Pearson, "Japan Uneasy over Dragon's Rise," *Australian Financial Review*, April 15, 2002.

[23] Terumasa Nakanishi and Kazuya Fukuda's "A Nuclear Declaration for Japan," quoted in Matthews, "Japan's New Nationalism," 82.

[24] Sheila A. Smith, "Japan's Future Strategic Options and the U.S.-Japan Alliance," in *Japan's Nuclear Option: Security, Politics, and Policy in the 21st Century*, ed. Benjamin L. Self and Jeffrey W. Thompson (Washington, D.C.: Henry L. Stimson Center, December 2003), 20.

[25] See "85% of Lawmakers Support Revising the Constitution," *Japan Times*, September 5, 2004.

[26] Similar arguments are made by Andrew L. Oros, "Godzilla's Return: The New Nuclear Politics in an Insecure Japan," in *Japan's Nuclear Option: Security, Politics, and Policy in the 21st Century*, ed. Benjamin L. Self and Jeffrey W. Thompson (Washington, D.C.: Henry L. Stimson Center, December 2003).

[27] Smith, "Japan's Future Strategic Options," 20.

[28] Center for Strategic and International Studies (CSIS), *Generational Change in Japan: Its Implications for U.S.-Japan Relations* (Washington, D.C.: CSIS, August 2002), 4.

[29] E-mail correspondence with a former foreign service national at U.S. Embassy Tokyo, January 4, 2004.

[30] Keizo Takemi was born in 1951. However, his stance on defense policies better qualifies him as a member of the Young Turks than the older generation of Diet members.

[31] "Non-partisan Lawmakers' Statement"; author's interview with LDP Upper House member, Tokyo, August 2003.

[32] Calculation based on a poll described in "Support for New Constitution," *Asahi Shimbun*, November 4, 2003.

[33] See "60 Percent of Young Lawmakers for Revising Constitution's Article 9," *Kyodo News Service*, June 9, 2003.

[34] Ibid.

[35] Cabinet Office, "Jieitai-bouei mondai ni kan suru seronchousa" (Opinion poll concerning the SDF and defense problems), in *Gekkan Seronchousa 29* (Public Opinion Poll Monthly), no. 10 (October 1997); and Cabinet Office, "Jieitai-bouei mondai ni kan suru seronchousa," in *Gekkan Seronchousa 35*, no. 6 (June 2003).

[36] "Poll on Japan's Constitution," *Yomiuri Shimbun*, April 8, 2005; untitled poll, *Mainichi Shimbun*, April 20, 2005.

[37] "Poll on Constitutional Revision," *Mainichi Shimbun*, September 29, 2003; and "Poll on Japan's Constitution," *Yomiuri Shimbun*, April 2, 2003.

[38] "Poll on Japan's Constitution," *Yomiuri Shimbun*, April 2, 2003.

[39] I arrived at these figures by multiplying the percentage of respondents who supported constitutional revision by the subset of respondents who favored defining the SDF through an amendment.

[40] "Poll on Japan's Constitution," *Yomiuri Shimbun*, April 8, 2005.

[41] These figures are adjusted as a percentage of all respondents. Untitled poll, *Mainichi Shimbun*, April 20, 2005.

[42] "Poll on Japan's Postwar Constitution," *Asahi Shimbun*, May 3, 2005.

[43] "Poll on Japan's Constitution," *Yomiuri Shimbun*, 2002–2005.

[44] Surveys predating 1969 do not contain data on foreign threats. All statistics on public threat perceptions are contained in Cabinet Office, "Jieitai-bouei mondai," 1997–2003.

[45] Author's interviews with Japanese academics, Tokyo, July 2003.

[46] CSIS, *Generational Change in Japan*, 6, 8–9, 12.

[47] Cabinet Office, "Jieitai-bouei mondai," 1997–2003.

[48] A similar age gap existed for poll questions on expanding the defense budget.

[49] Between 1997 and 2003, support for strengthening the SDF grew 117 percent among 20–29 year olds and 111 percent among the total population. The number of respondents who wanted to reduce the SDF's capabilities declined by 49 percent for individuals in their twenties and 46 percent for the general public. Cabinet Office, "Jieitai-bouei mondai," 1997–2003.

[50] "Poll on Japan's Constitution," *Yomiuri Shimbun*, April 8, 2005

[51] Sidney B. Westley, "Asia's Next Challenge: Caring for the Elderly," East-West Center's *Asia-Pacific Population and Policy*, no. 45 (April 1998): 1–2.

[52] "Table 1: Projected Future Population and Proportion by Age Group, 2000–2050: Medium Variant," in *Population Projections for Japan: 2001–2050* (Tokyo: National Institute of Population and Social Security Research, January 2002).

[53] These figures are for the Tokyo area. Andrew Saidel, "Japan 2003: The Politics of Aging," *AARP Global Aging Program*, September 25, 2003.

[54] Polls before 1997 do not contain a demographic breakdown of responses.

[55] Data on public attitudes toward China are from Cabinet Office, "Gaikou ni kan suru seronchousa" (Opinion poll concerning diplomacy), in *Gekkan Seronchousa* 25, no. 4 (April 1992); and Cabinet Office, "Gaikou ni kan

suru seronchousa," December 2004, http://www8.cao.go.jp/survey/h16/h16-gaikou/index.html.

[56] Calculations based on data from Cabinet Office, "Gaikou ni kan suru seronchousa," 1992–2004.

[57] Between 1992 and 2005, the proportion of total poll respondents who selected "no sense of closeness with China" increased 46 percent.

[58] Calculation based on data from Japan Statistical Yearbook, "Population by Age: 1920–2003," 2005, http://www.stat.go.jp/data/nenkan/zuhyou/y0206007.xls.

[59] Calculations based on "Poll on Japan's Constitution," *Yomiuri Shimbun*, 1998–2005.

4

Japan and September 11

Introduction: A Transitional Model

Japan's strategic transition is incomplete. Although increasingly realist in outlook, Tokyo's security policy remains subject to enduring, albeit weakened normative constraints. Nonetheless, the changes detailed in past chapters are significant. Since 2001 the SDF's roles and missions have expanded at an unprecedented rate. At the same time, a growing proportion of elites and the public have adopted more pragmatic views of national security. Furthermore, amending Article 9 is more or less an agenda item for all the major political parties. This transition from a norms-based to interest-based security policy is unlikely to reverse. Both demographics and geopolitical trends will continue to erode the normative foundations of Tokyo's defense strategy. And yet, a fundamental question remains unanswered: What variables underlie Japan's strategic evolution?

Tokyo's strategic transition is predicated on four factors: foreign threats, U.S. policy, prime ministerial leadership, and generational change. Together, these particular variables constitute a transitional model that optimizes the tradeoff between analytical parsimony and real-world accuracy. External threats and Washington's influence are fundamentally distinct, though at times the impact of each on Japan's security behavior may be

interlinked. Executive leadership and generational change similarly exist as separate, independent variables. Political leadership
is ultimately based on idiosyncratic characteristics—namely,
popularity and tolerance for risk. Generational change is a unique
structural process. One factor excluded from the transitional
model—public opinion—is significant. However, popular sentiment represents an intervening variable between foreign threats
and specific defense initiatives rather than a fully independent
factor.

The transitional model should explain Tokyo's response to
multiple foreign policy shocks: September 11, the North Korean
threat (BMD), and the Iraq War and postconflict reconstruction.
This is not to say that the relative weight of each variable must
remain static: the four factors should evolve alongside Japan's defense strategy. Indeed, over time, new variables may supersede individual components of the transitional model.

Unpacking Japan's Response to September 11

What factors motivated Japan's security behavior in the aftermath
of September 11? Of the four factors, only U.S. policy and prime
ministerial leadership exerted a decisive influence. The impact of
foreign threats is ambiguous. In public, Koizumi argued that international terrorism endangered Japan. Yet the prime minister
belonged to a minority within the government. Whether threat
perceptions enhanced popular support for the antiterrorism legislation is equally opaque. Widespread concern that a terror attack
could occur in Japan might have inspired the public to favor Tokyo's
participation in Operation Enduring Freedom. On the other hand, a
majority of the population feared that SDF dispatch would bring
about Al Qaeda's retaliation. In this sense, threat perceptions might
have deterred public support for the antiterrorism bill.

During the aftermath of September 11, U.S. policy occupied
a prominent position in Japan's security calculus. Washington's
representatives initially refrained from articulating overt expectations of Japan. Behind closed doors, however, the United States in
effect did call upon Japan to "show the flag." These exhortations
may have been unnecessary. The humiliation of the 1991 Gulf War
and subsequent milestones in Japan's defense policy led Tokyo to

internalize U.S. and international expectations. As a result, officials in the Ministry of Foreign Affairs (MOFA) and the JDA challenged constitutional restraints in their haste to demonstrate Japan's commitment to the bilateral alliance and global security. In hindsight, however, U.S. expectations could not ensure the full, rapid implementation of Tokyo's promised assistance. For example, the MSDF fleet dispatched to the Indian Ocean lacked an Aegis destroyer. And the SDF's operations in Pakistan fell short of Japan's initial pledge.

Executive leadership, along with outside expectations, played a critical role in shaping Tokyo's contribution to the war on terror. Koizumi circumvented his government's standard foreign policy making procedures to expedite Japan's antiterrorism contribution. The prime minister also used speeches and summit diplomacy to direct *naiatsu* against opponents of his seven-point assistance package. The speed with which the antiterrorism legislation passed the Diet—the bill became law in less than one month— stands as another testament to the importance of executive leadership. Additionally, Koizumi defused regional anxieties stemming from SDF dispatch and ensured early deployment of Japanese ships to the Indian Ocean. However, two critiques can be made of Koizumi's leadership. First, the prime minister failed to completely implement his antiterrorism package, and second, his decisive role might have related to earlier administrative reforms rather than personality.

Generational change exerted a negligible influence over Japan's response to September 11. Although young lawmakers in the DPJ initially pressured the party's leadership to support the antiterrorism legislation, they ultimately followed party line and voted against the bill.

Foreign Threats: Ambivalence in an Age of Terror

To U.S. policymakers, September 11 heralded a new international paradigm. In the wake of the terrorist attacks on New York and Washington, nonstate actors displaced rogue nations as the most pressing threat to U.S. security. Mass casualties, high profile targets, and the resulting change in U.S. strategy meant that September 11 inaugurated an age of global terror. This new age in part represented a U.S. construct: hostile neighbors rather than Islamic terrorists continued to preoccupy many states. Thus—in addition to threat perceptions—alliances, ties of friendship, U.S. power, or mere expedience led many countries to join the antiterror coalition.

Did Tokyo perceive terrorism as an urgent security threat and accordingly embrace Washington's vision of a new global paradigm? Or, instead, do other factors better account for Japan's response to September 11? On the surface, the threat of terrorism appears to have partly motivated Japan's security behavior. Throughout the months following September 11, Koizumi reiterated that terrorism endangered the "lives and lifestyles of the people all over the world and the peace and security of all countries . . . ."[1] The prime minister also described the war on terror as Japan's "own challenge."[2] Such statements suggest that Koizumi considered Al Qaeda a threat to Japan.

The prime minister's apparent sense of alarm belied the Japanese government's mixed sentiment: only certain elements within the bureaucracy considered Al Qaeda a direct security threat. In contrast to other major powers—Britain and Russia, for example—Japan had never experienced Islamic terrorism. Tokyo's cordial relations with the Arab world and calibrated neutrality in the Israeli-Palestinian conflict rendered Japan an unlikely target. To many JDA officials and Diet members, terrorism therefore imperiled Japanese nationals abroad, but posed a minimal danger to the Japanese homeland. In fact, lawmakers sometimes appeared more concerned by the economic cost of fighting global terror than by Al Qaeda. Prominent members of the LDP worried that by "lead[ing] Arab nations to believe that Japan has provided heavy military assistance," MSDF deployment to the Indian Ocean would undermine Tokyo's oil interests in the Middle East.[3] Fear of economic blowback compelled the Japanese government to dispatch former prime minister Ryutaro Hashimoto to the Middle East to downplay Tokyo's MSDF contribution.[4] In contrast to their JDA counterparts, officials within MOFA identified Al Qaeda as a direct threat.[5] This disagreement among the Japanese bureaucracy reflected the official and personal ties that linked MOFA to the U.S. government: Japanese diplomats were influenced by U.S. threat perceptions to a greater extent than other officials. Ultimately, both MOFA and the JDA dismissed the possibility that military assistance to Operation Enduring Freedom would provoke Al Qaeda's retaliation.[6] All in all, the Japanese government did not consider Al Qaeda and its ilk an immediate threat.

In this respect, public attitudes toward international terrorism more closely resembled Koizumi's viewpoint than did the attitudes of other government elites. After September 11, one representative poll conducted by *Asahi Shimbun* found that 81 percent of respondents were "uneasy that a terrorist incident may occur in Japan like in the U.S."[7] That the public responded strongly to September 11 should be expected. Having experienced a sarin attack at the hand of Aum Shinrikyo in 1995, Japan's population was already sensitive to the threat of terrorism.

The public's sense of unease did not automatically translate into support for government action, however. On the one hand, the anxiety engendered by September 11 might have prompted the public to favor participation in Operation Enduring Freedom. From this perspective, securing Japan against the threat of global terror required SDF dispatch. On the other hand, public threat perceptions might have actually deterred support for the antiterrorism legislation. After all, even a logistics contribution risked entrapment. By visibly joining the antiterror coalition, Japan became a target for Al Qaeda. Indeed, more than two-thirds of the public predicted that SDF dispatch would "likely bring about terrorism in Japan."[8] Nonetheless, fear of retaliation failed to decisively influence public opinion. A majority of Japanese—some 57 percent—of the population, backed the antiterrorism legislation. Whether this majority reflected threat perceptions or other factors such as U.S. expectations and prime ministerial leadership is impossible to ascertain, given the limited scope of opinion surveys. The 37 percent of Japanese who opposed the antiterrorism legislation did so for reasons other than potential retaliation. For example, left-wing constituencies opposed the bill on the grounds of Article 9.[9] In short, the impact of threat perceptions on public support for the antiterrorism legislation is indeterminant.

Could another foreign threat—say, North Korea—have influenced Japan's response to September 11? In the fall of 2001, the international community remained unaware of the DPRK's clandestine uranium enrichment program. Even so, Japan viewed North Korea as a security threat. The Taepo-dong missile launch in 1998 had shocked government officials as well as the larger public. And the 1999 spy boat incident further reinforced North Korea's hostile image.[10] In spite of this deteriorating security environment, Koizumi never cited the bilateral alliance's value as a rationale for joining the war on terror. The prime minister rarely mentioned the U.S.-Japan alliance at all—in sharp contrast to his later remarks on Iraq. Likewise, in private deliberations, the Japanese government did not perceive a link between antiterrorism cooperation and North Korea.[11]

Why did the DPRK occupy such a minor role in Japan's political calculus? In this case, the most obvious explanation is correct—that North Korea became an urgent threat only after the visit to Pyongyang in October 2002 by Assistant Secretary of State James Kelly. The DPRK's revived plutonium program greatly added to Japan's insecurity. Moreover, Kim Jong-il's admission that his regime had abducted Japanese nationals led the public to view the DPRK in a new, more critical light. Prior to October 2002, the DPRK remained a largely existential threat and consequently exercised a relatively lesser influence within Tokyo's strategic calculations.

U.S. Policy: The Appeal of Expectations

U.S. policy decisively shaped Tokyo's participation in the war on terror. In contrast to earlier decades, Washington relied primarily on expectations rather than *gaiatsu* to influence Japan's security behavior. Indeed, the phenomenon of internalized *gaiatsu* motivated Tokyo to offer visible antiterrorism support with comparatively little U.S. prompting.

"Show the Flag": Transmitting U.S. Expectations

Broadly speaking, in the wake of September 11 one watershed event underlay U.S. expectations for Japan—Tokyo's conduct during the 1991 Gulf War. To alliance managers in Washington, the Gulf War constituted a nadir in the bilateral relationship. Despite U.S. urgings, the Japanese government failed to provide logistics support in a conflict that clearly affected Tokyo's vital interests. Instead, Japan contributed $13 billion to defray the war's cost—a generous sum, but in the eyes of the world, no substitute for SDF participation. Although not irreparable, the damage to the U.S.-Japan alliance was substantial because the Gulf War cast doubt on Tokyo's dependability. Thus, in the aftermath of September 11, U.S. policymakers expected that Japan's contribution to the war on terror would encompass more than financial support. This belief was personally held by key members of the first Bush administration: Deputy Secretary of State Richard Armitage and Senior National Security Council Director for Asian Affairs Torkel Patterson. Having served in the U.S. government during the Gulf War, both officials "didn't want the same kind of controversy we'd had with Japan" and, to this end, strove to facilitate Tokyo's visible participation in Operation Enduring Freedom.[12]

Washington's expectations operated on two levels following September 11. In public forums the United States refrained from issuing specific demands.[13] At most, alliance managers on the U.S. side expressed their personal hopes regarding Japan's contribution to the war on terror. For example, to expedite the passage of the antiterrorism bill, Armitage told Japanese reporters: "I hope that both houses in the Diet will see this [logistic support in the war on terror] clearly."[14] Armitage's remarks, coming two weeks after Koizumi proposed SDF rear-area support, exemplified the tactfulness of U.S. policy. To avoid creating an impression of *gaiatsu*, Washington waited for the Koizumi government to determine Japan's antiterrorism role before publicly communicating its expectations. Indeed, U.S. officials actively challenged the perception that Tokyo's participation in Operation Enduring Freedom resulted from external pressure. When addressing the Japan National Press Club, then U.S ambassador Howard Baker vigorously denied that U.S. promptings had led Japan to join the antiterror coalition.

> It is not my purpose as American Ambassador, it is not the purpose of my government to tell you how you support the friendship and alliance between our nations. That is your judgment to make. And we have high confidence that you will make the right decisions, and that you will contribute not only in a meaningful way, but in a great way, to this new alliance against terrorism.[15]

Did government-to-government consultations match Ambassador Baker's discreet approach? Yes, despite the controversy surrounding Armitage's alleged "show the flag" comment. The deputy secretary's purported comment aroused accusations of *gaiatsu* among the Japanese media. But upon closer examination, the September 15 meeting between Armitage and Shunji Yanai, Japan's ambassador in Washington, bears little resemblance to a standard definition of *gaiatsu*—that is, official, explicit demands accompanied by political pressure. Whether Armitage even used the phrase "show the flag" is a matter of considerable doubt. In a later interview, the deputy secretary recalled telling Yanai that "you've got to show the flag and show the flag in far-flung locations from Japan."[16] However, according to Yanai, Armitage communicated "show the flag" without employing that particular phrase.[17]

The etymology of "show the flag" notwithstanding, the nature of the meeting between Armitage and Yanai also deviates from any traditional conception of *gaiatsu*. First, Yanai rather than Armitage initiated the conversation. Although still awaiting instructions from Tokyo, Yanai confided to Armitage that Japan would visibly contribute to the emerging war on terror. Second, the deputy secretary's comments did not reflect an official position. Both men discussed the details of Japan's antiterrorism contribution on an informal basis.[18] Third, Armitage refrained from issuing specific requests. Instead, he suggested that "it would be possible for SDF vessels and aircraft to cooperate with the U.S. military forces in the area of transportation."[19] The precise nature of Tokyo's security contribution—where the SDF would operate, what it would transport, and the number of troops deployed—remained the Japanese government's prerogative. Furthermore, Armitage's remarks delineated U.S. expectations in addition to presenting a general framework for Japan's security role. The deputy secretary told Ambassador Yanai that "I do not expect Japanese troops to play a combat role."[20]

Both senior and working-level consultations mirrored the exchange between Yanai and Armitage. The U.S. side clearly stated that Washington expected visible support in the war on terror and referred to the Gulf War as an outcome to avoid. However, rather than conveying official, specific requests, the U.S. government asked the GOJ to determine its own contribution.[21] In short, the U.S. side "believed that Japan could and should act more like a 'normal' nation and that if we treated Japan as an ally, then Japan would so respond."[22]

Whether by design or serendipity, this approach maximized Japan's contribution to the war on terror. Presenting Tokyo with a list of demands would have divided Japanese popular opinion and antagonized Diet members otherwise inclined to support the United States. Moreover, an overbearing approach would neither have befitted an equal alliance partner nor capitalized on the personal ties between Prime Minister Koizumi and President Bush. Instead, U.S. officials expressed broad, often vague expectations, thereby transferring responsibility onto Japan for deciding the exact nature of antiterrorism cooperation. By appealing to Tokyo's sense of alliance obligation and, in particular, to Koizumi's relationship with Bush, this approach engendered greater security cooperation than *gaiatsu* could have achieved. Indeed, although the dispatch of MSDF vessels to patrol the Indian Ocean would have satisfied Washington, the Japanese government spontaneously offered to refuel U.S. ships and to provide other forms of rear-area support.[23]

Internalizing U.S. Expectations: From the Gulf War to the Armitage-Nye Report

Expectations communicated in the wake of September 11 clearly influenced Japan's security policy. However, even without U.S. exhortations, Japan would still have visibly contributed to the war on terror. Why? Because Tokyo internalized Washington's expectations during the decade spanning the Gulf War and September 11. This process began in 1991, a watershed year for Japan's defense policy. The Gulf War painfully exposed the limitations of Tokyo's Cold War modus operandi—securing its overseas interests through the exercise of economic power. Pressured by the international community in 1991 to contribute rear-area support, the Japanese government attempted to pass enabling legislation. But the Diet balked at the prospect of SDF dispatch, forcing the government to withdraw the bill. As a consequence, Japan underwrote 20 percent of the war's expense, yet received neither gratitude nor respect.[24] Media accusations of "checkbook diplomacy" and "too little, too late" stung Japanese officials, many of whom had struggled in vain to implement SDF deployment. The

U.S. government's disappointment, though expressed in more diplomatic terms, constituted another source of humiliation. Finally, the Gulf War's ramifications extended beyond Japan's sense of wounded national pride. Tokyo feared for the bilateral alliance's future credibility, for why would Washington expend blood and treasure to protect a fair-weather ally?

Not surprisingly, then, the Gulf War led to a rethinking of Japan's defense policy. This reassessment inculcated several outside expectations. First, government officials accepted, and later embraced, the idea that Japan's global status required a significant international security role. Initially, the memory of Tokyo's 1991 humiliation led elites to internalize this concept. However, during the first year of Koizumi's tenure as prime minister, international responsibility became a value in itself. Whether stemming from ideals or a desire to uphold national pride, great power obligation meant the same in operational terms: SDF participation in UN peacekeeping efforts and, later, SDF logistics support for out-of-area U.S. missions. Second, Japanese policymakers adopted Washington's vision for the bilateral alliance—a relationship characterized by reciprocity and mutual reliability. Both expectations underlay U.S. frustration at Tokyo's paralysis during Desert Storm. In the Gulf War's aftermath, the Japanese government concluded that reciprocity entailed sharing physical risk in addition to financial burdens and that refusing to deploy the SDF overseas would consign Tokyo to the status of a junior partner indefinitely. U.S. expectations of reciprocity and reliability were of course inextricably linked. Without legal infrastructure to enable SDF deployment, a reciprocal security relationship would prove untenable.

The Gulf War rendered Japanese policymakers keenly sensitive to international and U.S. expectations. Nevertheless, it constituted only the beginning of a decade-long process. From 1991 to 2001, the International Peace Cooperation Law, the Higuchi Report, the Clinton-Hashimoto Joint Declaration, the revised U.S.-Japan Defense Guidelines, and the Armitage-Nye report marked the internalization and, at times, institutionalization of outside expectations.[25] Through each of these milestones, Japanese elites progressively embraced expectations set forth by the U.S. and international community. And yet, whether Tokyo could avoid a second Gulf War experience remained an open question. On the eve of September 11, no outline, much less legal framework, described logistics support for out-of-area U.S. military operations.

Internalized Gaiatsu or Why Tokyo Joined the War on Terror

The alignment between outside expectations of Japan and Tokyo's expectations of itself proved decisive in the weeks following September 11. Indeed, the major foreign policy organs of the Japanese government responded to September 11 on the basis of internalized expectations. Although the *Kantei*, the Diet, MOFA, and the JDA at times disagreed over the specifics of Japan's antiterrorism contribution, all held similar beliefs—that combating Al Qaeda required Japan to fulfill its international obligations and demonstrate alliance loyalty.

Expanding Japan's global security role and strengthening the U.S.-Japan alliance constituted two of Prime Minister Koizumi's foreign policy objectives before September 11. Not surprisingly, then, internalized expectations underlay the *Kantei*'s response to the attacks on New York and Washington. Koizumi expressed Japan's willingness to visibly join the antiterror coalition even before the conversation between Yanai and Armitage. On September 12, the prime minister pledged to cooperate with the "United States and other concerned nations to combat international terrorism."[26] Two days later, on September 14, Koizumi announced that Japan's support would comprise all measures short of combat.[27] Only on September 15 did the United States informally communicate expectations to Japan. Clearly, internalized expectations rather than Washington shaped Koizumi's initial response to September 11.

Internalized expectations exercised a dual influence over the *Kantei*'s deliberations. On the one hand, fulfilling Japan's international responsibility and alliance obligation promised significant rewards. Acting as a responsible great power provided the *Kantei* with an opportunity to enhance Japan's political and, to a lesser extent, military clout. More generally, helping to eradicate terrorism through noncombat support increased Tokyo's global prestige. Furthermore, demonstrating alliance loyalty opened the way for closer U.S.-Japan security relations. Tokyo could win greater equality within the alliance by expeditiously dispatching the SDF.

In short, meeting outside expectations advanced Japan's national interest. These benefits, however, exerted a secondary impact on the *Kantei*'s calculations. More often than not, the cost of failing to meet expectations preoccupied the Office of the Prime Minister. Like his cabinet, Koizumi feared a repeat of the Gulf War, noting that "if Japan fails to take a responsible action against this sort of terrorism, it will be left isolated in the international community."[28] The *Kantei* also viewed expectations surrounding the U.S.-Japan alliance in largely negative terms. Indeed, the *Kantei*'s logic was essentially fear of abandonment: "Should we fail to immediately indicate a set of support measures for the U.S., the Japan-U.S. alliance itself will be questioned."[29] Despite Koizumi's vision of an expanded security relationship, the *Kantei*'s rhetoric sounded more akin to damage control than alliance building.

The *Kantei*'s approach to September 11 offers valuable insights into the process by which Japanese elites embraced outside expectations. From 1991 to the eve of September 11, Tokyo internalized the values of great power responsibility and alliance loyalty. Yet, this process distorted outside expectations. To a substantial degree, Japanese elites internalized the cost of failure—a price measured in terms of national interest—without internalizing the benefits of success. Tokyo largely ignored the positive repercussions that flowed from meeting international and alliance commitments. Even Prime Minister Koizumi, a proponent of strengthening the bilateral relationship, reverted to worst-case logic when confronted by a crisis on the magnitude of September 11. The *Kantei*'s deliberations thus reveal a dynamic of internalized *gaiatsu*, a one-sided calculation of national interest. By fixating on the consequences that accompanied failure to meet outside expectations, the Japanese government generated sufficient internal pressure to motivate new defense initiatives.[30] As a result, traditional *gaiatsu*—pressure applied from without—reinforced, rather than induced, Tokyo's decision to participate in the war on terror.

Internalized *gaiatsu* played a similar role throughout the Japanese polity. Like the *Kantei*, Diet members largely focused on the negative dimension of great power responsibility and alliance obligation. LDP lawmakers feared that international isolation would ensue if the Diet failed to quickly enact antiterrorism legislation. But the possibility that mismanaging the antiterrorism bill would irreparably damage the U.S.-Japan alliance outweighed all other concerns. Even before Armitage's meeting with Yanai, lawmakers from the LDP Foreign Affairs Research Commission and the LDP National Defense Department concluded that "retaliation by the U.S. does not permit failure. Our country should take an action befitting of a U.S. ally."[31]

The DPJ, however, voted against the antiterrorism bill, claiming that it violated the prohibition on collective defense. In reality, the DPJ was subject to internalized *gaiatsu*, but less so than the ruling parties. As the opposition, the DPJ lacked a decisive vote. Unlike members of the ruling coalition, DPJ lawmakers could go against the antiterrorism bill without any real consequences for Japan. Regardless of the DPJ's support, the LDP coalition's numerical superiority guaranteed that the bill would pass and, by extension, that Tokyo would fulfill internal and external expectations, thereby securing its national interest.

Had the DPJ been a ruling party or possessed the ability to table legislation, would it have still voted against the antiterrorism bill? No. In all likelihood, the DPJ would have acted similarly to a minority party that *did* wield a decisive vote—New Komeito. Despite a pacifist constituency, New Komeito supported the antiterrorism legislation after achieving several modifications.[32] Political considerations aside, New Komeito's position on the bill derived from a sense of accountability. As the linchpin of the ruling coalition, New Komeito would have borne direct responsibility for the Japanese government's failure to visibly participate in the war on terror. Internalized *gaiatsu* therefore exercised greater influence over New Komeito lawmakers than their DPJ counterparts. Moreover, even in voting against the antiterrorism bill, the DPJ exhibited signs of internalized *gaiatsu*. The party's leadership reportedly worried that "if we oppose the new legislation, America would no longer think of us as a friend . . . ."[33] As a result, Yukio Hatoyama, then-DPJ president, met Ambassador Baker in order to explain the party's stance on the antiterrorism bill. Like the Diet as a whole, DPJ lawmakers fully grasped the negative dimension of alliance loyalty.

As the governmental actor most attuned to international and U.S. expectations, MOFA exhibited internalized *gaiatsu* to a degree unmatched by either the *Kantei* or the Diet. From the outset, MOFA officials resolved to dispatch the SDF in order to avert another Gulf War experience. This desire to contribute visibly to the antiterrorism coalition was, of course, not unique. Yet in contrast to other governmental actors, MOFA intended that Japan's assistance exceed the range of activities defined by the revised Defense Guidelines. First, MOFA wanted the antiterrorism bill to permit medical and humanitarian operations on behalf of U.S. forces and refugees. As originally proposed, the geographic scope of these SDF missions would have incorporated India and the Afghan-Pakistan border.[34] Second, and more notably, MOFA officials sought to "fly a Japanese flag in a battlefield" by extending medical activities into combat zones.[35] The latter form of assistance challenged existing constitutional restraints, and ultimately the Cabinet Legislation Bureau decided that such support would contravene Article 9.

MOFA's effort to expand Japan's security contribution beyond the Defense Guidelines attests to the strength of internalized *gaiatsu*. In the case of MOFA, internalized *gaiatsu* related to national interest and personal relationships. Relative to other bureaucrats and politicians, MOFA officials interacted more closely with members of the U.S. government. Consequently, to a proportion of Japan's diplomatic corps, demonstrating Tokyo's alliance commitment thus became a matter of personal obligation.[36]

The JDA, and to a lesser degree the SDF, advocated a visible troop contribution for many of the same reasons. JDA officials shared MOFA's desire to meet U.S. expectations and prove Japan's willingness to combat international terrorism. And like MOFA bureaucrats, JDA officials and some SDF officers (mainly in the MSDF) were motivated by a sense of obligation toward their counterparts in the U.S. government and military.[37] But although the JDA wanted to see "television pictures of [the] rising-sun flag flying in CNN news,"[38] it envisioned a maritime role for SDF forces. Unlike MOFA, the JDA clearly understood the operational difficulties of dispatching troops to conduct humanitarian missions. And the GSDF, citing safety concerns, expressed a marked reluctance to deploy along the Afghan-Pakistan border. Despite holding a different vision of Japan's antiterrorism role, the JDA proved as eager as MOFA to assist U.S. forces in the wake of September 11. On September 21, the JDA ordered four MSDF vessels to escort the USS *Kitty Hawk* from Yokosuka, a maneuver that constituted a de facto act of collective defense.[39] All the more remarkably, the JDA authorized the escort mission without fore-warning the *Kantei*.[40] In short, internalized *gaiatsu* led the JDA (and MSDF) to successfully subvert Article 9.

Internalized Gaiatsu: One Caveat

Although potent, the effect of internalized *gaiatsu* should not be overstated. Internalized *gaiatsu* motivated Japan's verbal support for the war on terror. But in retrospect, the connection between external expectations and national interest proved unable to ensure the full implementation of Tokyo's promised security assistance. Indeed, the uneven execution of the antiterrorism bill underscores the limits of internalized *gaiatsu*.

On the face of it, the Japanese government's inability to dispatch an Aegis destroyer in the fall of 2001 seems to confirm that internalized *gaiatsu* offered no insurance against implementation failure. In reality, the Aegis controversy should not be linked to Japan's execution of the antiterrorism legislation. Shortly after September 11, the MSDF initiated the Aegis controversy by calling on the government to dispatch Japan's most sophisticated naval asset. MOFA, eager to demonstrate Japan's commitment to the bilateral alliance, echoed the JDA's position.[41] At no time did the Japanese government officially pledge to contribute an Aegis vessel to the war on terror. The antiterrorism bill and subsequent basic plan described the maritime component of Tokyo's logistics support in general terms as "supply support ships and escort ships."[42] In sum, the Aegis episode attests to the limits of internalized *gaiatsu*, but falls short of demonstrating that Tokyo failed to implement the antiterrorism legislation.

Ironically, most accounts of Japan's initial antiterrorism role ignore true cases of implementation failure. Many of the SDF activities mandated by the antiterrorism legislation remained unrealized. SDF personnel neither provided medical services to U.S. soldiers nor carried out search and rescue operations. Moreover, Japanese forces never entered refugee camps to offer medical and other forms of humanitarian assistance.[43] In sum, Tokyo's contribution fell short of the official pledge contained in the antiterrorism legislation and basic plan.

Internalized *gaiatsu* failed to ensure full implementation because Japanese policymakers perceived few costs to national interest if the SDF eschewed on-the-ground missions. To the international community as a whole, and particularly the United States, dispatching the MSDF constituted a significant contribution in its own right.[44] Given Tokyo's concomitant financial donations to UNHCR (United Nations High Commissioner for Refugees) and emergency assistance to Pakistan, Japanese officials could rightly expect that the world would overlook the SDF's circumscribed on-the-ground role. This perception effectively disrupted the dynamic of internalized *gaiatsu*. Without the prospect of international rebuke—a diplomatic blow deemed inimical to national interest—Japanese officials were not subject to self-induced pressure and hence were unlikely to pursue new defense initiatives.

Executive Leadership: Koizumi's Expert Hand

Koizumi's leadership greatly shaped Tokyo's initial response to September 11. However, the prime minister's record did not constitute an unblemished success. Koizumi only succeeded in implementing the most visible elements of Japan's antiterrorism package.

A Tale of Political Acumen

Prime Minister Koizumi displayed leadership on multiple occasions in the wake of September 11, but the genesis of the antiterrorism legislation particularly reflected his political acumen. Convinced that Japan had to offer rapid, visible assistance to the United States and the international community, Koizumi circumvented his government's standard foreign policy making procedures. To expedite Japan's response to September 11, the prime minister established an emergency response office in the *Kantei* fewer than 24 hours after the Al Qaeda attacks. The emergency response office brought together *Kantei* officials and senior bureaucrats from MOFA and the JDA, thereby allowing Koizumi to centralize decisionmaking.[45] The prime minister's willingness to venture outside the traditional foreign policy making process did not end there. On September 19, he articulated a seven-point assistance package that later became the basis for the antiterrorism legislation. Although he consulted key LDP members before this speech, the prime minister neglected to confer with the Diet Committee on Foreign Affairs and Defense.[46] As a result, Koizumi pledged specific forms of security assistance, including SDF dispatch, without any assurance that requisite Diet support would be forthcoming. In announcing the seven-point package, the prime minister risked his credibility both at home and abroad.

Circumventing the Japanese government's foreign policy making procedures required a substantial degree of ingenuity and political bravery. But in the case of the September 19 announcement, doing so also constituted a shrewd political maneuver. Domestically, promising concrete forms of antiterrorism cooperation allowed Koizumi to direct *naiatsu* against obstinate elements within the government and the Diet. In effect, the prime minister used the threat of *gaiatsu*—failure to enact the seven-point declaration would incur U.S. and international condemnation—to compel support for his policies. Internationally, the seven assistance measures shielded Japan's security policy from possible *gaiatsu*. Swiftly articulating Japan's contribution permitted Koizumi to define the SDF's antiterrorism role on his own terms. Furthermore, demonstrating an early commitment to the war on terror might have defused any U.S. urge to fall back on *gaiatsu*.

The prime minister used summit diplomacy to similar political ends. When meeting with President Bush on September 25, Koizumi reiterated that Japan would "make all possible contributions [to the war on terror] that do not require the use of armed force."[47] Moreover, he clarified the scope of Japan's assistance by proclaiming that Tokyo "will no longer hold that the Self-Defense Forces should not be sent to danger spots."[48] The latter comment clearly outdistanced the Diet and, for that matter, Koizumi's own cabinet.[49] Having thus elevated U.S. expectations, Koizumi presented government elites with a fait accompli: failure to implement his pledge would bring about certain *gaiatsu*. Stated alternatively, Koizumi employed *naiatsu* to strengthen internalized *gaiatsu*, thereby obligating domestic elites to support his position.

Perhaps the most outstanding example of prime ministerial leadership, however, is the speed with which the antiterrorism bill became law. Koizumi shepherded the antiterrorism legislation through the Diet in record time. The 1992 International Peace Cooperation Law required nine months of debate, and Diet members considered the 1999 law on areas surrounding Japan for nearly one year. In contrast, lawmakers approved the antiterrorism bill in less than three weeks. The bill's swift passage should be directly attributed to Koizumi rather than his advisers. Indeed, the prime minister played an intimate role in steering the bill through both the government and the Diet. To avoid a protracted debate within the bureaucracy, Koizumi tasked then LDP secretary general Taku Yamasaki to determine whether antiterrorism cooperation would necessitate new legislation.[50] When an intragovernmental debate threatened to emerge, Koizumi intervened by ordering MOFA, the JDA, and Yamasaki to prepare a new antiterrorism bill authorizing SDF dispatch. The prime minister also shaped the government's strategy once the bill entered the Diet. Fearing that the unpredictable Makiko Tanaka would antagonize opposition lawmakers, Koizumi sidelined his foreign minister from Diet proceedings. Instead, then JDA chief Gen Nakatani served as the cabinet's spokesman. And finally, under Koizumi's guidance, the LDP granted New Komeito a series of tactical concessions that guaranteed the party's support for the antiterrorism legislation.[51]

Regional objections to SDF dispatch might have halted, or at least prolonged the bill's passage through the Diet. That Japan's neighbors expressed only muted concern at Tokyo's new antiterrorism role reflected Koizumi's skillful use of preventive diplomacy. In the weeks following September 11, the prime minister traveled to Beijing and Seoul to counter perceptions of renewed Japanese militarism. When meeting his Chinese and South Korean counterparts, Koizumi stressed that Tokyo's antiterrorism contribution would not involve the use of force. At the same time, he also addressed regional anxieties by visiting two symbols of Japan's imperialist past—the Marco Polo Bridge and the Sodaemun Independence Park. Although Koizumi's itinerary might have included both landmarks even in the absence of September 11, such visits constituted a particularly reassuring gesture at a time when Japanese forces ventured far abroad. Indeed, the prime minister's efforts resulted in an immediate diplomatic payoff. Chinese president Jiang Xemin found SDF dispatch "understandable," and South Korean President Kim Dae-jung agreed that Tokyo and Seoul should cooperate in the war on terror.[52]

Finally, Koizumi's leadership enabled timely deployment of the MSDF. The prime minister's determination to bring about SDF dispatch at the earliest possible date meant that Japanese vessels provided symbolic rear-area support to U.S. forces before the end of major hostilities in Afghanistan. Although still formulating a basic plan, the Japanese government achieved early dispatch through utilizing the 1954 Defense Agency Establishment Law.[53] As a result, the GOJ deployed three vessels to the Indian Ocean on November 9, 2001. At the same time, Koizumi's adept handling of the antiterrorism legislation allowed the cabinet to approve a basic plan by November 16. Three additional MSDF vessels then departed for the Indian Ocean on November 26. The original fleet reached the Indian Ocean on November 28; the second flotilla conducted the MSDF's first refueling operations on December 2.[54] In both cases, Japanese forces narrowly avoided arriving "too late," because the fall of Kandahar on December 7 signaled the collapse of the Taliban regime. If Koizumi had placed less emphasis on early SDF dispatch, Japanese forces would have been absent from the first, critical phase of Operation Enduring Freedom.

Koizumi's Leadership: Two Critiques

Japan's response to September 11 undoubtedly bears the mark of Koizumi's personal leadership. That being said, the prime minister on occasion failed to make good on his international commitments. Koizumi's September 19 announcement contained three antiterrorism measures involving SDF dispatch. Japan fully implemented only one of these pledges—rapidly deploying MSDF vessels to collect intelligence. The SDF's actual support for coalition forces fell short of Koizumi's initial statement: Japan provided transport but not medical services.[55] Furthermore, Tokyo fulfilled the letter but not the spirit of Koizumi's promise to assist Afghan refugees. The SDF conducted "drop and run" aid operations. Japanese C-130s deposited blankets and tents in Islamabad and returned home; SDF personnel remained hundreds of miles from the nearest refugee camp.[56] Consequently, Tokyo's response to September 11 belied Koizumi's assertion that the Japanese government would no longer regard "danger spots" as taboo when dispatching the SDF overseas. In practice, the policy of limiting SDF deployment to safe areas continued.

Nonetheless, these failures detract little from Koizumi's overall leadership. A potentially more damaging critique is that the prime minister's decisive role reflected administrative reforms rather than personality. Immediately before Koizumi began his tenure in office, the Japanese government enacted a series of measures to "strengthen the administrative leadership of the Cabinet and Prime Minister."[57] These reforms established the Cabinet Secretariat, a mechanism that enhanced the prime minister's ability to coordinate the bureaucracy and manage crises. Thus, unlike his predecessors, Koizumi benefited from new institutional arrangements that magnified his authority.

Does Koizumi's leadership then reflect the earlier restructuring of the Cabinet Office? To a certain extent, yes. The new Cabinet Secretariat likely enabled Koizumi to play a more active role in the policymaking process than would have otherwise been possible.[58] In particular, the Cabinet Secretariat increased the prime minister's influence over the creation of the antiterrorism bill. But ultimately, much of Koizumi's leadership in the wake of September 11 was unrelated to administrative reforms. That Koizumi circumvented normal government procedures and promised antiterrorism assistance without requisite domestic support reflected political courage, not institutional factors. Directing *naiatsu* against opponents of the seven-point assistance package constituted a display of personal ingenuity. Likewise, preventive diplomacy and early MSDF dispatch stemmed from Koizumi's initiative, not prior government restructuring. In short, under a different prime minister, the Cabinet Secretariat alone would not have guaranteed prompt, visible assistance to Operation Enduring Freedom.

Generational Change: The Triumph of Partisanship

Japan's response to September 11 evidenced generational change at the elite level. Yet in the end, demographic factors exerted little real impact on Japan's security behavior. Young lawmakers in both the LDP and the DPJ favored active participation in the war on terror. Moreover, the DPJ divided along generational lines when considering Koizumi's proposed antiterrorism package. Junior DPJ lawmakers supported some form of SDF dispatch. Like members of the ruling coalition, these young politicians believed that Japan's contribution to the war on terror needed to "exhibit willingness to expend sweat . . . ."[59] On the other hand, older DPJ lawmakers—former members of the Japan Socialist Party—approached SDF deployment with great reluctance.[60]

Ultimately, junior DPJ members were unable to deliver the party's support for the antiterrorism bill, though not for lack of effort. Although Yukio Hatoyama, then DPJ president, had initially favored close cooperation with the ruling coalition, he soon backpedaled under pressure from the party's left wing. In response, young DPJ lawmakers urged Hatoyama to change course and accommodate the government's proposed legislation. At the behest of these Young Turks, Hatoyama shifted once again, and on September 20 expressed his support for the antiterrorism legislation.[61] The influence of young DPJ members proved fleeting, however. Under continued pressure from his party's former socialists, Hatoyama attempted to reconcile both wings of the DPJ by setting forth a compromise position on Japan's security assistance.[62] When the ruling coalition refused to accept Hatoyama's proposal, the DPJ decided to oppose the government's antiterrorism bill.

The DPJ's position demonstrates that generational variation played a negligible role in facilitating Japan's response to September 11. First, despite generational change, the DPJ as a whole failed to endorse the antiterrorism bill. Second, although demographic differences existed within the DPJ, even young lawmakers eventually voted against the government's legislation. Party affiliation prevailed over generational solidarity.

The Nature of Japan's Strategic Transition

In broad terms, September 11 demonstrates that Japan's strategic evolution is to a substantial degree internally driven. Japanese policymakers viewed terrorism as an indirect danger. Nonetheless, Tokyo commenced to offer rapid, visible assistance to the war on terror. Internal factors consequently underlay Japan's security behavior in the wake of September 11. Washington's expectations exercised a decisive influence over Tokyo's foreign policy calculus, but U.S. policy acted from within rather than without. Internalized *gaiatsu*—a one-sided calculation of national interest—compelled Japanese officials to propose new forms of security cooperation to avoid the negative consequences of failing to meet outside expectations. Finally, Koizumi's leadership had a powerful impact on Japan's antiterrorism contribution. Although SDF dispatch might have occurred in his absence, the rapidity by which Tokyo deployed forces overseas is due to the prime minister's initiative.

Tokyo's initial participation in the war on terror also reveals significant continuity in Japan's defense strategy. Even when confronted by a major foreign policy shock, Japanese officials barely strayed from existing legal frameworks. Despite some discussion of revising Article 9 or abolishing the prohibition on collective defense, policymakers ultimately utilized existing legal precedents to implement SDF dispatch. Koizumi's rhetoric aside, SDF personnel never assisted U.S. forces in "dangerous areas." Yet, Tokyo's response to September 11 represents a turning point in Japan's transition from a norms-based to interest-based defense strategy. Before the attacks on New York and Washington, Japan's strategic evolution could be described as a punctuated equilibrium. Episodes of rapid change gave way to political exhaustion and periods of policy stasis. After September 11, however, Tokyo's defense strategy no longer conformed to this cycle. Rather, change became constant, and shows no sign of abating.[63]

Notes

[1] Cabinet Office, "Statement by Prime Minister Junichiro Koizumi," October 8, 2001, http://www.kantei.go.jp/foreign/koizumispeech/2001/1008danwa_e.html.

[2] Ibid.

[3] Koichi Kato quoted in Heginbotham and Samuels, "Japan," 102.

[4] Ibid.

[5] MOFA and JDA officials disagreed about the nature of the terror threat after September 11. However, following the March 11, 2004, bombings in Madrid, both MOFA and JDA officials concurred that terrorism directly threatens Japan. Author's interviews, Tokyo, March 2004.

[6] During four meetings with MOFA and JDA officials, only one interviewee claimed that some (not a majority) of GOJ officials feared possible Al Qaeda retaliation. Author's interviews, Tokyo, March 2004.

[7] "Poll on Koizumi Cabinet, Political Parties, SDF Backup Legislation," *Asahi Shimbun*, October 1, 2001.

[8] "Poll on U.S. Antiterror Action, SDF Backup Legislation," *Mainichi Shimbun*, October 16, 2001.

[9] Christopher Hughes, "Japan's Security Policy and the War on Terror: Steady Incrementalism or Radical Leap?" (working paper published by the Centre for the Study of Globalisation and Regionalisation, University of Warwick, United Kingdom, August 2002), 26.

[10] Matake Kamiya, "A Disillusioned Japan Confronts North Korea," *Arms Control Today* 33, no. 4 (May 2003).

[11] Author's interview with a retired senior MOFA official, Tokyo, March 2004.

[12] Richard Armitage interviewed by Edward Stourton, BBC Radio, "With Us or without Us," April 10, 2002, http://www.bbc.co.uk/radio4/news/withus/armitage.pdf.

[13] Hughes, "Japan's Security Policy and the War on Terror," 30.

[14] "Armitage Seeks Early Enactment of Japan's Antiterrorism Bills," *Japan Economic Newswire*, October 5, 2001.

[15] U.S. Embassy Tokyo, "Transcript: Ambassador Baker Says U.S., Japan Allied against Terrorism," October 5, 2001, http://japan.usembassy.gov/e/amb/tamb-0016.html.

[16] Stourton, "With Us or without Us."

[17] Author's interview with Shunji Yanai, Tokyo, April 19, 2005.

[18] Ibid.

[19] Gaku Shibata, "Japan Perspective: Japanese Media Stuck up the Flagpole," *Yomiuri Shimbun*, October 30, 2001.

[20] Ibid.

[21] In separate meetings, observers on the U.S. and Japanese sides stated that this constituted Washington's approach in the wake of September 11. Author's interviews, Tokyo, March 2004.

[22] E-mail correspondence with U.S. official, April 19, 2004.

[23] Author's interview with U.S. official, Tokyo, March 2004.

[24] For example, Kuwaiti advertisements placed in U.S. newspapers did not recognize Japan as a contributor to liberation.

[25] For more information on these milestones, see Michael J. Green, "Balance of Power," in *U.S.-Japan Relations in a Changing World*, ed. Steven K. Vogel (Washington, D.C.: Brookings Institution, 2002), 9–34; Akio Watanabe and Hisayoshi Ina, "Changing Security Environments and Their Impacts on U.S.-Japan relations," in *Redefining the Partnership: The United States and Japan in East Asia*, ed. Chihiro Hosoya and Tomohito Shinoda (Lanham, Maryland: University Press of America, Inc., 1998), 15–28; Ralph A. Cossa,

"U.S.-Japan Security Relations: Separating Fact from Fiction," in *Restructuring the U.S.-Japan Alliance: Toward a More Equal Partnership*, ed. Ralph A. Cossa (Washington, D.C.: CSIS Press, 1997), 31–49; and Matake Kamiya, "Reforming the U.S.-Japan Alliance: What Should be Done?" in *Reinventing the Alliance: U.S.-Japan Security Partnership in an Era of Change*, ed. G. John Ikenberry and Takashi Inoguchi (New York: Palgrave Macmillan, 2003), 91–116.

[26] Cabinet Office, "Statement by Prime Minister Junichiro Koizumi at the Press Conference," September 12, 2001, http://www.kantei.go.jp/foreign/koizumispeech/2001/0912kaiken_e.html.

[27] "Japan Will Support the U.S.—but without Force, Says Koizumi," *Deutsche Presse-Agentur*, September 14, 2001.

[28] "Japan Mulling a Best Option of Contribution," *Asahi Shimbun*, September 18, 2001.

[29] "Facing the Question of 'Who Is a Real Ally,' Prime Minister Was Hasty in Announcing a Set of Assistance Measures," *Nihon Keizai Shimbun*, September 20, 2001.

[30] As a form of self-generated pressure, internalized *gaiatsu* differs from the political phenomenon termed *naiatsu*. *Naiatsu* occurs when one element of the Japanese government directs the threat of *gaiatsu* against an individual policymaker or a bureaucracy. The two phenomena can, and do, simultaneously exist. On *gaiatsu* and *naiatsu*, see Leonard Schoppa, "Two-Level Games and Bargaining Outcomes: Why *Gaiatsu* Succeeds in Some Cases but Not Others," *International Organization* 47, no. 3 (Summer 1993): 353–386.

[31] "Japan to Consider Ways to Support the U.S. as Ally," *Asahi Shimbun*, September 13, 2001.

[32] Hughes, "Japan's Security Policy and the War on Terror," 25–27.

[33] "Security Debate Getting down into Specifics," *Asahi Shimbun*, October 19, 2001.

[34] Hughes, "Japan's Security Policy and the War on Terror," 11, 15.

[35] Unnamed MOFA official quoted in "Simultaneous terrorist attacks—Crisis and Japan: Gap between Defense Agency and MSDF, Foreign Ministry," *Asahi Shimbun*, September 28, 2001.

[36] Author's interview with MOFA official, Tokyo, March 2004.

[37] Author's interview with SDF officer, Tokyo, March 2004.

[38] Senior JDA official quoted in "Voices of Skepticism Heard about Scope and Effectiveness of SDF Rear-Area Support," *Asahi Shimbun*, September 19, 2001.

[39] The JDA initially claimed that the MSDF had accompanied the USS *Kitty Hawk* as part of an intelligence gathering mission rather than for the

aircraft carrier's protection, and therefore, did not violate the prohibition on collective defense. Hughes, "Japan's Security Policy and the War on Terror," 16–17.

[40] "Simultaneous Terrorist Attacks—Crisis and Japan: Gap between Defense Agency and MSDF, Foreign Ministry," *Asahi Shimbun*, September 28, 2001.

[41] Hughes, "Japan's Security Policy and the War on Terror," 17–20.

[42] Ministry of Foreign Affairs, "Basic Plan Regarding Response Measures Based on the Anti-Terrorism Special Measures Law," November 16, 2001, http://www.mofa.go.jp/region/n-america/us/terro0109/policy/plan.html.

[43] Heginbotham and Samuels, "Japan," 104.

[44] The U.S. government would have been satisfied with MSDF dispatch alone. Author's interview with U.S. official, Tokyo, March 2004.

[45] Hughes, "Japan's Security Policy and the War on Terror," 9, 14.

[46] This is usually a standard procedure for any major foreign policy speech. Author's interview with MOFA official, Tokyo, August 2003.

[47] "Major Exchanges at Japan, U.S. Summit Meeting," *Asahi Shimbun*, September 27, 2001.

[48] Koizumi quoted in Cossa, "U.S.-Japan Defense Cooperation."

[49] "Prime Minister's Remarks of 'Dangerous Areas' Perplex the SDF," *Asahi Shimbun*, September 26, 2001.

[50] "Facing the Question of 'Who Is a Real Ally,' Prime Minister Was Hasty in Announcing a Set of Assistance Measures," *Nihon Keizai Shimbun*, September 20, 2001.

[51] These concessions included limiting the bill's lifespan to two years and eliminating the transport and supply of weapons from possible SDF activities. Hughes, "Japan's Security Policy and the War on Terror," 13–14, 24–25.

[52] Ministry of Foreign Affairs, "Visit to the People's Republic of China by Prime Minister Junichiro Koizumi," October 8, 2001, http://www.mofa.go.jp/region/asia-paci/china/pmv0110/meet-2.html; and "Japan-Republic of Korea Summit Meeting," October 16, 2001, http://www.mofa.go.jp/region/asia-paci/korea/pmv0110/outline.html.

[53] The MSDF staff office suggested that the GOJ use the Defense Agency Establishment Law to effect an early dispatch. Author's interview with MSDF officer, Tokyo, March 2004.

[54] Ibid.

[55] On Koizumi's seven-point assistance package, see Cabinet Office, "Opening Statement by Prime Minister Junichiro Koizumi at the Press

Conference," September 19, 2001, http://www.kantei.go.jp/foreign/koizumispeech/2001/0919sourikaiken_e.html.

[56] Heginbotham and Samuels, "Japan," 104.

[57] Cabinet Office, "Establishing a System with More Effective Political Leadership," January 2001, http://www.kantei.go.jp/foreign/central_government/frame.html.

[58] Author's interview with Japanese academic, Tokyo, July 2003.

[59] "Interview with Seiji Maehara," *Mainichi Shimbun*, September 27, 2001.

[60] DPJ supporters of the antiterrorism bill comprised members of the older generation—former LDP members—in addition to junior lawmakers who joined the party since the mid-1990s. E-mail correspondence with DPJ policy staffer, April 13, 2004.

[61] "Hatoyama Strengthening Support for U.S. Cooperation, Pressed by Junior Lawmakers in the Party," *Yomiuri Shimbun*, September 21, 2001.

[62] Hughes, "Japan's Security Policy and the War on Terror," 26.

[63] A senior U.S. official brought this cycle to my attention. Author's interview, Washington, D.C., September 2003.

5

Under North Korea's Shadow: Japan and Missile Defense

Tokyo's response to September 11 indicates that prime ministerial leadership and Washington's expectations constitute key factors behind Japan's strategic evolution. Do the four components of the transitional model—foreign threats, U.S. policy, executive leadership, and generational change—function similarly in another context: the Koizumi administration's decision to introduce missile defense? BMD serves as a particularly useful contrast to other foreign policy shocks. Both September 11 and Iraq reconstruction involved high-profile overseas deployments, whereas missile defense constituted a procurement decision with long-term strategic ramifications.

It should come as no surprise that the GOJ moved to acquire missile defense in response to North Korea. The DPRK's No-dong missile represented one rationale for introducing BMD. However, other dimensions of the North Korean threat exerted a more profound influence over the fate of missile defense. The prospect of Pyongyang's developing an operational nuclear arsenal motivated the GOJ to discard its original time line for BMD in favor of an off-the-shelf purchase from the United States. Spy ship intrusions and, to a much greater extent, Pyongyang's history of abducting Japanese nationals fundamentally altered popular perceptions of the DPRK. The public's acute anxiety—"North Korea–phobia"—compelled politicians and bureaucrats to support missile defense. As a result, the Japanese government rapidly overcame once formidable barriers to BMD, such as questions of technical feasibility, cost, and legality. In short, the North Korean threat transformed the environment in which elites and the public considered missile defense.[1]

Other constituent variables of the transitional model exerted a minor or negligible influence over Tokyo's decision to introduce BMD. Historically, U.S. efforts to expedite the GOJ's consideration of missile defense have ended in failure. After October 2002, Washington's urgings merely echoed the Japanese government's independent desire to deploy BMD. Furthermore, prime ministerial leadership was absent from the decisionmaking process on missile defense. Koizumi assumed a peripheral role, while then JDA chief Ishiba constituted BMD's main public advocate. Finally, generational change, though in evidence, was overshadowed by North Korea. Compared with older lawmakers, the Young Turks displayed greater support for BMD prior to Pyongyang's fall 2002 bombshells involving the abductees and uranium enrichment. However, as the DPRK stepped up its nuclear program, missile defense became an item of cross-generational consensus.

Foreign Threats: Good (De)Fences Make Good Neighbors

North Korea as a Multidimensional Threat

North Korea poses a multidimensional threat to Japan. These dimensions include the DPRK's deployment of medium-range missiles, its nuclear weapons program, the intrusion of North Korean spy ships into Tokyo's territorial waters, and Pyongyang's abduction of Japanese nationals. How did each of these threats influence the GOJ's decision to deploy a missile defense system? The turning point in Japan's consideration of BMD, October 2002 through December 2003, contains the answer. During 14 months, the Japanese government discarded plans for a jointly produced BMD system in favor of purchasing missile defense from the United States. Doing so ensured Tokyo an initial missile defense capability by 2007, but entailed a large opportunity cost: U.S. companies would receive the lion's share of BMD-related contracts. This economic sacrifice attests to the urgency with which Tokyo perceived the North Korean threat.

Japan Awakens to the No-dong. On the face of it, Tokyo's decision to field BMD appears to be a response to Pyongyang's growing arsenal of medium-range missiles. Upon declaring Japan's intention to deploy missile defense, then chief cabinet secretary Fukuda noted that the system was a "purely defensive measure, without alternatives, to protect life and property of the citizens of Japan against ballistic missile attacks . . . ."[2] Naoto Kan, the president of the DPJ, articulated the motivating role of the No-dong in more explicit terms: "North Korea's Rodong and Taepodong missiles pose a threat . . . isn't there room for Japan to discuss . . . the development of missile defense."[3] Yet, the number of No-dongs fielded by the DPRK increased slowly between October 2002 and December 2003. North Korea also refrained from launching another Taepo-dong: the DPRK continued to maintain the letter, though not the spirit, of its self-imposed testing moratorium.[4] Nor did a collective revelation about North Korean missiles occur among Japanese security elites. Policymaking circles have long realized that the No-dong, if fitted with a nuclear warhead, represents a high-casualty, low-probability threat.

What changed since October 2002 was that political elites and the public joined government officials in recognizing the danger posed by North Korea's missile buildup. The technical specifications of the No-dong render Japan the missile's only viable target. With a range of 1,000 kilometers, the No-dong would overfly South Korea. China and the Russian Far East are unlikely targets, and the missile cannot reach the United States.[5] Nevertheless, prior to October 2002, Japanese politicians and the general populace overlooked the hostile intentions communicated by North Korea's medium-range missile. The roots of this naiveté were primarily domestic. Chosen Soren, a pro-Pyongyang organization for Koreans residing in Japan, forestalled criticism of the DPRK by courting LDP politicians. The organization also directly supported the Socialist Democratic Party of Japan (SDPJ), a left-wing party sympathetic to Pyongyang. Chosen Soren's political influence declined in the mid-1990s as Japan's economic recession undermined many of the group's core businesses such as pachinko (pinball-type gambling). Additionally, the collapse of the SDPJ in 1996 further weakened Chosen Soren's ability to serve as the DPRK's domestic lobby.[6] Still, the outcome of Chosen Soren's political activities—a partial whitewashing of North

Korea's image—persisted through the advent of the Koizumi administration.

Politicians and the public fully recognized the nature of the Kim Jong-il regime after October 2002. Within elite and popular discourse, the No-dong came to signify the DPRK's malevolent designs. North Korea's use of the testing moratorium as a bargaining chip for progress in the normalization talks antagonized elites and the larger public. Even so, the intentions attached to the No-dong related more to other factors than the capability itself. In isolation, Pyongyang's missile diplomacy would not have transformed Japanese perceptions of the DPRK. Indeed, in the context of the normalization talks, government elites might have considered North Korea's missile-rattling as nothing more than a crude negotiating tactic. However, elite (and public) perceptions of the No-dong threat were (and are) embedded in the larger state of Japan-DPRK relations. From October 2002 on, this relationship rose to new levels of acrimony. Virtually all major bilateral issues—nuclear weapons, spy ship intrusions, and the abductees—appeared to demonstrate Pyongyang's hostility. The intentions communicated by these issues colored Japanese perceptions of the No-dong. Thus, capabilities and behavior that elites and the public might have previously dismissed became evidence for a dire missile threat.

Pyongyang and the Bomb. Compared to the No-dong threat, the DPRK's nuclear program played a more critical role in Tokyo's decision to introduce missile defense. Excluding domestic factors, the severity of the missile threat has always depended on Pyongyang's unconventional capabilities. If armed with regular explosives, 100 No-dongs would inflict a relatively low number of casualties. An attack utilizing conventional warheads would also lack the destructive force to disrupt Japan's economy or cripple vital infrastructure. North Korea did possess weapons of mass destruction before October 2002.[7] According to CIA estimates, Pyongyang had produced one or two nuclear bombs from plutonium reprocessed during the early 1990s. However, most experts discounted the operational utility of these nuclear devices. Without testing, Kim Jong-il could have little confidence in his arsenal. In addition, the DPRK faced major technical hurdles in miniaturizing a nuclear warhead to deploy atop the No-dong.[8]

The character of the missile threat changed qualitatively between October 2002 and December 2003 as North Korea developed an operational nuclear force. It is worth noting that the uranium enrichment program that sparked the Korean nuclear crisis had few immediate ramifications for Japan. Still in its early stages, the program would begin yielding bomb-grade material only after 2005. Had Pyongyang refrained from escalating its nuclear activities beyond the uranium enrichment program, the Japanese government might have proceeded more slowly toward introducing BMD. That being said, North Korea's move to reprocess used plutonium represented a pressing threat. The 8,000 spent fuel rods stored in Yongbyong constituted an "overnight" nuclear capability. After reprocessing, they provided enough plutonium to construct five nuclear weapons within a year.[9] These additional warheads mitigated operational constraints on the DPRK's nuclear arsenal: North Korea could test a weapon and still retain a minimal deterrent; even without testing, the regime could assume that at least one or two bombs out of five would successfully detonate. Furthermore, by June 2003, Pyongyang reportedly overcame the final barrier to developing useable nuclear weapons—a smaller warhead.[10] Thus, within the space of nine months, the No-dong became the delivery vehicle for a nuclear attack.

The Japanese government responded to Pyongyang's operational nuclear arsenal by introducing missile defense. Indeed, an almost linear relationship existed between the GOJ's steps toward purchasing BMD and major developments in the North Korean nuclear program. Tokyo learned of the DPRK's uranium enrichment program in the first weeks of October 2002. Less than one month later, JDA chief Ishiba called for moving BMD cooperation to the development phase. On December 12, 2002, North Korea announced that it would resume operating all nuclear facilities. Five days after Pyongyang's statement, Ishiba communicated to U.S. officials that Japan would study the development *and* deployment of missile defense. North Korea withdrew from the NPT in January 2003. The following month, the GOJ requested detailed information on U.S.-designed missile defense systems. In February and March 2003, the DPRK restarted the Yongbyong reactor complex and began to reprocess spent fuel rods. During April 2003, newspaper reports indicated that the GOJ had begun to study purchasing missile defense. In July 2003, Pyongyang warned that it had reprocessed the 8,000 spent fuel rods and claimed to possess sufficient plutonium to produce six nuclear weapons. At the end of August, the JDA requested that the Diet earmark $1.2 billion for missile defense starting in fiscal year 2004. Finally, in mid-October 2003, North Korea threatened to test a nuclear bomb. Within two months the Japanese government formally decided to introduce BMD. Clearly, Pyongyang's growing nuclear capabilities motivated the GOJ to purchase missile defense.

The impact of the DPRK nuclear program is even greater than this chronology would suggest. Contrary to past accounts, the Koizumi administration began considering BMD development and deployment as early as December 2002. At a meeting of the U.S.-Japan Security Consultative Committee on December 17, 2002, Ishiba told Defense Secretary Donald Rumsfeld that Japan would "study the [joint missile defense program] with an eye toward a future move to development and deployment."[11] Shortly thereafter, Chief Cabinet Secretary Fukuda refuted Ishiba's statement and claimed that the Japanese government had yet to determine the necessity of BMD.[12]

Most Japanese newspapers and outside observers took Fukuda's denial at face value. In reality, the cabinet had approved Ishiba's remarks. Instead of deviating from the government's position, the JDA chief actually enunciated the cabinet's inclination to move forward on missile defense. The logic behind this apparent deception is as follows. Ishiba served a vital role in the Koizumi administration. By articulating cabinet decisions as personal statements, the JDA chief allowed the government to gauge the public and Diet reaction on controversial defense issues. If the public and lawmakers appeared receptive, the cabinet would announce its decision as official policy. Conversely, if both groups responded unfavorably, the Koizumi administration would downplay Ishiba's remarks.[13] Thus, in mid-December 2002, the cabinet used Ishiba to test the waters on missile defense. Uncertain that political support existed for moving ahead on BMD and perhaps still hopeful that diplomacy could resolve the North Korean crisis, the cabinet decided to refute the JDA chief. Nonetheless, this episode demonstrates that the Koizumi administration had begun to revise the time line for missile defense less than a week after the announced restoration of North Korea's plutonium program.

Spy Ships: A Tangible Threat. From 1999 on, North Korean spy ships repeatedly infiltrated Japanese waters. These maritime intrusions cast the DPRK as a tangible security threat. In particular, the display of a salvaged North Korean vessel sunk by the Japanese Coast Guard in 2001 added to the public's growing sense of anxiety. When exhibited in early 2003, the spy ship display attracted 20,000 visitors its first weekend. The vessel's armament—rocket launchers, machine guns, an antiaircraft gun, and two antiaircraft missile launchers—shocked the Japanese public.[14] Although not a main impetus behind missile defense, the spy ship intrusions contributed to the popular belief that Pyongyang constituted an erratic, menacing regime.

The Abductions: Japan Discovers an "Evil Empire" Next Door. By fundamentally changing popular perceptions of North Korea, the plight of the abductees prepared the Japanese public to accept, if not demand, missile defense. Before the Pyongyang summit in September 2002, most Japanese viewed the DPRK with relative ambivalence. Kim Jong-il's admission that his country had kidnapped Japanese citizens provoked a wave of anger against North Korea. Rather than subsiding, antipathy for the DPRK actually deepened as more information emerged about the abductions. Of the thirteen Japanese nationals kidnapped by North Korean agents, eight died under mysterious circumstances—gas poisoning, automobile crashes, drowning, heart attacks, and suicide. Adding to popular suspicions, all abductees received death certificates from the same hospital, although they allegedly perished in different locations.[15] Based on this evidence, the public concluded that North Korea murdered many of the Japanese citizens it kidnapped. As if Pyongyang's culpability in the deaths of eight Japanese was insufficient to inflame popular sentiment, the DPRK refused to release the families of the five abductees who returned to Japan in October 2002. The Japanese government sought to use the Six-Party Talks and bilateral channels to unite the families, but until May 2004, these efforts were to no avail.[16] Finally, the number of potential abductions more than doubled after the establishment of the Investigation Commission on Missing Japanese Probably Related to North Korea (COMJAN). By December 2003, COMJAN had investigated 370 missing person cases, of which 16 appeared to involve Pyongyang.

The plight of the abductees engendered a popular backlash against North Korea that had at least three ramifications for missile defense. First, the abductions sounded a death knell for *Chosen Soren*'s influence in Japanese politics. *Chosen Soren* became the focus of popular hatred to such a degree that the government reportedly deployed riot police to prevent attacks on the organization's facilities. Prior to September 2002, major LDP politicians had routinely attended *Chosen Soren*'s founding day banquet, an event that commemorated the DPRK's creation. After the abduction issue came to light, public outrage prevented even representatives of the Japanese Communist Party from participating in this annual rite.[17] In short, *Chosen Soren* became a pariah among elites and the public. As a result, measures directed against North Korea—missile defense—encountered minimal domestic opposition.

Second, emotions stemming from the abduction issue rendered the public receptive to BMD. Japanese media coverage of the abductees dramatically revealed the DPRK's brutality and aggressiveness. Psychologically, the public linked these kidnappings to North Korea's military capabilities: both appeared to demonstrate Pyongyang's inherent hostility toward Japan. As a result, North Korea's growing arsenal of missiles, nuclear program, and spy boat intrusions became more than just an existential danger. In light of the abductions, the public perceived North Korean capabilities as a tangible security threat.

Third, the plight of the abductees led popular opinion to support a hard-line approach to North Korea's nuclear program. The kidnapping of Japanese nationals created a general sense of loathing toward "sending rice and money"—Tokyo's former policy for managing its relations with the DPRK. Thus, as attempts to reunify the abductees and their families proved fruitless, the public increasingly favored aggressive methods to resolve the nuclear crisis. In a January 2003 survey conducted by *Mainichi Shimbun*, 25 percent of poll recipients supported a "hard-line stance" toward North Korea, while 65 percent called for "dialogue." By June 2003, those favoring hard-line economic measures or U.S. military pressure to disarm Pyongyang composed a majority of survey participants—44 percent and 9 percent, respectively. Slightly more than a third of respondents continued to support dialogue as a strategy for dismantling the DPRK's nuclear program.[18] Neither of these *Mainichi Shimbun* polls explicitly referred to missile defense. Even so, popular backing for hard-line measures likely translated into support for BMD.

Of course, these survey results reflect more than the impact of the abductions. North Korea's intransigence on the nuclear front and its test-firing of short-range missiles also contributed to a hardening of popular sentiment. In fact, as the saga of the abductees and the nuclear crisis unfolded simultaneously, the distinction between the kidnappings and traditional security concerns became increasingly blurred.

No-dongs, Nukes, and North Korea–Phobia

The fusion of the abduction issue and military threats gave birth to a new political force—"North Korea–phobia." This phenomenon, characterized by acute public anxiety, created unparalleled opportunities for proponents of BMD. Fear of a North Korean attack increased substantially after September 2002. Before Koizumi's Pyongyang summit, the general populace considered security matters a low priority within Japan-DPRK relations. In a poll conducted by *Tokyo Shimbun* on September 7, 2002, only 13.1 percent of respondents deemed "North Korea's suspected development of nuclear weapons and missiles" the bilateral issue of greatest concern.[19] If measured through public support for missile defense cooperation, popular anxiety regarding the DPRK's military capabilities actually declined in the late 1990s. After the Taepo-dong launch in 1998, 32 percent of the Japanese public remained opposed to BMD development. Two years later, this proportion had risen to 46 percent, while those who favored cooperation stood at 41 percent.[20] Popular ambivalence toward the DPRK's military capabilities thus posed a major challenge for advocates of missile defense before October 2002.

Public indifference became outright alarm in the wake of Assistant Secretary of State Kelly's visit to Pyongyang. An *Asahi Shimbun* poll taken one month later found that 95 percent of respondents expressed "concern" at North Korea's nuclear program.[21] Unlike 1998, repeated DPRK provocations sustained the public's sense of insecurity over a prolonged time period. As a result, between November 2002 and April 2003, the proportion of Japanese who felt "somewhat uneasy" or "very uneasy" about North Korea's military capabilities remained close to 90 percent. In fact, individuals professing the most severe anxiety predominated and by April 2003 constituted 65 percent of all respondents.[22] The public's heightened sense of insecurity impressed itself on members of the Japanese government. One anecdote provided by a JDA official is worth retelling. When lecturing to audiences across Japan, the official encountered a surprising level of public unease. Groups typically removed from national security debates—housewives, for example—seemed genuinely afraid of a North Korean attack.[23] Clearly, North Korea–phobia had become widespread.

Popular anxiety regarding Pyongyang's military capabilities was largely a natural reaction. No public could easily disregard an emotional issue like the abductees when evaluating the intentions behind a foreign state's military posture. That being said, Japanese politicians actively blurred the distinction between the intentions conveyed by the abductions and the aims underlying North Korea's missile and nuclear buildup.

Statements by then JDA chief Ishiba encouraged the public to view the abductions and the DPRK's military capabilities as one and the same. In November 2002, Ishiba argued that "missile defense is one option in dealing with an adventurous state that is not affected by deterrence."[24] Ishiba made this assertion despite the fact that his own defense analysts considered a North Korean attack deterrable under most circumstances.[25] Moreover, Pyongyang's most "adventurous" security behavior lay in the future: the DPRK began to reprocess spent fuel rods after December 2002. Whether deliberate or not, the adventurism referred to by Ishiba evoked the abduction issue. For most Japanese, the abductions highlighted the hostile, seemingly irrational nature of the North Korean regime. Ishiba's comments therefore reinforced the public's natural tendency to believe that the intentions communicated by the abduction issue signaled North Korea's willingness to use missiles and nuclear weapons against Japan.

Multiple politicians seized upon the abduction issue to advocate BMD. To the right of Ishiba, political figures like Tokyo governor Ishihara Shintaro blatantly manipulated the abductions to exploit the public's North Korea–phobia. At times, Ishihara's statements verged on demagoguery:

> We are under threat ourselves from another terrorist state, North Korea, which has kidnapped 150 of our citizens. 150 people! I don't think any of them are alive. Pyongyang is also sending boatloads of drugs to Japan to harm our youngsters, and

it has missiles ready to hit 15 Japanese cities . . . . This is the country that says it is ready to deliver a "sea of fire" over Japan.[26]

By framing the DPRK in terms of the abductions, Ishihara conveyed a clear message to the Japanese public: the intentions underlying North Korea's missile and nuclear buildup are unpredictable and aggressive. Moreover, Ishihara's statement carried an additional subtext. If Kim Jong-il's regime constituted a "terrorist state," Tokyo's only recourse would be enhanced military capabilities. As demonstrated by Ishihara and Ishiba, the confluence of Pyongyang's missile rattling, nuclear provocations, and the abduction issue provided a golden opportunity for proponents of a "normal" Japan.

North Korea–Phobia as a Catalyst for BMD

Popular fear of a North Korean attack—whether spontaneous or the product of elite rhetoric—decisively influenced the fate of Japanese BMD. As the public's sense of insecurity deepened, the political imperative to deploy a missile defense system grew accordingly. Thus, North Korea–phobia overrode many of the obstacles that had previously hindered Tokyo's consideration of BMD.[27]

Technical Feasibility: Hitting a Bullet with a Bullet. Prior to October 2002, questions of technical feasibility precluded Japanese development or deployment of missile defense. Political elites doubted whether BMD systems designed by the United States could function in the narrow time frame created by Japan's geography.[28] Another criticism of BMD was that the underlying technology would become mature long after Japan resolved current missile threats.[29] Furthermore, Japanese politicians held extremely high expectations for BMD's performance effectiveness. Because Japan's population is distributed among a handful of large urban centers, leakage by even one missile armed with a nuclear weapon could result in mass casualties. In mid-2002, Japanese missile defense needed to approach a 100 percent interception rate to be politically viable.[30]

Thirteen months after North Korea's nuclear revelation, the GOJ professed complete faith in BMD's technical feasibility. Upon announcing the Japanese government's decision to purchase missile defense, then chief cabinet secretary Fukuda offered several explanations for this apparent conversion. Fukuda cited the success of "interception tests and various performance evaluations in the United States and . . . our own simulation results."[31] He also justified the cabinet's decision by noting that the U.S. government had deemed BMD technology mature enough to deploy. In the past, the progress noted by Fukuda would not have dispelled Japanese skepticism toward missile defense technology. The United States conducted three flight tests of Aegis BMD between October 2002 and December 2003. Two of the three trials resulted in a successful intercept, a far cry from 100 percent effectiveness. Additionally, many U.S.-based security experts considered these flight tests heavily scripted: interceptions occurred under conditions that bore little resemblance to real combat. Thus, although the U.S. government opted to deploy BMD, the system's technical feasibility remained in doubt.

Fukuda's statement therefore reflected a key development in the GOJ's approach to missile defense: the watering down of once rigorous criteria for technical feasibility. Popular opinion led the Japanese government to adopt less stringent expectations for BMD's performance effectiveness. Given the public's rising sense of insecurity, failure to address North Korea's nuclear and missile buildup would have undermined the GOJ's legitimacy. By introducing BMD, the Japanese government could visibly demonstrate its responsiveness to the DPRK threat.[32] Thus, even after Tokyo decided to purchase missile defense, JDA officials and SDF personnel continued to (privately) recognize the system's technical limitations. Performance effectiveness, though still important, had become secondary to a new political criterion—restoring the public's sense of physical security.[33]

BMD and the Defense Budget. Until the advent of North Korea–phobia, financial considerations constituted a significant challenge to deploying missile defense. In Japan's case, economic weakness transformed defense allocations into a zero-sum game. Faced with ever higher social security payouts, declining revenue, and a national debt exceeding 150 percent of GDP, the Japanese government lacked the resources to finance BMD outside existing defense budgets.[34] However, the 2000 Mid-Term Defense Program could not accommodate missile defense. Funding for the procurement of new equipment related solely to weapon modernization programs. Consequently, missile defense presented the JDA and the SDF in particular with a painful choice—sacrificing conventional force upgrades to fund BMD. To say that the SDF services were reluctant to forgo mainstream procurements for missile defense would be an understatement. In 2002, BMD contained the potential to unleash an interservice struggle over the distribution of program cuts.[35]

Yet, by September 2003, the JDA opted to fund missile defense through reducing conventional procurements.[36] Moreover, the decision to introduce BMD resulted in a minimum of interservice rivalry.[37] Public opinion constituted one reason behind the JDA's increasing willingness to postpone force modernization. As popular fear of a North Korean attack intensified, the acceptable cost of BMD—in monetary terms and conventional procurements—rose proportionally. This dynamic stemmed from the same political logic that lowered government expectations of BMD's performance effectiveness. At the same time, other factors beside public sentiment enabled the JDA to fund missile defense. Reprioritization of SDF roles and missions was a more critical factor. The cost savings that resulted from purchasing missile defense off-the-shelf also rendered BMD more palatable from a budgetary perspective.

Promoting Diet Support for BMD. Popular opinion exerted a major, perhaps decisive influence over the Diet's treatment of BMD. North Korea–phobia compelled Japan's major political parties to endorse missile defense. Before October 2002, neither the LDP nor the DPJ had firmly supported BMD development or deployment. Although most LDP members favored some form of missile defense, questions of technical feasibility, cost, and legality inhibited active support. Furthermore, some LDP legislators opposed BMD on the grounds that the system would destabilize Japan's relationship with China. This group included the once dominant Hashimoto faction. Unlike the LDP, the DPJ lacked even a rough consensus on missile defense.[38] The party's former socialist wing opposed missile defense, while LDP defectors viewed BMD more positively. Then DPJ president Yukio Hatoyama embodied his party's schizophrenic attitude toward missile defense. During the prelude to the 2000 Upper House elections, Hatoyama characterized BMD as an attempt by Washington to gain access to Japanese technology. In the election's aftermath, however, Hatoyama asserted that he would support exercising the right of collective defense, a position held by most proponents of BMD.[39]

Clearly, no observer in 2002 would have predicted that *both* the LDP and the DPJ would endorse missile defense less than two years later. Public fear of a North Korean attack overrode lawmakers' earlier concerns. Neither party could ignore the Japanese people's acute sense of insecurity. To appear passive in the face of North Korean provocations risked electoral defeat.[40] This was particularly true for the DPJ, a party seeking to establish itself as a viable alternative to LDP rule. Endorsing missile defense allowed the DPJ to act as a responsible opposition party capable of assuming the reins of government. Hence, Naoto Kan, who succeeded Hatoyama as DPJ president, chose to signal his support for BMD two months after North Korea withdrew from the Nuclear Non-Proliferation Treaty.[41]

The political imperative created by North Korea–phobia served in another capacity to expedite the Diet's consideration of BMD. Lawmakers acceded to, indeed condoned, the Koizumi administration's efforts to roll back legal hurdles associated with missile defense. In mid-2002, the prohibition on collective defense constituted an intractable barrier to deploying BMD. The government's legal interpretation prevented the exchange of theater-area information between the U.S. military and the SDF.[42] As a result, the robust C4I infrastructure needed for an effective missile defense system appeared unrealizable. Additionally, the ban on collective defense precluded the integration of Japanese BMD assets into the Pentagon's global missile defense architecture.[43] Given that most Diet members lacked any familiarity with the technical and strategic aspects of missile defense, national security elites expected that the right of collective defense would dominate legislative proceedings on BMD.[44]

To the contrary, the legality of missile defense became a nonissue under the political landscape created by the North Korean threat. When Fukuda announced the government's decision to purchase BMD, only the remnants of Japan's once powerful Left raised the issue of collective defense. Equally notable, the GOJ expanded the definition of self-defense to circumvent constitutional restrictions on BMD without provoking a reaction from the Diet. To overcome one hurdle to Tokyo's participation in a global missile defense architecture—the possible use of Japanese BMD assets to defend U.S. territory—the Cabinet Legislation Bureau ruled that intercepting a missile "judged to have a significant probability of targeting Japan . . . will be considered to have justified our right to self-defense."[45] This ruling meant that inadvertently protecting the U.S. homeland from missile attack fell within the interpreted scope of Article 9.[46] In the past, the constitutional implications of the Cabinet Legislation Bureau's statement would have aroused significant controversy. However, as Diet members sought to reassure constituents frightened by North Korea, the Koizumi administration's subversion of Article 9 went largely unchallenged.

The government's effort to broaden the definition of self-defense also included the exchange of theater-area information. In January 2004, the Cabinet Legislation Bureau held that "it's necessary to share intelligence between our two countries to guarantee Japan's security. Doing so does not constitute an attempt to gather intelligence for the purposes of supporting U.S. military actions."[47] This ruling signaled a subtle, but important deviation from the government's past interpretation of collective defense. The GOJ recognized that a global missile defense architecture would incorporate data from Japanese sensors.[48] Thus the Cabinet Legislation Bureau asserted that in the case of BMD, constitutionality depended on the intent rather than the outcome of intelligence sharing. In the political climate that existed prior to October 2002, this de facto, albeit narrowly oriented reinterpretation of collective defense would have ignited fierce debate within the Diet. That it did not is testimony to the transformation wrought by popular fear of North Korea.

U.S. Policy: "Pushing an Open Door"

U.S. policy played a minimal role in the Japanese government's decision to purchase missile defense. In fact, the North Korean threat prevailed over Washington's influence before and after October 2002. Until 1994, the Japanese government refused to even participate in bilateral studies of missiles defense. Instead, the GOJ outsourced the "Western Pacific Basin Architecture Study" to private companies. Japan's initial wariness of BMD stemmed from two concerns: First, Tokyo feared that missile defense would serve as a pretext for technology transfer and reducing the bilateral trade deficit. Second, the weaponization of space associated with the Reagan-era "Star Wars" program rendered BMD politically unattractive. The Japanese government embarked on the Bilateral Study on BMD in 1994. Not coincidentally, this insourcing of missile defense followed the DPRK's test of a No-dong, the first North Korean missile capable of reaching Japan. Washington continued to press Tokyo to participate in BMD research after 1994.[49] For example, in 1995 the U.S. government approached MOFA to discuss advancing missile defense beyond the bilateral study. MOFA declined.[50] Although the Japanese government agreed to joint research three years later, it did so in response to the Taepo-dong flyover. In the absence of further North Korean provocations, Washington's later efforts to expand BMD cooperation met with little success.[51]

Despite the advent of North Korea–phobia, U.S. policy continued to occupy a backseat position in Japanese considerations of BMD. Between October 2002 and December 2003, Washington's representatives at both the working and senior levels urged Tokyo to move forward on missile defense.[52] But bilateral meetings merely confirmed the GOJ's desire to adopt a new, accelerated time line for BMD. Confronted by a nuclear-armed North Korea, JDA officials proved as eager as their U.S. counterparts to advance beyond joint BMD research. Given the Japanese side's enthusiasm, Washington's emissaries found that urging Tokyo to deploy missile defense was like "pushing an open door."[53] Similar to the 1990s, the North Korean threat rather than U.S. policy prompted Japanese support for BMD.

However, U.S. influence has more subtle manifestations. Did general expectations surrounding the bilateral alliance underpin Tokyo's decision to introduce BMD? No, because from the fall of 2001 to December 2003, the impact of alliance expectations on missile defense actually declined. Following September 11, and particularly during and after the Iraq War, other security issues superseded BMD at the forefront of the alliance agenda. MSDF dispatch to the Indian Ocean and Japanese support on Iraq became U.S. priorities. Under these circumstances, resisting Washington's calls for greater BMD cooperation had few repercussions for the alliance, provided that Tokyo assisted the United States on more important fronts. Without the prospect of outside punishment, internalized *gaiatsu* operated weakly, if at all. Conversely, Japan possessed a wealth of opportunities to strengthen the alliance post-September 11. Missile defense presented Tokyo with the highest financial cost for the least alliance payoff. Thus, in contrast to the cases of September 11 or Iraq, U.S. expectations seldom entered into the Japanese government's final decision on BMD.

Executive Leadership: Missile Defense as the JDA's Initiative

In marked contrast to September 11, prime ministerial leadership was generally absent from the GOJ's consideration of missile defense. The technical nature of BMD naturally ensured the JDA a prominent decisionmaking role. However, technical complexity alone did not preclude the prime minister from seizing the initiative on missile defense. Indeed, one previous Japanese executive—Prime Minister Hashimoto—played an active part in securing funds for joint BMD research. Nevertheless, Hashimoto delegated most responsibilities for missile defense to his subordinates. Direct prime ministerial involvement declined with subsequent administrations. Keizo Obuchi's chief cabinet secretary, Hiromu Nonaka, garnered Diet support for BMD research, and under Yoshiro Mori, missile defense became the JDA's sole jurisdiction.[54] Much like his predecessors, Koizumi remained a marginal player in the government's evaluation of BMD. Political considerations may have dictated the prime minister's hands-off approach; given that BMD constituted a low-profile, relatively noncontroversial defense issue, Koizumi could invest his political capital in more contentious security debates like Iraq. Furthermore, the prime minister lacked strong convictions either for or against deployment.[55] The JDA thus took the lead on missile defense throughout Koizumi's tenure. For example, at the Crawford summit in May 2003, the prime minister announced that Japan would accelerate consideration of BMD, yet the JDA had already done so months earlier.[56] Rather than outdistancing the government's position on missile defense, Koizumi merely gave retroactive confirmation to policies undertaken by the JDA.

If any official deserves credit for facilitating Japan's decision to acquire BMD, that individual is Shigeru Ishiba.[57] Unlike the previous JDA chief, Ishiba viewed the prohibition on collective defense as a barrier that could (and should) be overcome to permit new SDF roles and capabilities—BMD included.[58] During the last months of 2002, Ishiba deviated from the government's public line and advocated missile defense. Although the JDA chief's "personal" comments received the cabinet's tacit approval, he still risked criticism by the media and the Diet. Calling on the government to expedite its consideration of BMD thus required a degree of political courage. In sum, the leadership that expedited BMD occurred at the cabinet level of government.

Generational Change: Toward a BMD Consensus

The DPRK threat eliminated generational differences on missile defense. Before the advent of the North Korean nuclear crisis, junior lawmakers viewed BMD more positively than their older colleagues.[59] Senior legislator's ambivalence or opposition to missile defense stemmed from a number of factors—legality, cost, and the impact of BMD on Sino-Japanese relations. Generational differences within the DPJ were especially pronounced because the party's older membership hailed from the left-wing Social Democratic Party.[60] Once the DPRK's nuclear program came to light, however, generational variation surrounding BMD decreased substantially. China's reaction and the prohibition on collective defense—concerns once held by older legislators—largely disappeared from political discourse. The majority of senior Diet members embraced, or at least accepted, missile defense.

Japan's Strategic Evolution: Kim Jong-il in the Driver's Seat?

Tokyo's decision to introduce BMD offers multiple insights into Japan's strategic evolution. Missile defense reveals that foreign threats, if sufficiently urgent, can transform the framework by which politicians and the public evaluate security issues. Prior to October 2002, the Japanese government's approach to BMD typified that of a norms-based defense policy. Rather than calibrating the SDF's future capabilities to existing or expected threats, politicians agonized over the constitutionality of missile defense. More generally, domestic issues preoccupied the Diet's initial deliberations on BMD. Yet, when North Korea emerged as a nuclear threat, Tokyo's assessment of missile defense assumed an entirely different character—that of an interest-based security strategy. Neutralizing the DPRK's missile and nuclear buildup rapidly trumped constitutional concerns. Indeed, that the public and the Diet failed to react as the Koizumi administration achieved a de facto reinterpretation of collective defense indicates that institutionalized and internalized norms are less deeply embedded than once thought.

Calculations of national and political interest compelled the GOJ to acquire missile defense. By raising the Japanese public's sense of insecurity to unprecedented levels, Pyongyang transformed BMD into a political issue. Diet members opposing missile defense after October 2002 risked electoral punishment, because vocal objections to BMD would appear as appeasement in the face of North Korean provocations. The political classes responded to and also influenced popular opinion on missile defense. Public fear of a North Korean attack arose primarily as a spontaneous reaction to the abductions and the DPRK's revived nuclear program. At the same time, politicians manipulated North Korea–phobia to generate support for BMD. This dynamic illustrates the dual impact of foreign threats on Japan's body politic. External threats promote realist values both directly and through strengthening political elements that already favor a "normal" defense policy.

Finally, missile defense contradicts a key insight derived from Japan's response to September 11—that Tokyo's strategic transition is internally driven. BMD suggests precisely the opposite. The North Korean threat, an exogenous variable, decisively influenced Japan's consideration of missile defense. In a historic irony, Kim Jong-il constituted BMD's most effective advocate.

Notes

[1] Although some Japanese officials viewed BMD as a useful hedge against China's future security behavior, the PRC played a minimal role in expediting Tokyo's consideration of missile defense. Author's interview with JDA official, Tokyo, March 2004.

[2] Cabinet Office, "Statement by the Chief Cabinet Secretary," December 19, 2003, http://www.kantei.go.jp/foreign/tyokan/2003/1219danwa_e.html.

[3] "Argument Supportive of Missile Defense Gaining Momentum among Minshuto," *Asahi Shimbun*, April 3, 2003.

[4] North Korea threatened to lift the missile moratorium if Japan failed to move forward on normalizing bilateral relations. The DPRK also tested surface-to-ship missiles that fell below the range stipulated in the moratorium.

[5] Nuclear Threat Initiative, "North Korea Profile: Missile Overview," August 2004, http://www.nti.org/e_research/profiles/NK/Missile/index.html.

[6] Barbara Wanner, "Japan-North Korea Relations Improving but Formal Ties Remain Uncertain," *Japan Economic Institute Report*, no. 44 (November 21, 1997), http://www.jei.org/Archive/JEIR97/9744f.html#Heading2.

[7] I omit the DPRK's chemical and biological capabilities because they do not compare, in resulting casualties or psychological effect on Japan, to the impact of a nuclear weapon.

[8] Nuclear Threat Initiative, "North Korea Profile: Nuclear Overview," May 2005, http://www.nti.org/e_research/profiles/NK/Nuclear/index.html.

[9] Mid-range estimate cited in Jon B. Wolfsthal, "Estimates of North Korea's Unchecked Nuclear Weapons Production Potential" (working paper from Non-Proliferation Project, Carnegie Endowment for International Peace, Washington, D.C., July 2003), 2.

[10] "U.S. Told Japan that North Korea Has Several Nuclear Warheads," *Agence France Presse*, June 21, 2003.

[11] David Fouse, "Japan Gets Serious about Missile Defense," *Asia-Pacific Security Studies* 2, no. 4 (June 2003): 2.

[12] "Jumping the Gun on Missile Defense," *Mainichi Shimbun*, December 20, 2002.

[13] Author's interview with JDA staffer, Tokyo, March 2004.

[14] Mark E. Manyin, "Japan–North Korea Relations: Selected Issues," CRS Report for Congress RL32161, Washington, D.C., November 26, 2003, 11.

[15] Ministry of Foreign Affairs, "Abductions of Japanese Citizens by North Korea," n.d., http://www.mofa.go.jp/region/asia-paci/n_korea/abduction.pdf.

[16] The May 2004 summit between Koizumi and Kim Jong-il secured the release of five of the abductees' children. In July 2004, the husband of Hitomi Soga—Charles Jenkins—and their two daughters were repatriated to Japan via Indonesia.

[17] James Brooke, "North Korea Birthday Party in Japan Illustrates Strains," *New York Times*, September 9, 2003.

[18] Although the two polls conducted by *Mainichi Shimbun* differ somewhat in wording, the questions are similar enough to demonstrate that popular attitudes toward North Korea hardened after January 2003. "Poll on Koizumi Cabinet, Political Parties," *Mainichi Shimbun*, January 28, 2003; and "Poll on Koizumi Cabinet, Political Parties, SARS, Emergency Legislation, North Korea," *Mainichi Shimbun*, June 2, 2003.

[19] "Poll on Koizumi Cabinet, Political Parties, North Korea Ties," *Tokyo Shimbun*, September 7, 2002.

[20] Poll conducted by the United States Information Agency cited in Richard P. Cronin, "Japan-U.S. Cooperation on Ballistic Missile Defense: Issues and Prospects," CRS Report for Congress RL31337, Washington, D.C., March 19, 2002, 21.

[21] *Asahi Shimbun* poll cited in James Brooke, "A Missile Shield Appeals to a Worried Japan," *New York Times*, November 10, 2002.

[22] "Poll on Koizumi Cabinet, Political Parties, Iraq, and North Korea," *Yomiuri Shimbun*, March 25, 2003; and "Poll on Iraq Issues," *Yomiuri Shimbun*, April 21, 2003.

[23] Author's interview with JDA official, Tokyo, March 2004.

[24] "As North Korea Talks Stall, Calls Grow for Missile Defense," *Asahi Shimbun*, November 19, 2002.

[25] Author's interview with JDA official, Tokyo, March 2004.

[26] Ishihara Shintaro quoted in Victor D. Cha, "Containment Lite," *Comparative Connections* 5, no. 2 (April–June 2003): 119–126.

[27] This section draws upon Kliman, "U.S.-Japan Missile Defense Cooperation."

[28] Author's interview with former Japanese minister of foreign affairs, Tokyo, July 2002.

[29] "As North Korea Talks Stall, Calls Grow for Missile Defense," *Asahi Shimbun*, November 19, 2002.

[30] Author's interview with JDA official, Tokyo, August 2002.

[31] Cabinet Office, "Statement by the Chief Cabinet Secretary," December 19, 2003.

[32] Author's interview with MSDF officer, Tokyo, March 2004.

[33] Author's interviews with JDA officials and MSDF officer, Tokyo, March 2004.

[34] Michael Swaine, Rachel Swanger, and Takashi Kawakami, *Japan and Ballistic Missile Defense* (Santa Monica: RAND Corporation, 2001), 67.

[35] Author's interview with JDA official, Tokyo, August 2002.

[36] "Japan to Cut Defense Buildup Target to Fund Missile System," *Jiji Press*, September 1, 2003.

[37] E-mail correspondence with SDF officer, May 12, 2004.

[38] Cronin, "Japan-U.S. Cooperation on Ballistic Missile Defense," 18.

[39] Swaine et al., *Japan and Ballistic Missile Defense*, 57, 59.

[40] Author's interview with LDP Upper House member, Tokyo, August 2003.

[41] "Argument Supportive of Missile Defense Gaining Momentum in Minshuto," *Asahi Shimbun*, April 3, 2003.

[42] Mark T. Staples, "Legal Reform of the Self-Defense Forces," in *United States–Japan Strategic Dialogue: Beyond the Defense Guidelines*, ed. Brad Glosserman et al. (Honolulu: Pacific Forum CSIS, 2001), 46.

[43] Author's interview with MOFA official, Tokyo, July 2002.

[44] Author's interview with JDA official, Tokyo, August 2002.

[45] "Ishiba: Japan to 'Counterattack' if N. Korea Prepares to Attack," *Yomiuri Shimbun*, January 25, 2003.

[46] In reality, the trajectory of a missile aimed at the United States would be easily differentiable from that of a missile targeted at Japan. However, Japan could conceivably provide early warning data on a missile destined for U.S. territory, an act that would have previously qualified as collective defense. Trajectory information from e-mail correspondence with Dean Wilkening, Stanford University, January 26, 2003.

[47] "Successful Missile Defense Requires Close U.S. Support," *Yomiuri Shimbun*, March 29, 2004.

[48] "Japan, U.S. to Share Radar Defense Data," *Yomiuri Shimbun*, March 29, 2004.

[49] Cronin, "Japan-U.S. Cooperation on Ballistic Missile Defense"; and Swaine et al., *Japan and Ballistic Missile Defense*, 20–21.

[50] Author's interview with former Japanese minister for foreign affairs, Tokyo, July 2002.

[51] Japan never acted on the U.S. request to expand joint BMD cooperation to include radar-tracking technology. "U.S. Seeks More Japan Missile Input," *Asahi Shimbun*, June 2, 2001.

[52] U.S. Department of Defense, "Under Secretary Feith Roundtable with Japanese, U.S., and International Media," November 8, 2002, http://www.defense.gov/transcripts/2002/t11122002_t1108feith.html; and "Japan Urged to Adopt U.S. Missile Defense System," *Japan Times*, June 14, 2003.

[53] Author's interview with U.S. official, Tokyo, March 2004.

[54] Swaine et al., *Japan and Ballistic Missile Defense*, 42–43.

[55] Author's interview with JDA official, Tokyo, March 2004.

[56] The White House, "President Bush Meets with Japanese Prime Minister Koizumi," May 23, 2003, http://www.whitehouse.gov/news/releases/2003/05/20030523-4.html.

[57] Author's interview with JDA official, Tokyo, March 2004.

[58] Fouse, "Japan Gets Serious about Missile Defense."

[59] Author's interview with LDP Upper House member, Tokyo, March 2004.

[60] Author's interview with former Japanese minister for foreign affairs, Tokyo, July 2002.

6

Japan, the Iraq War, and Postconflict Reconstruction

Compared to other foreign policy shocks, the Iraq War led to the most dramatic shift in Japan's defense policy. Three of the four factors that make up the transitional model—foreign threats, U.S. policy, and executive leadership—significantly influenced Japan's response to the removal of Saddam Hussein and postconflict reconstruction. However, actual and apparent manifestations of these variables sometimes differed. The gap between articulated and perceived threats embodies this disparity. Koizumi's public rationale for supporting the U.S. attack on Iraq highlighted the threat created by the proliferation of WMD. After the war's conclusion, the prime minister cited the danger of a destabilized Middle East to justify SDF participation in the rebuilding of Iraq. But in reality, the main foreign threat that entered into Japan's Iraq calculus was North Korea.

Like external threats, U.S. policy played a vital role in shaping Japan's approach to Iraq. As before, Washington's representatives relied primarily on broad expectations to influence Tokyo's security behavior. Whether in public forums or private consultations, U.S. officials refused to articulate a vision of Japan's wartime support. Although Tokyo's assistance to postwar Iraq reflected more overt manifestations of U.S. influence, Washington couched its expectations in vague concepts like international responsibility. To describe the impact of U.S. policy as internalized *gaiatsu* would be misleading. At the outbreak of the Iraq War, Japan also evaluated the benefits of meeting international and alliance expectations. By March 2003, fulfilling outside expectations offered a significant payoff: deterring North Korea through strengthening the bilateral alliance. Thus, Japanese policymakers met and at times exceeded U.S. expectations.

Japan's response to the Iraq crisis also reflected Koizumi's leadership. As in the aftermath of September 11, the prime minister decided Japan's security policy in consultation with only a few key advisers. When the opposition parties balked, the prime minister used the ruling coalition to force Iraq dispatch legislation through the Diet. Equally notable, Koizumi dared to defy public opinion by supporting U.S. action against Iraq and later deploying SDF peacekeepers. Rather than reaping the whirlwind of plunging opinion ratings, Koizumi endured only a temporary downturn in popular support. The prime minister's leadership was lacking in only one respect; Koizumi could disregard, but not *shape*, public opinion.

Finally, demographic factors exerted a negligible impact on Japan's Iraq policy. At the elite level, Japan's approach to the Iraq crisis contradicted the standard hypothesis of generational change. Throughout the Diet's deliberations, party affiliation rather than age divided lawmakers.

Foreign Threats: Looking Close to Home

What threats motivated Japan's response to the Iraq War and postconflict reconstruction? Like its U.S. counterpart, did the Koizumi administration perceive Iraq's purported WMD programs as a "grave and growing" danger?[1] After the war's denouement, did the scenario of a destabilized Middle East lead the Japanese government to dispatch SDF peacekeepers? Or rather, did the specter of a nuclear North Korea overshadow Tokyo's Iraq policy?

Iraqi WMD: Peril and Pretext

When addressing the public, members of the Japanese government professed great anxiety over Saddam Hussein's covert WMD programs. As war appeared imminent, Prime Minister Koizumi dwelt on the threat posed by Iraq's biological, chemical,

and latent nuclear capabilities. In particular, Koizumi emphasized that Iraqi WMD endangered more than U.S. interests:
"What would be the consequences were dangerous weapons of
mass destruction to fall into the hands of a dangerous dictator?
Any consequences would certainly not be limited to the people of
the United States. This is not a matter without implications for Japan either."[2] Like Bush, Koizumi highlighted the proliferation
threat posed by the nexus of international terrorism and Iraqi
WMD. Although stopping short of claiming that Saddam's regime
had active ties with Al Qaeda, Koizumi forcefully articulated the
perils of national WMD programs in a world beset by terrorism:
"The international community has become keenly aware of the
horror of nuclear materials, biological weapons, and chemical
weapons falling into the hands of terrorists. In the world today,
the question of whether you possess weapons of mass destruction
or not is not something that could be left unanswered."[3]

In public, at least, the Japanese government in the person of
Prime Minister Koizumi clearly viewed Iraqi WMD as a threat
meriting U.S. military action. And yet, a cynical observer might
rightly question the prime minister's sincerity. After all, by endorsing a U.S. attack on Iraq, Koizumi flouted public opinion. At one
point 80 percent of Japanese opposed the war.[4] To explain such
an unpopular decision, what skilled politician would not seize
upon any and all possible justifications?

This cynicism is largely unfounded. Koizumi genuinely believed that Iraq possessed WMD. U.S. intelligence convinced the
prime minister that Baghdad maintained covert WMD programs.[5] Moreover, the prime minister and the GOJ as a whole put
equal or greater store in Iraq's refusal to comply with multiple UN
Security Council resolutions. To Japanese policymakers, this track
record suggested that Saddam's regime had something to hide—
namely, WMD.[6] Thus, both Koizumi and the larger government
considered Iraqi WMD a likely probability. However, neither the
prime minister nor the GOJ viewed Iraqi WMD as a direct threat.
Japan's geographic distance from the Middle East naturally precluded an Iraqi attack.[7] Koizumi's rhetoric aside, the Japanese
government also held few concerns that Baghdad's chemical, biological, or nuclear stockpile might fall into the hands of terrorists.
On the contrary, the JDA projected that Saddam would retain
control over his WMD arsenal.[8] And furthermore, the possibility

that Iraq might transfer WMD to a third country engendered little anxiety in Tokyo. The one state in Japan's proximity that would seek such weapons—North Korea—already possessed them.[9]

Then what, if any, threat did Iraqi WMD pose to Japan? Tokyo perceived Iraq's defiance of the UN Security Council as related to other cases of WMD proliferation. If the international community successfully dealt with Baghdad's intransigence, other proliferators would be deterred. Alternatively, if the world proved unable or unwilling to confront Iraq on WMD, such a failure would "give a green light" to other rogue states. This logic surfaced during internal MOFA deliberations and, not surprisingly, pertained to North Korea. Interestingly, MOFA decided to exclude this link between Iraq and North Korea from Koizumi's talking points on WMD. Instead, the ministry opted for a vague statement that merely cited WMD's relevance to the "Asian region."[10] Nonetheless, the belief that disarming Baghdad would have positive repercussions vis-à-vis North Korea informed Koizumi's consideration of WMD.[11]

Unlike government officials, most Diet members ignored WMD when formulating a position on Iraq.[12] In fact, lawmakers seldom, if ever, perceived Iraqi WMD as a potential threat to Japan. The results of three *Asahi Shimbun* polls are striking in this regard. Each survey queried the same 20 legislators whose party affiliation mirrored that of the actual Diet. A total of 12 lawmakers consistently "supported" or "understood" the U.S. strategy toward Iraq. Yet across the three surveys, only one of thirty-six positive responses cited WMD as a rationale for endorsing the U.S. position. And the threat posed by WMD was merely implied by Taro Nakayama, who stated that "Iraq must prove its scrapping of WMD before the international community."[13] Members of the LDP failed to echo the prime minister's assertion that Iraqi WMD would endanger the international community and Japan. Even specialists in defense and foreign affairs, Gen Nakatani and Yoshimasa Hayashi respectively, were silent on the proliferation threat posed by Saddam's unconventional arsenal. Instead, many of the 12 lawmakers identified the U.S.-Japan alliance and North Korea as factors warranting Tokyo's support for Iraqi regime change.

In sum, government officials and legislators never viewed Saddam's acquisition of WMD as a direct threat to Japan's security. Instead, Iraqi WMD mainly threatened Japan via North Korea.

Stabilizing the Middle East

As Operation Iraqi Freedom commenced on March 20, 2003, the Japanese government began to indicate that reconstruction assistance would be forthcoming after the war's conclusion. To justify his government's postwar contribution, Prime Minister Koizumi again invoked a threat to Japan's national security—instability in the Middle East. At the outset, Koizumi offered little explanation to back up his assertion that "peace and stability in the Middle East region is a matter of significance to Japan directly linked to its peace and prosperity."[14] In all likelihood, the prime minister considered this generic rationale more than adequate, given initial public sentiment toward SDF dispatch. For in the wake of the Iraq War, a majority of Japanese actually supported contributing peacekeepers.[15]

However, unforeseen shifts in public opinion compelled the prime minister to elaborate on the implications of a destabilized Middle East. When proposing SDF dispatch, the Koizumi administration had assumed that on-the-ground security would improve, not deteriorate, as the occupation of Iraq continued. Events proved otherwise. As U.S. casualties mounted, most Japanese came to perceive Iraq as a country of endemic bombings and terrorist attacks. The murder of two Japanese diplomats in November 2003 further soured public attitudes toward SDF deployment.[16] Therefore, as the government's deadline for SDF deployment drew near, Prime Minister Koizumi articulated a more nuanced argument linking Middle East stability, oil security, and terrorism.

> The achievement of a stable and democratic administration in Iraq is extremely important for the international community and Japan, which relies for the large part on the Middle East for its energy. In the midst of the ongoing fight against terrorism by the international community, if we were to now yield to terrorism, allowing Iraq to become a base for terrorism, the threat of terrorism would hang not only over Iraq, but also over the entire world.[17]

Is Koizumi's statement simply rhetoric? Because Japan is dependent on the Middle East for 88 percent of its crude oil, it probably is not.[18] An Iraqi civil war or the ascension of a fundamentalist regime in Baghdad would threaten a region vital to Tokyo's national interest.[19] Furthermore, a stable Iraq might provide Japan with a secure source of energy to replace a less reliable Middle Eastern supplier—Iran. Arguably, rebuilt Iraqi oilfields might substitute for Iran's untapped reserves. Such a shift in energy imports would have been desirable from Koizumi's perspective, given that U.S. concern over Iran's nuclear program had complicated Japanese attempts to develop the Azadegan oilfields.[20]

Although recognizing the Middle East's importance to Japan, the impact of Tokyo's troop contribution on Middle East stability is questionable. At the time of SDF dispatch, coalition forces stationed in Iraq numbered more than 140,000. The introduction of fewer than 1,000 additional peacekeepers would not dramatically enhance Iraq's future prospects. Indeed, in this respect, Japan's financial contribution—both grant aid and debt relief—would exert a more decisive impact. But SDF peacekeepers could (and did) prove a major boon to the U.S.-Japan alliance and hence strengthen Tokyo's position vis-à-vis the DPRK.

The Specter of North Korea

The threats that outwardly motivated Japan's Iraq policy pertained to WMD proliferation and, later, a destabilized Middle East. In fact, the Japanese government looked closer to home when formulating a position on Iraq. As mentioned previously, the GOJ feared that Baghdad's WMD programs, if unchecked, would inspire further North Korean provocations. Middle East stability, though a genuine concern, also served as pretext for Tokyo to deepen the bilateral alliance. Clearly, North Korea and Iraq were linked in the eyes of Japan's leadership. Yet, observers have misconstrued the nature of this connection. Before and after the Iraq War, some Japanese newspapers accused the government of blindly supporting the United States because of North Korea. In reality, the link between the DPRK and Japan's Iraq policy was more nuanced.

From Koizumi downward, the GOJ recognized that standing with the United States on Iraq would enhance extended deterrence against North Korea. By responding to a global crisis in close coordination with Washington, Tokyo could demonstrate the alliance's dynamism to Pyongyang. On the flip side, Japanese policymakers worried that failure to support the United States on Iraq would undermine extended deterrence. Regardless of reality, North Korea would perceive a U.S.-Japan rift over Iraq as signaling a weakened alliance. Government officials feared that this change in perception might lead the DPRK toward more adventurous behavior, thereby endangering Japan's security.[21]

The extent to which the GOJ considered Washington's support against Pyongyang as contingent upon Tokyo's cooperation in Iraq is less clear. Some Japanese officials foresaw that a mishandled Iraq policy would diminish U.S. backing on issues related to the DPRK, but whether these officials represented a near majority or small minority is a matter of dispute.[22] Fear of abandonment that did exist within the Japanese government related to nonmilitary matters. For example, some GOJ officials believed that Tokyo's voice during a North Korean contingency would be diminished if Japan failed to stand with the United States on Iraq.[23] That Washington might become a less forceful advocate of Japanese interests in the Six-Party Talks constituted another item of concern. However, government circles dismissed the idea that U.S. military aid against a North Korean attack would depend upon Japan's approach to Iraq. In the event of armed conflict, the Japanese government viewed North Korea as distinct from Iraq because the Mutual Security Treaty would obligate U.S. military support.[24]

In bilateral consultations, the GOJ never expressed concern that U.S. policy had linked Iraq to the DPRK.[25] Yet in public, Prime Minister Koizumi implicitly framed the U.S. security guarantee as contingent upon Japan's contribution to Iraq.

> We can never be sure when the threat will fall upon Japan. In the event that Japan's own responses are inadequate, we must make full efforts to ensure the security of the Japanese nationals based on the strong *relationship of trust* [italics mine] under the Japan-U.S. Security Treaty and Japan-U.S. alliance . . . . The people of Japan should not forget that the fact that the United States deems the attack to Japan as an attack to itself is serving as a great deterrence against any country attempting to attack Japan.[26]

To Koizumi's domestic audience, the DPRK constituted the only threat likely to "fall upon Japan." Moreover, Japanese listeners would envisage North Korea as the target of U.S. deterrence. Other neighboring states capable of attacking Japan—China and Russia—do not inspire similar anxiety. In this sense, Koizumi's statement referred to North Korea in all but name. The juxtaposition of "relationship of trust" established a connection between Japan's Iraq policy and U.S. support against North Korea. In effect, Koizumi conveyed a belief rejected by his own government— that Washington's willingness to defend Japan was predicated upon endorsing the invasion of Iraq.

Did Koizumi in fact doubt the U.S. security guarantee? No. Instead, the link between Iraq and North Korea served as a form of political cover.[27] Although the public might oppose the government's position on Iraq, the Japanese people would forgive the prime minister because geopolitical realities had left him with little room to maneuver. As a shield against negative opinion, the Iraq-DPRK connection proved highly effective. Two days after Koizumi's press conference, *Mainichi Shimbun* found that 49 percent of poll respondents who favored the government's Iraq policy did so because "U.S. military power is needed to vie with the threat posed by North Korea."[28] Furthermore, Koizumi's overall popularity barely declined despite his support for the U.S. invasion. Convinced that failure to endorse Operation Iraqi Freedom might jeopardize the U.S. security guarantee, the Japanese public absolved the prime minister of all responsibility.

Even more than Koizumi, lawmakers expressed forthright concern that Japan's response to the Iraq War would determine later U.S. support against North Korea. The three *Asahi Shimbun* polls offer a vivid example of the degree to which Diet members outwardly feared abandonment. Of the 12 lawmakers who "supported" or "understood" the U.S. position on Iraq, one third alluded to North Korea.[29] However, explanations of the link between Iraq and North Korea varied considerably. Former JDA chief Gen Nakatani cited national interest, arguing that "given North Korea's nuclear threat to Japan, it's not within Japan's interests that Japan takes a view or attitudes different from those of the U.S."[30] Other Diet members, specifically former prime minister Yoshiro Mori, described the connection more explicitly. "If we on the part of Japan did not support the U.S. this time, we would face a severe U.S. public opinion to [sic] Japan when we seek support from the U.S. in the event of contingencies caused by North

Korea." Such rhetoric notwithstanding, few lawmakers genuinely worried that missteps on Iraq would reduce U.S. military aid during a DPRK attack.[31] Instead, many Diet members simply followed Koizumi in using the supposed link between Iraq and North Korea as a form of political cover.

U.S. Policy: The Alignment of Expectations and National Interest

U.S. influence played a pivotal role in shaping Japan's response to the Iraq crisis. Expectations, rather than *gaiatsu*, characterized Washington's efforts to win Tokyo's support. The confluence of foreign threats, historical precedent, and domestic politics rendered Japan's security behavior more sensitive to U.S. expectations than during any prior time period, including the aftermath of September 11. First, the growing threat posed by North Korea inclined Japan's leadership to shun policies that risked straining the bilateral alliance. Second, recently established historical precedent intensified U.S. expectations in the run-up to the Iraq War: by dispatching MSDF vessels to the Indian Ocean, Japan's leadership had raised the bar for future security cooperation. And third, the Koizumi-Bush friendship had attained a new level of intimacy as Japan contributed to Operation Enduring Freedom. With many of Koizumi's economic reforms stalled or unrealized, the prime minister's rapport with President Bush constituted one of his chief political assets on the eve of the U.S. invasion. In sum, the intervening period between September 11 and the Iraq War had heightened Tokyo's receptivity to Washington's desires.

The Iraq War

Compared to September 11 and Iraq reconstruction, overt manifestations of U.S. influence were largely absent from the months preceding the Iraq War. Put simply, the U.S. invasion of Iraq lacked a policy catchphrase. Operation Enduring Freedom was synonymous with "show the flag." "Boots on the ground" evoked SDF dispatch to postwar Iraq.[32] However, no equivalent encapsulation of U.S. policy described Washington's expectation that Japan would support regime change in Baghdad. The absence of a policy catchphrase was not coincidental. U.S. officials deliberately refused to articulate expectations of Japan's security behavior.[33] For example, during a press briefing in August 2002, Armitage underscored that Tokyo, not Washington, would determine Japan's position on Iraq: "If President Bush decides to attack Iraq, what would we expect the government of Japan to do? Well, I think I'd refer you to the government of Japan. I shouldn't make a prediction on what any sovereign government would do or not do."[34]

Government-to-government consultations paralleled Armitage's public approach. In private, senior U.S. officials rarely, if ever, conveyed verbal requests to their Japanese counterparts.[35] Instead, Washington asked the Japanese government to explore what kind of support it could offer during an Iraq conflict. U.S. expectations provided such vague guidance that high- and mid-level Japanese officials visited Washington to clarify the Bush administration's position. These delegations returned empty-handed. U.S. alliance managers simply reiterated that the Japanese government should independently decide Tokyo's role in the Iraq War.[36] During the prelude to the invasion of Iraq, Japanese officials thus confronted U.S. inscrutability rather than pressure. In fact, Washington's unreadability generated frustration on the Japanese side.[37]

The United States did, on one occasion at least, issue a written request to the Japanese government. In mid-November 2002, the United States formally asked that Japan support the invasion of Iraq if Saddam's regime failed to comply with UN Security Council Resolution 1441. Washington's request contained three separate proposals: Japan would politically endorse a U.S. attack on Iraq; Japan would consider ways to support U.S. military operations; and, finally, Japan would "study" diplomatic and material contributions to postwar reconstruction.[38] Although the first item explicitly stated U.S. expectations, the second and third proposals coincided with Armitage's public (and private) ambiguity. The request lacked any reference to SDF deployment and merely called on Japan to "study" wartime and postconflict assistance.[39]

Why did the United States generally refrain from voicing expectations in public or private? Although the U.S. government "had a certain faith that they would do the right thing," Washington never considered Japanese support for the war a foregone conclusion.[40] Moreover, until Koizumi's speech on March 20, 2003, the U.S. government could only speculate as to the nature of

Japanese backing.[41] A display of U.S. expectations might have catalyzed an earlier declaration of Japanese support. But the Bush administration decided against pressuring Tokyo through overt expectations. Several considerations underlay this decision. First, overthrowing Saddam enjoyed little backing among the Japanese people, 80 percent of whom opposed a U.S.-led invasion.[42] By conveying its expectations in public, the U.S. government would have merely reinforced the popular impression that *gaiatsu* dictated Japan's position on Iraq. Second, the Gulf War had impressed upon Washington that direct pressure constituted a poor tool for influencing the GOJ. In the run-up to the invasion of Iraq, U.S. officials therefore viewed specific requests for assistance as unproductive.[43] Third, Armitage and other alliance managers recognized that U.S. expectations were a prominent variable in Tokyo's strategic calculus. Given that Koizumi viewed damaging the bilateral alliance as inimical to Japan's national interest, U.S. officials rightfully believed that support for an invasion of Iraq, though not assured, would be likely.

Washington's conviction that alliance considerations would shape Tokyo's response proved remarkably prescient. Indeed, throughout the lead-up to the Iraq War, the GOJ considered only one policy option—standing with the United States.[44] Even more striking, elements of the Japanese government sought to provide SDF support for Operation Iraqi Freedom. Despite Washington's November 2002 request that Japan study wartime assistance, U.S. officials held no expectations that Tokyo's participation in the conflict would extend beyond a declaration of political backing.[45] The GOJ, accurately perceiving the U.S. position, determined that a verbal endorsement would satisfy Washington.[46] Nonetheless, within the Japanese government, the JDA advocated wartime SDF dispatch. At Ishiba's behest, the GSDF and MSDF drafted plans to deploy a makeshift hospital ship to the Persian Gulf.[47] In addition, the JDA proposed dispatching minesweepers during the conflict.[48] For its part, MOFA also considered utilizing the SDF to support coalition forces during the Iraq War. Ultimately, the brevity of the conflict brought the JDA's hopes to naught. MOFA officials decided even before the initiation of hostilities that Japan lacked the legal infrastructure to implement a wartime deployment.[49]

That the Japanese government, on its own initiative, discussed wartime SDF dispatch reveals a change in Tokyo's strategic calculus. The concern that failure to match outside expectations would harm national interest underlay Japan's response to September 11. To a certain extent, similar anxieties motivated political support for the Iraq War. But discussion of SDF dispatch to assist U.S. forces in the Middle East stemmed from an assessment of national interest that transcended internalized *gaiatsu*. By the Iraq War, the Japanese government viewed its alliance obligations as carrying benefits, not merely potential costs. In the months preceding the invasion of Iraq, Tokyo focused on the positive dimension of fulfilling U.S. expectations: strengthening the bilateral alliance enhanced Japan's national security. As a consequence, segments of the Japanese government spontaneously chose to examine and, in the JDA's case, to advocate wartime deployment.

Koizumi's comments at the outbreak of the Iraq War were emblematic of Tokyo's new strategic calculus. On March 18, 2003, the prime minister justified his decision to support the United States by voicing an argument derived from internalized *gaiatsu*: "Damaging the confidence on the Japan-U.S. relationship . . . would go against the national interest of Japan."[50] But Koizumi's view of the bilateral relationship also included positive dimensions of alliance responsibility. When speaking to the public, the prime minister implied that a sense of shared values, purpose, and friendship should motivate Tokyo's support for the U.S. attack on Iraq. "At a time when the United States is about to make a tremendous sacrifice for the great cause of the international community, it is Japan's *duty* [italics mine], and is all too natural, that Japan should provide support as much as it can."[51]

The prime minister's reference to "Japan's duty" did not result from feelings of personal friendship for President Bush. Koizumi's use of alliance loyalty, and indeed Tokyo's new strategic calculus as a whole, stemmed from fundamentally realist considerations. In the absence of an immediate threat, strengthening the U.S.-Japan alliance had promised few clear benefits. Between 2002 and early 2003, however, North Korea's revived nuclear program greatly increased the Japanese government's sense of insecurity. Thus, during the run-up to the Iraq War, enhancing the bilateral security relationship offered tangible rewards—mitigating the North Korean threat. During the prelude to the Iraq War—in contrast to September 11—intragovernment discussions concentrated on deepening the alliance rather than avoiding policy missteps.[52]

Postwar Reconstruction

Japan's contribution to postwar reconstruction featured more overt manifestations of U.S. influence. Indeed, among most Japanese, the phrase "boots on the ground" became synonymous with Washington's desire for SDF personnel to participate in the rebuilding of Iraq. The public display of U.S. expectations that occurred after the Iraq War's denouement reflected several factors. At least initially, Japanese popular opinion appeared receptive to Washington's expectations; until July 2003, the public was evenly split between supporters and opponents of SDF deployment.[53] Thus, in contrast to the Iraq War, U.S. officials could overtly request Tokyo's support without antagonizing a majority of the Japanese populace. After July 2003, however, public articulation of U.S. expectations became necessary to shore up Tokyo's weakening resolve, a product of deteriorating security conditions in Iraq and the November 2003 Lower House elections.[54]

One comment on the timing and nature of U.S. expectations is in order. Washington directly requested SDF dispatch only after the Japanese government had decided to commit troops. During the summer of 2002, MOFA began to internally discuss the SDF's role in postwar Iraq. In December 2002, the Cabinet Office ordered MOFA to begin preparing legislation to enable SDF deployment.[55] At the Crawford Summit in May 2003, Koizumi assured Bush that Japan's involvement in the rebuilding of Iraq would include SDF dispatch. Only after receiving the prime minister's reassurance did the U.S. government officially request SDF deployment to Iraq.[56] In fact, Koizumi's reputation as a man of his word set the tone for later U.S. expectations. Washington's representatives trusted the prime minister, and although Koizumi's pledge lacked concrete details, they believed that Japan's troop contribution would be forthcoming.[57] Thus, in August 2003, Washington relied mainly on positive reinforcement when responding to Tokyo's postponement of SDF dispatch. In public, U.S. alliance managers emphasized Japan's great power obligations. Likewise, in government-to-government consultations, U.S. diplomats conveyed Washington's belief that Tokyo would "do the right thing."[58]

Japan's International Responsibility. Between June 2003 and February 2004, Washington's representatives embedded the SDF's dispatch to Iraq within a generic expectation—that Japan should assume a leadership role on the stage of international politics. Armitage's remarks on June 10, 2003, embodied this belief: "I'm hoping that Japan, as a political matter, will decide to involve herself in the great issues of the day and, if she chooses, as a practical matter, to allow SDF forces to go into Iraq . . . . I think that'd be a great statement of Japan's willingness to take part in arduous activities around the world."[59] Six months later, Ambassador Baker echoed the deputy secretary when addressing the Foreign Correspondents' Club of Japan: "You [Japan] have much to bring to that leadership role. But there are many responsibilities that go with it. Among those responsibilities is to participate fully and freely in the efforts of free nations to try to bring peace and stability . . . ."[60]

This rhetoric reflected both a political strategy and the sincere conviction of U.S. officials. Advocating SDF dispatch under the rubric of Japan's international responsibility represented the most tactful form of public persuasion available to Washington. Furthermore, U.S. officials could at least hope that stressing Tokyo's great power obligations rather than the bilateral alliance would minimize public impressions of heavy-handed *gaiatsu*. At the same time, alliance managers on the U.S. side genuinely believed that Japan should assume a leadership role in world affairs or, to borrow the metaphor coined by Armitage, that Japan should "quit paying to see the baseball game and get down on the baseball diamond and play . . . ."[61]

Washington's expectation—that Japan should approach Iraq reconstruction as a full-fledged member of the international community—resonated with Prime Minister Koizumi. From the outset of his administration, Koizumi had sought to accelerate Japan's becoming a "normal" nation. Dispatching the SDF to Iraq served this objective. As a result, the prime minister echoed Armitage and Baker when calling on Japan to support Iraq reconstruction. Indeed, by March 2003, the prime minister had already adopted the language of international responsibility to justify Japan's participation in the rebuilding of Iraq. "Japan must fulfill its responsibility as a member of the international community, through coordination with the international community to see what can be done for the people of Iraq . . . ."[62] As the domestic debate on SDF deployment intensified, Koizumi began to explicitly link troop contributions to

Japan's great power obligations. "If we were to leave the personnel contribution to other countries for possibility of danger, and thus limit the contribution to provision of materials, it can not be said that Japan is fulfilling its responsibilities as a member of the international community."[63]

Koizumi's emphasis on international responsibility could have stemmed from political calculations. Deploying troops to a violence-wracked occupation might have been more palatable to the public when euphemized as Japan's global duty. Although a factor behind Koizumi's choice of diction, "international responsibility" did not arise primarily out of political considerations. Instead, senior members of the Japanese government had internalized Washington's desire that Tokyo "take part in all the great efforts and great events of our day."[64] For example, Ishiba viewed Iraq as an opportunity to demonstrate Japan's dedication to the maintenance of global order.[65] Other key members of Koizumi's national security team felt similarly. Thus, within the highest levels of the Japanese government, "almost everybody" advocated SDF participation in the rebuilding of Iraq.[66]

Like alliance obligations, the idea of international responsibility underwent a transformation following September 11. Until the U.S. invasion of Iraq, the legacy of the Gulf War meant that Tokyo internalized the costs but not the benefits associated with international responsibility. By appearing to defer its great power obligations to others, Japan lost credibility in the eyes of the world, a result adverse to national interest. This logic emerged in Koizumi's speeches on Iraq and undoubtedly influenced the Japanese government's decision to contribute troops to reconstruction. But the prime minister also dwelt on the positive repercussions of meeting international expectations. Koizumi argued that SDF deployment would stabilize the Middle East, thereby securing Tokyo's energy interests. Moreover, when addressing the Diet, the prime minister implied that SDF dispatch would improve Japan's prospects of attaining a permanent seat on the UN Security Council: "I hope Japan can make appropriate contributions even under the restrictions of the current Constitution and I'm in a position that (while making contributions) Japan should discuss in a dignified manner that the present structure of the Security Council is not fair and it could be reformed."[67]

Clearly, Koizumi perceived fulfilling Tokyo's great power obligations as an avenue for advancing Japan's national interest, not merely an exercise in damage control. In this respect, the prime minister and his cabinet were unexceptional. Similar sentiment existed at the working level of the Japanese government.[68] As in the case of alliance expectations, Tokyo's strategic calculus had expanded beyond the narrow lens of internalized *gaiatsu*.

Alliance Considerations: Expectations and National Interest. One topic is conspicuously absent from U.S. statements on Japan's contribution to postwar Iraq—the bilateral security relationship. In fact, only after SDF peacekeepers had literally put their "boots on the ground" did Washington begin to comment publicly on the alliance dimension of Iraq reconstruction.[69] The absence of such statements notwithstanding, expectations surrounding the U.S.-Japan alliance played a determinative role in Tokyo's decision to contribute peacekeepers to Iraq. To begin with, Tokyo's 1991 humiliation and Washington's ensuing criticism continued to exercise residual influence over the Koizumi administration. More important was the continuing alignment between Japan's national interest and U.S. expectations. The Six-Party Talks with Japan's truculent neighbor, North Korea, stood at an impasse. And as the Japanese government considered SDF dispatch, Pyongyang broadcasted that it had nearly reprocessed 8,000 spent fuel rods.[70] Consequently, strengthening the bilateral alliance—demonstrating Tokyo's reliability through troop contributions—became even more pressing.

When explaining SDF dispatch to the public, Koizumi highlighted the link between Tokyo's personnel contribution and the U.S.-Japan alliance. In his press conference on December 9, 2003, the prime minister emphasized that the well-being of the alliance required a relationship of mutual trust. "I believe now is the time indeed when we are to be tested, not only in our words, but in our deeds . . . . The United States is Japan's ally, and I believe that Japan must also be a trustworthy ally for the United States."[71] Similarly, Koizumi cited the bilateral security relationship when advocating SDF dispatch in Diet hearings. Given this relatively more private setting, the prime minister offered a much blunter assessment of Japan's dependency on the United States.

Both France and Germany have a collective security mechanism, NATO. France has nuclear weapons. If you oppose everything, how do you think Japan can build up the confidence of the U.S.-Japan alliance? How do you think Japan can preserve its peace and security? . . . It is only the U.S. that we have an alliance with . . . . How can we hesitate from supporting the reconstruction of Iraq?[72]

Japan's dependence on the United States in part motivated SDF dispatch to Iraq. And yet, the asymmetry between Tokyo and Washington could have equally generated resentment and foot-dragging rather than cooperation. Japan's leadership could have viewed Iraq reconstruction as a form of alliance entrapment. Although compelled by national interest to deploy peacekeepers, Tokyo might have satisficed U.S. expectations with a token on-the-ground presence. But it did not. Instead, Koizumi coupled Japan's dependence on the United States to a positive, expanded vision of the bilateral alliance. Deploying the SDF to Iraq constituted a mechanism to *build up* [italics mine] the confidence of the U.S.-Japan alliance," and was not simply a gesture to avert a possible crisis in the bilateral security relationship. Furthermore, at the Crawford Summit in May 2003, Koizumi described bilateral relations as the "Japan-U.S. alliance in the global context."[73] This principle recognized the reality of bilateral security cooperation: since 2001, the U.S.-Japan alliance had become global in scope. In subsequent meetings and phone conversations with Bush, Koizumi described Japan's participation in the rebuilding of Iraq from the standpoint of a world-encompassing alliance.[74] Rather than dwelling on the obligatory nature of Japanese support, Koizumi used SDF dispatch as a vehicle to formalize the global nature of the U.S.-Japan security relationship.

Executive Leadership: "The Tony Blair of East Asia"

Given another prime minister, would Japan's response to the Iraq crisis have been different? The answer to this counterfactual is yes. Koizumi's leadership took three distinct forms: shaping Japan's Iraq policy, managing the Iraq reconstruction assistance bill, and swaying public opinion. The prime minister proved adept at the former two, while the latter demonstrated the limits of Koizumi's charisma.

Koizumi's "Presidential" Style

Koizumi exercised significant control over Japan's approach to the Iraq War and postconflict reconstruction. Along with a small coterie of advisers, he largely bypassed the bureaucracy and the Diet to determine the broad outlines of Japan's Iraq policy. Although MOFA and the JDA influenced Tokyo's position on Iraq, both bureaucracies did so mainly at the level of implementation and timing.[75]

The Japanese government's decision to support the U.S. invasion of Iraq indicates the bureaucracy's diminished position in the foreign policy making process. Before President Bush issued an ultimatum to Saddam Hussein on March 17, 2003, MOFA officials presented the prime minister with recommendations for a public speech to be made at the war's outbreak. Koizumi, however, felt that MOFA's statement lacked a concrete declaration of support for the United States. Rather than use the talking points provided by MOFA, the prime minister chose to draft his own speech instead.[76] In this sense, Japan's position on the Iraq War bore Koizumi's personal mark.

How did Koizumi, who lacked a strong base within the LDP, seize the reins of power on Japan's Iraq policy? In the past, even LDP prime ministers who enjoyed the backing of a strong faction left national security to the bureaucracy. Unlike his predecessors, Koizumi began his term in office with a resounding popular mandate. Although this mandate initially corresponded to reforming the Japanese economy, public support translated into power over other policy areas. Indeed, because foreign policy affected fewer entrenched domestic interests, high approval ratings provided Koizumi with the greatest direct influence over security issues.

Legislating SDF Dispatch

Although Koizumi could formulate Japan's Iraq policy, authorizing SDF dispatch required legislative action. Normally, deploying the SDF overseas would have entailed the passage of a special measures bill, often a laborious process. The nature of the Iraq dispatch—sending the SDF to an occupation zone—added a new layer of complexity. Previously, Japan had deployed peacekeepers under the aegis of the UN. In addition, SDF dispatch had required host country consent. Postwar Iraq, however, lacked both a UN mission and a national government. This meant that Koizumi's bill on Iraq reconstruction set a new legal precedent—SDF deployment based solely on UN resolutions.[77]

But the historic nature of the bill constituted the least of Koizumi's worries. Ambivalence, if not outright concern, characterized New Komeito's initial reaction to sending peacekeepers to Iraq.[78] Moreover, within the opposition parties, antipathy toward SDF dispatch ran high. The DPJ's position on the Iraq bill represented a combination of principle and politics. Members of Japan's largest opposition party viewed the U.S. attack on Iraq as lacking international legitimacy. Many also feared for the safety of SDF personnel.[79] Of course, political considerations underlay the DPJ's opposition to the Iraq bill. With one eye on the November 2003 Lower House elections, the DPJ's leadership sought to differentiate their party from the LDP.[80] The remaining opposition parties—all left-wing—resisted SDF deployment largely on constitutional grounds. To the Japanese Communist Party and the Social Democratic Party, dispatching troops to Iraq violated Article 9.

Under these circumstances, the speed by which the Iraq bill passed the Diet stands as a testament to Koizumi's leadership. On June 13, 2003, the cabinet approved legislation to permit Japan's involvement in Iraq reconstruction. Less than a month later, on July 4, the Lower House passed the Iraq dispatch bill. The bill finally became law on July 25 after gaining the Upper House's signature.[81] In the process, Koizumi overrode a no-confidence motion and other eleventh-hour filibuster tactics.[82] This legislative feat is particularly impressive when compared with the record of other prime ministers.

The content of the Iraq bill, or rather, the lack thereof, also reflected Koizumi's political acumen. Through calculated ambiguity, the Iraq legislation concentrated decisionmaking power in the hands of the *Kantei* and the JDA. First, the bill left the definition of "noncombat zones" to the government's discretion. The Koizumi cabinet, not the Diet, would determine whether areas of Iraq were safe for SDF deployment. Second, the Iraq law refrained from defining the SDF's activities. Specific roles and missions would be included in a basic plan formulated and approved by the cabinet alone. Thus, Koizumi shielded a host of potential controversies—the transportation of weapons and the SDF's rules of engagement—from the Diet's close scrutiny. Ultimately, the Iraq law required the Diet's approval within 20 days of SDF dispatch, so Koizumi was not completely unaccountable.[83] Nonetheless, the prime minister's deliberate vagueness accelerated the pace of SDF deployment.

Wooing the Public, Defying the Public

The analogy between Tony Blair and Junichiro Koizumi is particularly appropriate when discussing popular opinion. Like Blair, Koizumi disregarded domestic sentiment by positioning his country in the pro-war camp. In February and March 2003, approximately 80 percent of the Japanese public opposed a U.S. attack on Iraq.[84] Throughout the ensuing conflict, this proportion never fell below 60 percent.[85] Yet, despite the risk of alienating his electorate, Koizumi remained one of Washington's most steadfast supporters. The prime minister chose to defy public opinion, explaining in his own words: "When asked which you choose, war or peace, everybody naturally chooses peace. But when the government conducts the affairs of state in compliance with public opinion, it might make mistakes in some cases. History proves this."[86] The North Korean threat and U.S. expectations underlay the prime minister's assertion. Rather than accommodating popular opinion, Koizumi opted to pursue Japan's national interest. In short, the prime minister placed Japan's security above his own political future.

When advocating SDF participation in the rebuilding of Iraq, Koizumi again flouted popular sentiment. Initially favorable, public opinion toward SDF dispatch rapidly soured as attacks on U.S. forces in Iraq became a daily occurrence. Thus, from late July to December 2003, approximately 55 percent of the Japanese public opposed contributing troops to Iraq. Over the same time period, supporters of SDF dispatch stood at about 33 percent of the population.[87] The assassination of two Japanese diplomats on November 30, 2003, only reinforced the public's impressions that Iraq remained a war zone. And yet, ten days later, Koizumi announced a basic plan, confirming the government's decision to deploy the SDF.

Although matching Blair as a stalwart ally of the United States, Koizumi differed from the British prime minister in one notable aspect. Unlike Blair, Koizumi disregarded public opinion and escaped relatively unscathed. Between January and late March 2003, Koizumi's popular support declined from 47 percent to 42 percent. Over the same time period, his disapproval rating rose from 35 percent to 45 percent. When compared to the depth of Japanese antiwar sentiment, the decline in Koizumi's popularity is negligible. Even more remarkable, the prime minister enjoyed rising public support in the wake of the Iraq War. From April to September 2003, Koizumi's approval rating increased from 43 percent to 59 percent. Simultaneously, his disapproval rating fell from 42 percent to 25 percent.[88] Evidently, neither the reconstruction bill nor the absence of Iraqi WMD had any impact on Koizumi's popularity. In contrast, Blair's disapproval rating soared to 64 percent by September 2003 as the British public became increasingly disillusioned with his Iraq *casus belli*.[89]

Koizumi's Teflon armor was not completely impervious, however. In the months before SDF deployment to Iraq, the prime minister's popularity underwent a substantial decline. Between September and December 2003, Koizumi's public support dropped 18 points to 41 percent. At the same time, his disapproval rating rose 16 points to 41 percent. This downturn likely reflected popular opposition to Iraq dispatch and the public's reaction to the murder of Japanese diplomats Katsuhiko Oku and Masamori Inoue. But once again, the slump in Koizumi's popularity proved short-lived. By January 2004, the prime minister's approval rating had begun to recover.[90]

Should Koizumi's buoyant popularity be attributed to political leadership? Yes, to a point. Through speeches and press conferences, the prime minister communicated the necessity of supporting U.S. military action and participating in Iraq reconstruction. Additionally, by intimating that Washington linked North Korea and Iraq, Koizumi absolved himself of responsibility for Japan's foreign policy. Then again, the prime minister's Teflon-like quality also reflected exogenous factors—most Japanese perceived the Iraq War and postconflict reconstruction as relatively unimportant. In polls conducted by *Yomiuri Shimbun* between February 2003 and January 2004, more than 70 percent of respondents consistently cited "economic boosting measures" as the Koizumi cabinet's most pressing responsibility. The proportion that identified Iraq never exceeded 45 percent.[91] The prime minister's buoyant popularity was thus a product of both political acumen and public apathy.

Koizumi's leadership faltered in only one respect: he could not *shape* popular opinion. This weakness is particularly apparent when assessing Koizumi's press conference on March 20, 2003. One month earlier, 52 percent of the public had opposed Japan's supporting a U.S. attack on Iraq. Conversely, 37 percent of the population wanted the government to back the United States. One week after Koizumi's press conference, these proportions stood at 53 percent and 36 percent respectively.[92] Despite an eloquent defense of the GOJ's position, the prime minister failed to sway public opinion. And according to a later poll, 62 percent of Japanese found Koizumi's explanation "hard to understand."[93] To his credit, Koizumi probably faced an impossible task when justifying his decision to endorse the U.S. invasion of Iraq; most Japanese who opposed the U.S. attack did so "because I'm against any war."[94] Thus, in the case of the Iraq War, public opinion may have been unresponsive to any appeal.

However, SDF dispatch is another matter. Unlike the Iraq War, Koizumi at first benefited from favorable public opinion. But he allowed the specter of SDF casualties to undermine popular support for Japan's peacekeeping contribution. Furthermore, Koizumi's press conference on December 9, 2003, failed to rally the public behind SDF deployment. After the press conference, popular backing for SDF dispatch to Iraq increased a mere two points, from 32 percent to 34 percent.[95] Once more, the Japanese people found Koizumi unconvincing.

In late January 2004, newspaper polls revealed increasing popular support for SDF deployment. This change had little relation to the prime minister's leadership. By the end of January, the first SDF units had entered Iraq. The Japanese press gave substantial, positive coverage to the welcome these peacekeepers received. More broadly, the media emphasized the humanitarian nature of the SDF's assignment.[96] Of greatest importance, no attacks or casualties occurred, partly dispelling the public's perception of Iraq as a free-fire zone. In sum, SDF dispatch itself ultimately persuaded the Japanese people to support contributing troops to Iraq reconstruction.

Generational Change: The Young Turks Divided

Reminiscent of September 11, Japan's response to the Iraq War and postconflict reconstruction demonstrates that at the level of specific policy initiatives, generational change is an indeterminant factor. When addressing Iraq, junior lawmakers divided along party lines. Cleavages within the Young Turks first emerged during the lead-up to the Iraq War. Junior lawmakers within the LDP generally supported Koizumi's position. However, young DPJ lawmakers opposed U.S. military action. As the Iraq War commenced, junior DPJ members echoed then party president Naoto Kan. Like Kan, the DPJ's Young Turks argued that continued inspections might have peacefully disarmed Saddam's regime. Many also considered the U.S. attack illegitimate given the absence of a new UN resolution.

The Young Turks remained divided throughout the Diet debate on Iraq reconstruction. Although junior LDP lawmakers favored contributing peacekeepers, the young generation within the DPJ claimed that instability in Iraq precluded SDF dispatch.[97] Junior DPJ politicians also argued that prior to any Japanese deployment, the United States needed to cede authority in Iraq to the UN and an indigenous government.[98] Thus, when deciding the fate of the Iraq legislation, young DPJ lawmakers voted in opposition to their LDP counterparts. Along with the rest of the party, the DPJ's Young Turks boycotted the Lower House plenary session that gave ex post approval to SDF dispatch.[99]

However, opposition to deploying the SDF was neither uniform, nor solely inspired by a divergent outlook on the legitimacy of the Iraq War. Within the DPJ, some party members actually wished to support SDF involvement in the rebuilding of Iraq without preconditions. And a few DPJ lawmakers even attended the farewell ceremony for SDF personnel deployed to Iraq. These cleavages were generational.[100] Moreover, the DPJ's Young Turks may have opposed SDF dispatch partly on the grounds of domestic politics. As the November 2003 Lower House election neared, the DPJ needed to differentiate itself from the LDP. Finally, party members believed that SDF casualties in Iraq would provoke a public backlash against the LDP-led government. To avoid becoming a target of popular anger and, conversely, to capitalize on the

LDP's potential misfortune, the DPJ vocally opposed an SDF role in Iraq reconstruction.[101]

Japan's New Realpolitik

What do the Iraq War and postconflict reconstruction reveal about Japan's strategic evolution? To begin with, the Koizumi administration's approach to Iraq represents Japan's transition from a norms-based to interest-based security policy. North Korea, an urgent regional threat, compelled the Koizumi administration to formulate an Iraq policy with one objective in mind—strengthening the U.S.-Japan alliance.

Public statements notwithstanding, the Japanese government derived little immediate anxiety from Saddam's purported WMD programs. Stabilizing the Middle East, though important to Japan's national interest, could have been accomplished through means other than SDF dispatch. In reality, concerns surrounding the North Korean threat underlay Japan's Iraq policy. Standing with the United States allowed the Japanese government to demonstrate the vitality of the bilateral alliance. Thus, Iraq provided the GOJ with an opportunity to enhance extended deterrence against Pyongyang.

Like September 11, the Iraq crisis also confirms that U.S. policy and Japan's prime ministerial leadership constitute key variables behind Japan's security behavior. Generic U.S. expectations—Japan as a reliable alliance partner and responsible great power—led Tokyo to join the pro-war coalition and later to contribute military personnel to reconstruction. But disentangling Washington's influence from Tokyo's strategic calculations is a difficult, perhaps impossible task. Indeed, the alignment of U.S. expectations and Japan's national interest was, and is, a potent catalyst for change in Tokyo's security policy. And yet, under a different prime minister, this alignment alone might have proved insufficient. Therefore, the Iraq War and its aftermath suggest that Japan's strategic evolution rests on the confluence of three factors—overseas threats, U.S. influence, and prime ministerial leadership.

Notes

[1] The White House, "President: Iraqi Regime Danger to America Is 'Grave and Growing,'" October 5, 2002, http://www.whitehouse.gov/news/releases/2002/10/20021005.html.

[2] Cabinet Office, "Press Conference by Prime Minister Junichiro Koizumi on the Issue of Iraq," March 20, 2003, http://www.kantei.go.jp/foreign/koizumispeech/2003/03/20kaiken_e.html.

[3] Cabinet Office, "Prime Minister Koizumi's Report on Japan's Measures in Response to the Situation Following the Use of Force against Iraq," March 20, 2003, http://www.kantei.go.jp/foreign/koizumispeech/2003/03/20houkoku_e.html.

[4] "Poll on Koizumi Cabinet, Political Parties," *Mainichi Shimbun*, March 3, 2003.

[5] Author's interview with MOFA official, Tokyo, March 2004.

[6] The Japanese government possessed no independent means of verifying U.S. intelligence. Thus, many GOJ officials found Iraq's noncompliance with multiple UN Security Council resolutions more compelling evidence for WMD. Author's interviews with MOFA official, JDA official, and U.S. official, Tokyo, March 2004.

[7] Author's interviews with MOFA official and JDA staffer, Tokyo, March 2004.

[8] Author's interview with JDA official, Tokyo, March 2004.

[9] Author's interview with JDA official, Tokyo, March 2004.

[10] Author's interview with MOFA official, Tokyo, March 2004.

[11] Author's interview with MOFA official, Tokyo, March 2004.

[12] Author's interview with LDP Upper House member, Tokyo, March 2004.

[13] Taro Nakayama quoted in "Diet Poll on Iraq Attack," *Asahi Shimbun*, February 28, 2003. Data also from "Poll of 20 Lawmakers on the Pros and Cons of an Iraq War," *Asahi Shimbun*, March 12, 2003; and "Opinion Survey Conducted with 20 Lawmakers on War in Iraq," *Asahi Shimbun*, March 25, 2003.

[14] Cabinet Office, "Prime Minister Koizumi's Report," March 20, 2003.

[15] In April 2003, 56 percent of Japanese favored SDF dispatch to Iraq based on a UN resolution. An additional 20 percent of respondents backed SDF dispatch even without a resolution. "Poll on Koizumi Cabinet, Political Parties, Iraq War," *Mainichi Shimbun*, April 21, 2003.

[16] Between July and December 2003, the proportion of Japanese favoring SDF dispatch declined from 46 percent to 34 percent, while opposition to the Iraq deployment increased from 43 percent to 55 percent. "Poll: Koizumi

Cabinet, Political Parties, Iraq Bill," *Asahi Shimbun*, July 1, 2003; and "Poll on Koizumi Cabinet, Political Parties, SDF Iraq Dispatch," *Asahi Shimbun*, December 13, 2003.

[17] Ministry of Foreign Affairs, "General Policy Speech by Prime Minister Junichiro Koizumi in the 159th Session of the Diet," January 19, 2004, http://www.mofa.go.jp/announce/pm/koizumi/speech040119.html.

[18] Japan Agency for Natural Resources and Energy, "Fundamental Concepts Underpinning Japan's Oil Policy: Securing a Stable and Efficient Supply," 1999, http://www.enecho.meti.go.jp/english/energy/oil/policy.html.

[19] Author's interviews with MOFA and JDA officials, Tokyo, March 2004.

[20] To accommodate U.S. pressure, a Japanese consortium refrained from signing a deal with Iran on the Azadegan oilfields in June 2003. As a result, the Japanese consortium lost exclusive rights to the oilfields.

[21] Author's interviews with retired senior MOFA official and JDA official, Tokyo, March 2004.

[22] Interviews provided conflicting accounts as to the number of officials who feared a loss of U.S. support against the DPRK.

[23] Author's interview with JDA staffer, Tokyo, March 2004.

[24] Author's interview with MOFA official, Tokyo, March 2004.

[25] Author's interview with U.S. official, Tokyo, March 2004.

[26] Cabinet Office, "Press Conference by Prime Minister Junichiro Koizumi," March 20, 2003.

[27] Author's interview with U.S. official, Tokyo, March 2004.

[28] "Poll on Koizumi Cabinet, Political Parties, Iraq Attack," *Mainichi Shimbun*, March 22, 2003.

[29] Any lawmaker who cited North Korea in at least one poll is part of this fraction.

[30] "Poll of 20 Lawmakers on the Pros and Cons of an Iraq War," *Asahi Shimbun*, March 12, 2003.

[31] Author's interview with MOFA official, Tokyo, March 2004.

[32] The coining of this phrase has been wrongly attributed to Armitage. Author's interviews with U.S. official and JDA staffer, Tokyo, March 2004.

[33] Author's interviews with U.S. officials, Tokyo, March 2004.

[34] U.S. Embassy Tokyo, "Transcript: Armitage Fields Questions on North Korea, Iraq," August 28, 2002, http://japan.usembassy.gov/e/p/tp-se1636.html.

[35] Author's interviews with U.S. and MOFA officials, Tokyo, March 2004.

[36] Author's interview with JDA staffer, Tokyo, March 2004.

[37] Author's interview with U.S. official, Tokyo, March 2004.

[38] Gaku Shibata, "U.S. Asks Japan to Back Possible Attack on Iraq," *Yomiuri Shimbun*, November 22, 2002.

[39] This assertion is inferred from comments by U.S. and Japanese officials. Author's interviews, Tokyo, March 2004.

[40] Author's interview with U.S. official, Tokyo, March 2004.

[41] Author's interviews with U.S. officials, Tokyo, March 2004.

[42] "Poll on Koizumi Cabinet, Political Parties," *Mainichi Shimbun*, March 3, 2003.

[43] Author's interview with U.S. official, Tokyo, March 2004.

[44] Author's interviews with MOFA officials, Tokyo, March 2004.

[45] Author's interviews with U.S. officials, Tokyo, March 2004.

[46] The Japanese side did not possess the same certainty with respect to the SDF's postwar role. Author's interviews with JDA official, Tokyo, March 2004.

[47] Author's interview with JDA staffer, Tokyo, March 2004.

[48] This plan was rejected by then chief cabinet secretary Fukuda as unfeasible. Author's interview with GOJ official, Tokyo, March 2004.

[49] Author's interview with MOFA official, Tokyo, March 2004.

[50] Cabinet Office, "Prime Minister Junichiro Koizumi's Interview on the Issue of Iraq," March 18, 2003, http://www.kantei.go.jp/foreign/koizumispeech/2003/03/18interview_e.html.

[51] Cabinet Office, "Prime Minister Koizumi's Report," March 20, 2003.

[52] Author's interview with MOFA official, Tokyo, March 2004.

[53] "Poll: Koizumi Cabinet, Political Parties, Iraq Bill," *Asahi Shimbun*, July 1, 2003.

[54] Brad Glosserman, "The Primacy of Politics?" *Comparative Connections* 5, no. 3 (July–September 2003): 21–31.

[55] Author's interviews with MOFA official, Tokyo, August 2003 and March 2004.

[56] The United States requested SDF dispatch at a working-level meeting on June 11, 2003. "Pentagon Requests SDF Air, Ground Units for Iraq," *Japan Times*, June 28, 2003.

[57] Author's interview with U.S. official, Tokyo, March 2004.

[58] Author's interview with U.S. official, Tokyo, March 2004.

[59] U.S. Department of State, "Interview with CNN with Tokyo Bureau Chief Rebecca McKinnon," June 10, 2003, http://www.state.gov/s/d/former/armitage/remarks/21416.htm.

[60] U.S. Embassy Tokyo, "Baker Lauds Japan's Help in Iraq, Anti-terror Efforts," December 4, 2003, http://japan.usembassy.gov/e/p/tp-20031205-11.html.

[61] U.S. Embassy Tokyo, "Armitage Calls for Multilateral Pressure on North Korea," June 9, 2003, http://japan.usembassy.gov/e/p/tp-20030610a1.html.

[62] Cabinet Office, "Press Conference by Prime Minister Junichiro Koizumi," March 20, 2003.

[63] Cabinet Office, "General Policy Speech by Prime Minister Junichiro Koizumi," January 19, 2004.

[64] U.S. Embassy Tokyo, "Armitage Says Multilateral Talks on North Korea Likely," June 10, 2003, http://japan.usembassy.gov/e/p/tp-20030611a2.html.

[65] Author's interview with JDA staffer, Tokyo, March 2004.

[66] E-mail correspondence with senior U.S. official, February 10, 2004.

[67] Koizumi in minutes of the 157th Diet Session Upper House Special Committee on the Prevention of International Terrorism and Japan's Cooperation Assistance Measures and Humanitarian Reconstruction Support for Iraq, October 6, 2003, http://kokkai.ndl.go.jp/cgi-bin/KENSAKU/swk_dispdoc.cgi?SESSION=7527&SAVED_RID=1&PAGE=0&POS=0&TOTAL=0&SRV_ID=8&DOC_ID=8140&DPAGE=1&DTOTAL=2&DPOS=2&SORT_DIR=1&SORT_TYPE=0&MODE=1&DMY=7910. Translation by Yuichi Nakai.

[68] Author's interview with MOFA official, Tokyo, March 2004.

[69] On February 2, 2004, Armitage told an audience in Tokyo that "Japan can count on America, and increasingly, America can count on Japan." U.S. Embassy Tokyo, "Armitage Praises Japan's Increasing Role in Global Security," February 2, 2003, http://japan.usembassy.gov/e/p/tp-20040203-21.html.

[70] Jun Kwanwoo, "North Korea Says Nearly Finished Reprocessing 8,000 Nuclear Rods: U.S. Team," *Agence France Presse*, June 2, 2003.

[71] Cabinet Office, "Press Conference by Prime Minister Junichiro Koizumi," December 9, 2003, http://www.kantei.go.jp/foreign/koizumispeech/2003/12/09press_e.html.

[72] Koizumi in minutes of the 158th Diet Session Lower House Special Committee on the Prevention of International Terrorism and Japan's Cooperation Assistance Measures and Humanitarian Reconstruction Support for Iraq, December 15, 2003, http://www.shugiin.go.jp/itdb_kaigiroku.nsf/html/kaigiroku/013315820031215003.htm. Translation by Yuichi Nakai.

[73] Ministry of Foreign Affairs, "Overview of Japan-U.S. Summit Meeting," May 26, 2003, http://www.mofa.go.jp/region/n-america/us/pmv0305/overview.html.

[74] Ministry of Foreign Affairs, "Japan-U.S. Summit Telephone Call," July 28, 2003, http://www.mofa.go.jp/region/n-america/us/summit0307.html; and

"Japan-U.S. Summit Meeting (Summary)," October 17, 2003, http://www.mofa.go.jp/region/n-america/us/summit0310.html.

[75] Author's interview with retired senior MOFA official, Tokyo, March 2004.

[76] Author's interviews with U.S. official and MOFA official, Tokyo, March 2004.

[77] The Iraq reconstruction law cited UN Security Council Resolutions 678, 687, 1441, and 1483.

[78] New Komeito maintained that a new UN Security Council resolution was necessary before passing the Iraq bill. The UN Security Council approved Resolution 1483 before Iraq legislation went to the Diet. "UNSC Resolution Boosts Govt Efforts on Passage of Iraq Bill," *Yomiuri Shimbun*, May 24, 2003.

[79] "Diet Debate on Iraq Legislation," *Yomiuri Shimbun*, June 26, 2003.

[80] Author's interview with DPJ policy staffer, Tokyo, August 2003.

[81] Brad Glosserman, "Still on a Roll," *Comparative Connections* 5, no. 2 (April–June 2003): 21–30; and Glosserman, "The Primacy of Politics."

[82] Reiji Yoshida, "Opposition Parties Try to Block SDF Bill," *Japan Times*, July 25, 2003.

[83] Yoichiro Sato, "The GSDF Will Go to Iraq without a Blue Helmet," *PacNet Newsletter*, no. 32 (July 31, 2003).

[84] "Poll on Koizumi Cabinet, Political Parties," *Mainichi Shimbun*, March 3, 2003; and "Poll on Koizumi Cabinet, Political Parties," *Asahi Shimbun*, February 26, 2003.

[85] "Poll on Koizumi Cabinet, Political Parties," *Mainichi Shimbun*, March 22, 2003; and "Poll on Koizumi Cabinet, Political Parties, Iraq War," *Mainichi Shimbun*, April 21, 2003.

[86] Koizumi quoted in "Is the Prime Minister Turning His Back on the Public on the Iraq Issue?" *Mainichi Shimbun*, March 6, 2003.

[87] "Poll: Koizumi Cabinet, Political Parties, Iraq," *Asahi Shimbun*, July 23, 2003; and "Poll on Koizumi Cabinet, Political Parties, SDF Iraq dispatch," *Asahi Shimbun*, December 13, 2003.

[88] "Poll on Koizumi Cabinet, Political Parties," *Asahi Shimbun*, February 26, 2003; "Poll on Koizumi Cabinet, Political Parties," *Asahi Shimbun*, April 1, 2003; and graph titled, "Saikin no Koizumi naikaku shijiritsu" (Koizumi cabinet's recent approval rating), *Asahi Shimbun*, n.d., http://www.asahi.com/special/shijiritsu/.

[89] The figure cited relates to job performance. "Half of Britons Think Blair Should Quit: Poll," *Agence France Presse*, September 27, 2003.

[90] "Poll on Koizumi Cabinet, Political Parties, SDF Iraq Dispatch," *Asahi Shimbun*, December 13, 2003; "Poll on Koizumi Cabinet, Political Parties, SDF Dispatch to Iraq," *Asahi Shimbun*, January 20, 2004.

[91] "Poll on Koizumi Cabinet, Political Parties, Iraq and North Korea," *Yomiuri Shimbun*, March 25, 2003; "Poll on Koizumi Cabinet, Political Parties, Iraq and North Korea," *Yomiuri Shimbun*, June 17, 2003; "Poll on Koizumi Cabinet, Political Parties," *Yomiuri Shimbun*, October 21, 2003; and "Poll on Koizumi Cabinet, Political Parties, SDF Iraq Dispatch, North Korea policy," *Yomiuri Shimbun*, January 27, 2004.

[92] "Poll on Koizumi Cabinet, Political Parties," *Asahi Shimbun*, February 26, 2003; and "Poll on Koizumi Cabinet, Political Parties," *Asahi Shimbun*, April 1, 2003.

[93] "Poll: Koizumi Cabinet after 2 Years," *Asahi Shimbun*, April 25, 2003.

[94] For example, see "Poll on Koizumi Cabinet, Political Parties," *Mainichi Shimbun*, March 3, 2003.

[95] "Poll on Koizumi Cabinet, Political Parties, SDF Iraq Dispatch," *Asahi Shimbun*, December 13, 2003

[96] David Pilling, "Opposition Boycott Overshadows Japan Troops Vote," *Financial Times*, February 2, 2004.

[97] For example, DPJ member Seiji Maehara told Koizumi in a Diet hearing that "it's a fiction to distinguish combat areas from noncombat areas." "Diet Debate on Iraq Legislation," *Yomiuri Shimbun*, June 26, 2003.

[98] E-mail correspondences with DPJ policy staffer, April 13–14, 2003.

[99] Pilling, "Opposition Boycott Overshadows Japan Troops Vote."

[100] Author's interview with MOFA official, Tokyo, March 2004.

[101] Author's interview with Japanese academic, Tokyo, March 2004.

7

Transitional Realism

Are external threats, U.S. policy, executive leadership, and generational change—the transitional model—relevant across multiple foreign policy shocks? Is the relative weight of each factor exogenously determined or instead dependent upon the strength of other endogenous variables? Will the same factors influence Japan's defense posture in the foreseeable future? At first glance, each case study appears to offer differing insights into the sources of Japan's strategic transition.

September 11 suggested that U.S. policy and prime ministerial leadership play a decisive role in shaping Tokyo's security behavior. Internalized expectations or, more precisely, the understanding that failure to meet outside expectations would damage national interest prompted Japan to dispatch the MSDF to the Indian Ocean. However, the timing and scale of this deployment reflected prime ministerial leadership. In contrast to later crises, the impact of foreign threats on Japan's defense policy was ambiguous. Although Koizumi may have considered terrorism an urgent threat, the majority of his government did not. Finally, generational change failed to overcome partisan disputes over the nature of Tokyo's antiterrorism support.

The GOJ's decision to deploy missile defense offered a different set of insights into Japan's strategic transition. BMD revealed that foreign threats can fundamentally alter the environment in which elites and the public consider a security issue. Aside from the danger posed by North Korea, other variables played a minimal role in facilitating missile defense. Washington's urgings were largely redundant because the Japanese government already sought to introduce BMD. Instead of Koizumi, then JDA chief Ishiba served as BMD's most public advocate. And ultimately, the DPRK threat engendered a crossgenerational consensus on missile defense, trumping earlier demographic differences.

Japan's approach to Iraq was decisively influenced by U.S. policy and prime ministerial leadership. By March 2003, the GOJ assessed *both* the costs and benefits associated with U.S. expectations. Standing with the United States on Iraq therefore promised a significant payoff—strengthening extended deterrence vis-à-vis a nuclear DPRK. Much like September 11, Koizumi acted as a policy entrepreneur, in this case engineering Tokyo's pro-war orientation and postwar troop contribution. Foreign threats influenced Japan's approach to Iraq, but concern over Saddam's alleged WMD related mainly to North Korea. Finally, the impact of generational change was negligible: the Young Turks divided over endorsing the Iraq War and participating in postconflict reconstruction.

The Transitional Model

The significance of foreign threats, U.S. policy, and executive leadership varied across each case study, while the impact of generational change remained minimal throughout (see table 7.1). Although at times conflicting, these findings illuminate deeper patterns in Tokyo's evolving defense strategy.

Foreign Threats

Overseas threats serve a vital, albeit sometimes indirect, role in catalyzing Japan's strategic evolution. The impact of external threats is twofold. First, if a neighboring regime poses an urgent danger, the Japanese government rapidly embraces defense policies designed to offset the state's threatening capabilities. In the language of economics, security initiatives tailored to a specific state are highly elastic to that regime's capabilities and perceived intent. On its face, this observation appears less than profound, but in Japan's case, the matching of national capabilities to external threats signals a changed outlook on security. Second, the impact of

Table 7.1. Relative Weight of Each Factor by Case Study

Variable/ Case Study	September 11	Missile Defense	Iraq War/ Reconstruction
Foreign threats	Ambiguous	Decisive	Ambiguous
U.S. policy	Decisive (internalized costs)	Minimal	Decisive (internalized costs and benefits)
Individual leadership	Important	Absent	Decisive
Generational change	Minimal	Minimal	Minimal

foreign threats also relates to the nature of Tokyo's strategic calculus. Specifically, the utility Tokyo assigns to fulfilling U.S. expectations is a function of the security environment. Neither September 11 nor the Iraq War involved a direct security threat to Japan. Nonetheless, in both cases, external threats led the GOJ to place a premium on strong alliance relations, thereby magnifying U.S. influence. In the aftermath of September 11, the alliance primarily served as a hedge against an uncertain future. Yet, even as a form of geopolitical insurance, the alliance wedded Japan's national interest to Washington's expectations. Deepening the bilateral security relationship assumed a new degree of urgency as North Korea emerged as a nuclear power. The utility of meeting U.S. expectations thus rose accordingly. Viewed in this light, Washington's influence constitutes an intervening variable between the threat environment and Japan's security behavior.

A combination of exogenous and endogenous factors determines the relative weight of foreign threats in Japan's strategic calculus. On the one hand, Tokyo evaluates external threats via a state's military posture and communicated intentions. Although political elites may mistake or deliberately misconstrue capabilities and signaling, these "facts" originate from an outside source. On the other hand, perceptions of foreign threats—what actually motivates new security initiatives—are an endogenous construct. Personal ideologies and political agendas lead elites to selectively interpret changes in the security environment. Moreover, public threat perceptions exhibit great volatility. Although popular memory of the 1998 Taepo-dong launch rapidly faded, the DPRK's nuclear program has engendered an altogether different reaction. The duration and intensity of North Korea–phobia reflects the abduction issue as much as Pyongyang's military capabilities.

Over time, foreign threats may assume even greater significance as Japan progressively abandons the vestiges of a norms-based defense policy. Given the geopolitical landscape of Northeast Asia, Tokyo will not lack extant or potential threats. In the short term, North Korea's military capabilities will continue to destabilize the region. Even if the DPRK peacefully dismantles its nuclear arsenal and production facilities, other foreign threats now loom on Japan's security horizon. The orientation of a unified Korea remains uncertain. If the peninsula tilted toward China, or exited from the U.S. network of global alliances, Korea might once again become a "dagger pointed at Japan's heart." At a minimum, lingering historical tensions will cause Japanese leaders to view a unified Korea with some trepidation. Regardless of developments on the peninsula, the PRC's rise as East Asia's preeminent military, political, and economic power will continue to disconcert Japanese elites and the public. Although cordial Sino-Japanese relations would mitigate Tokyo's anxiety, a sharp power inversion will still pose a source of insecurity to a "normal" Japan.

U.S. Policy

In the past four years, U.S. influence, more than any other factor, has directly shaped Japan's strategic transition. Whether in the form of *gaiatsu* or expectations, U.S. policy constitutes a key variable in Japanese calculations of national interest. Indeed, Japan's reaction to September 11 and the Iraq War demonstrates that U.S. influence may induce policy outcomes that, all things being equal, would not have occurred otherwise. The bilateral alliance aside, dispatching the MSDF to the Indian Ocean and backing the United States on Iraq provided few benefits to Japan. In the case of the Iraq War and reconstruction, supporting the United States actually entailed potential costs. As one of the few major countries to endorse the invasion, Japan risked international isolation. Moreover, by deploying the SDF to engage in postconflict reconstruction, Tokyo's neutral image in the Arab world might have become that of an occupier. At the level of domestic politics, joining the pro-war camp pitted the government against popular opinion. Dispatching the SDF to Iraq also exposed the Koizumi administration to geopolitical risk: the deaths of SDF personnel and, in particular, terrorist retaliation against the Japanese homeland could have brought down the LDP government.[1] The Koizumi administration accepted these risks because supporting the United States offered expected benefits to national interest that consistently outweighed potential costs.

The extent to which U.S. policy shapes Japan's defense strategy is a function of endogenous and exogenous factors. To a significant degree, foreign threats dictate the relative weight of U.S. influence. However, exogenous factors—the delivery and content of expectations—also determine the effectiveness of U.S. policy. Washington's influence is greatest when its representatives tactfully convey broad expectations. This style, typified by Armitage and Baker, resonates with Tokyo's sense of alliance obligation and international responsibility. Conversely, issuing concrete demands lessens the impact of U.S. policy. At best, the Japanese government fulfills, rather than exceeds, U.S. requests. At worst, direct *gaiatsu* promotes foot-dragging and acrimony. The content of Washington's expectations also determines the effectiveness of U.S. policy. Requests pertaining to issues at the forefront of the alliance agenda naturally exert a greater weight in Tokyo's strategic calculations, while secondary priorities within the bilateral relationship provide a weak foundation for U.S. influence. After October 2002, Tokyo could resist Washington's calls for greater BMD cooperation with impunity, provided that it met more important U.S. objectives. In short, U.S. influence is only decisive on issues central to the health of the bilateral alliance.

The future security environment of East Asia will likely ensure that U.S. expectations retain a prominent position in Japan's strategic calculus. That being said, several countertrends exist. U.S. policy will remain effective as long as Tokyo perceives close alliance relations as enhancing its own national interest. If U.S. actions once again alienate the world community, Tokyo may come to see the security relationship as one of diminishing returns: by drawing closer to the United States, Japan would become internationally isolated. Strengthening the alliance might thus entail prohibitive costs to national interest, and fear of entrapment would lead Japan to pursue greater distance in the bilateral relationship.

The perceived benefits of fulfilling U.S. expectations could also decline in the future. Iraq may presage this development. If Iraq's nascent democracy fails, Japanese policymakers and the larger public would question the benefits of meeting Washington's expectations: Why sacrifice blood, treasure, and political capital to support an ally's likely misadventures? Additionally, the U.S. reliance on coalitions of the willing may obscure the benefits of strengthening the alliance. By subordinating institutionalized security arrangements to expediency, coalitions of the willing disassociate "voice" from alliance loyalty. Should this policy endure, Tokyo may begin to discount the advantages that accrue from deepening the bilateral alliance.

Executive Leadership

Of the four factors underlying Japan's strategic transition, prime ministerial leadership displayed the greatest variation. This indicates that executive leadership, though potentially decisive, is not necessarily a prerequisite for major defense initiatives. Political courage and popularity provide the basis for leadership. Koizumi undeniably possessed both these traits, and yet he exercised direct control over only a subset of defense issues. The prime minister's intervention in policy debates depended upon two considerations. First, public visibility, an exogenous factor, dictated Koizumi's approach. Low-profile security initiatives that enjoyed popular support, or at least indifference, could be delegated to subordinates. Indeed, between 2001 and 2004, the JDA assumed a leading role on a number of defense issues: missile defense, the Proliferation Security Initiative, and the new National Defense Program Guidelines. However, highly visible, controversial security initiatives required the prime minister's firm hand. Thus, Koizumi played an intimate role in initiating and then promoting the dispatch of Japanese forces abroad.

Koizumi's leadership was also based on an endogenous variable—foreign threats. On the one hand, the JDA could independently advocate defense policies that clearly addressed an immediate threat. Growing realism among the public and the Diet assured support for such policies. On the other hand, defense initiatives outwardly divorced from urgent threats compelled Koizumi to act as a policy entrepreneur. Only through prime ministerial leadership would support emerge for deploying the SDF to Iraq. As a leader, Koizumi's behavior was that of an astute politician. The prime minister husbanded his political capital and chose to expend it only when doing so would decisively alter Japan's security behavior.

Is Koizumi's leadership replicable? Or will future prime ministers lack political courage and charisma? In the context of Japan's postwar history, Koizumi is an anomaly. Although other leaders have experienced ephemeral periods of popularity, only Koizumi enjoyed years of sustained public support. Moreover, unlike his predecessors, the current prime minister repeatedly defied popular opinion on security issues without lasting consequences. Even so, Koizumi may represent the forerunner of a new breed of Japanese executive. During Koizumi's tenure, the LDP's factions have become progressively weaker. Within the LDP, future would-be prime ministers may look to popularity as a springboard for electoral success. Additionally, Koizumi may provide a model for his successors to emulate—be they from the LDP or DPJ. By championing controversial defense initiatives while retaining popular approval, Koizumi demonstrated that strong leadership appeals to the Japanese public. Furthermore, his foreign policy victories compensated for early defeats on a host of domestic issues, particularly economic reform. Although future prime ministers may fall short of Koizumi's standing, Japan's political system appears increasingly conducive to the emergence of dynamic leaders.

Generational Change

Diverse foreign policy crises sharply highlight the limitations of generational change. Attitudinal variation clearly exists among different age cohorts within the Diet. Yet, generational change has exerted a minimal influence over the outcomes of specific policy debates. In the wake of September 11, the DPJ's Young Turks voted against the antiterrorism legislation, albeit reluctantly. After October 2002, the North Korean threat produced a crossgenerational consensus on missile defense. Finally, in the case of the Iraq War and reconstruction, partisanship triumphed over generational cohesion. When evaluated in the context of foreign policy shocks, demographic variation constitutes an indeterminant variable.

Rather than dictating singular defense initiatives, generational change alters the conceptual framework by which elites and the public approach national security. Generational turnover expands the menu of acceptable policy options, but other variables determine the security initiative Japan actually adopts.

Unlike other factors underlying Japan's strategic evolution, the significance of generational change is temporally delineated. The older generation of elites constitutes a steadily diminishing proportion of the Diet. Once the Young Turks become fully ascendant, demographic turnover will cease to represent a driving force behind Japan's strategic transition. In fact, the generational dynamic may cease to function even before older lawmakers exit politics en masse. Although based on historical experience, attitudinal variation among age cohorts is not immutable. As shown by missile defense, foreign threats may reduce or even eliminate previous demographic differences. Creeping realism will thus ensure that members of the older generation who remain in politics increasingly resemble their younger peers.

A Generalizable Model?

Are the four factors applicable to other national settings? Yes, in a narrow subset of states. The confluence of foreign threats, executive leadership, and generational change is relatively common in the international system. Few countries, however, share Japan's one-sided dependence on the United States for security. Most European nations are allied with the United States in the context of NATO, and large developing countries like China and India may pursue national security through self-help. Along with Japan, only South Korea, Taiwan, and Israel rely exclusively on U.S. alliances (formal or de facto) for security against urgent threats. But as demonstrated by the Republic of Korea (ROK), the four factor model can yield wildly different strategic trajectories. Since the commencement of the sunshine policy in the late 1990s, the ROK's leadership has discounted the threat posed by North Korea. At the popular level, threat perceptions have actually shifted against the United States. Despite the DPRK's nuclear program, the South Korean public has come to perceive Washington, not Pyongyang, as the principal source of instability on the peninsula.[2] Although Seoul supports the Six-Party framework, the United States has failed to persuade the ROK to adopt a uniformly hard-line approach to North Korea. Indeed, U.S. influence over South Korea appears to be on the decline. In stark contrast to Koizumi, the ROK's leadership has downplayed its alliance with Washington and, by seeking closer relations with North Korea, has distanced itself from the United States. Finally, generational change in the context of the ROK has widened the gap between U.S. and South Korean perceptions of Pyongyang. The younger generation of South Koreans also exhibits greater nationalism and anti-Americanism.

Why would such divergent results occur within relationships of dependence? Three factors explain variation among states that otherwise occupy roughly similar positions in the international system. First, the degree to which states rely upon Washington for security is neither uniform nor static. Although Japan and Taiwan have become increasingly dependent on the United States, South Korea's experience has been the opposite. Because Japan continues to forgo nuclear weapons, North Korea's growing missile and nuclear capabilities have rendered U.S. extended deterrence even more critical. In the case of Taiwan, the PRC's military deployments have steadily shifted the cross-strait balance in China's favor. On the other hand, the ROK has enjoyed tremendous gains against its principal adversary, North Korea. Since 1990, the DPRK's military has become outmoded. At the same time, South Korean forces incorporated the latest U.S. equipment, further widening the ROK's lead in military strength.[3] In short, South Korea's reliance on the United States for security has clearly declined, both in relative and absolute terms.

Second, threat perceptions introduce variation among states characterized by security dependence. As before, Japan and Taiwan diverge from South Korea. Tokyo now perceives the DPRK as an urgent threat. Similarly, Taiwanese perceptions of China have hardened as the PRC's military exercises, deployment of missiles, and rhetoric communicate hostile intent. The sunshine policy transformed South Korean perceptions of the DPRK along opposite lines. No longer an archenemy, North Korea became a wayward, but ultimately harmless brother. Seoul's changed threat perceptions thus magnified variation stemming from an actual lessening of security dependence.

Third, domestic politics, or more precisely, the ruling party's orientation toward Washington, accounts for these states' different strategic trajectories. In the case of Japan, the major political parties favor close bilateral ties. The LDP strongly supports the United States. In spite of calling for a more independent foreign policy, the DPJ also places great value in maintaining the alliance. Like their Japanese counterparts, Taiwan's mainstream parties— the Democratic Progressive Party and the Kuomintang—favor close bilateral relations. In contrast, South Korea's major parties are clearly differentiated by attitudes toward the United States. The Grand National Party that long dominated South Korea's legislature supported U.S. policy. However, the governing Uri party regards Washington with ambivalence. The alternation of pro-U.S. and nonaligned parties thus introduces even greater variation into relationships of one-sided dependency. In sum, although the transitional model is generalizable beyond Japan, the impact of each variable is state-specific.

International Relations Theory and Japan's Defense Policy Revisited

Thus far, I have borrowed Michael Green's concept of "reluctant realism" without fully developing it into a coherent theory. Indeed, "reluctant realism" has been treated as a sort of black box: I have highlighted trends in elite and public opinion that indicate growing pragmatism across all segments of Japanese society; I have reiterated that the pace of creeping realism has accelerated since the fall of 2001; and I have noted that the phenomenon of "reluctant realism" is emblematic of Japan's transition from a norms-based to interest-based defense strategy. However, several key questions remain unaddressed. Where is "reluctant realism" located along the spectrum of international relations theory? Why did Japan's defense policy exhibit "reluctant realism" starting in the 1990s? And not the least important, does "reluctant realism" provide predictive insights into the problem of strategic change?

"Reluctant Realism" as Learned Behavior

On its face, "reluctant realism" is a Frankensteinian theory that grafts elements of realism onto the body of cultural norms. Although possessing a long half-life, internalized norms and ultimately the institutions that inculcated them are superseded by realist calculations of national interest. In this sense, "reluctant realism" is a transitional theory, an uneasy amalgamation of norms and realpolitik that climaxes in the ascension of one theoretical paradigm over the other.

Articulated as such, "reluctant realism" suffers from the same weaknesses as other theoretical approaches to national strategy. In fact, this conception of "reluctant realism" would simply aggregate the flaws that separately characterize normative and realist explanations of strategic evolution. The theory of cultural norms illuminates the origins of a state's current security approach, but lacks an endogenous mechanism that can, with some accuracy, predict future directions of strategic change. The above definition of "reluctant realism" is similarly static. If a state's defense policy is initially dictated by internalized norms, shifts in the geopolitical landscape should have a minimal impact on national strategy. Consequently, "reluctant realism" does not contain a trigger that initiates the transition from a norms-based to interest-based security policy. During the shift to a realpolitik defense strategy, "reluctant realism" suffers from a different weakness, one that typically plagues explanations founded on neorealism. Neorealism permits strategic evolution through changes in the balance of power, but has limited ability to predict those changes except in rare cases of sudden power inversion. If the balance of power changes gradually, neorealism cannot describe how or when a state's security strategy will evolve. Likewise, apart from an abrupt, sweeping change in a nation's security environment, "reluctant realism" offers no guidance as to the speed or degree by which a state discards a normative defense policy in favor of realpolitik.

Clearly, the dichotomy of realism and cultural norms provides a poor framework for embedding "reluctant realism" within international relations theory. Instead, constructivism constitutes a more appropriate theoretical structure. According to one variant of constructivism, state behavior is learned. Nations are socialized by the existing world system.[4] In effect, the state is a *tabula rasa* that, depending on the threat environment, may subscribe to realpolitik or adopt a norms-based defense strategy. Viewed through this analytical lens, "reluctant realism"—or more accurately, "transitional realism"—is the process of resocialization into a changed global order. When the international system shifts along certain lines—a state socialized in a benign global order is suddenly confronted by a new environment that features hostile neighbors and other urgent threats—transitional realism will ensue.

Japan's Resocialization into a Dangerous World

The timing of Japan's evolution from a norms-based to an interest-based defense policy becomes obvious when examined through the perspective of learned behavior. The collapse of the Soviet Union, combined with the rise of China, marked the end of the postwar order in Northeast Asia. This environment had socialized Japan into the international system following military defeat and occupation. The postwar security landscape in Northeast Asia led Tokyo to adopt a normative approach to national security. Cocooned by its U.S. alliance, Japan alone among the major powers faced no immediate foreign threats. Although a belligerent in the Korean War, Maoist China soon turned inward and after 1958 was riven by economic and political turmoil. The Soviet Union, a hypothetical danger, was largely preoccupied with Europe until the mid-1960s, and North Korea lacked the means to directly threaten the Japanese homeland. This comparatively benign security environment encouraged Japan to focus on internal political and economic development. Domestic norms therefore played an intimate role in shaping Tokyo's defense strategy, and not surprisingly then, normative theories could generally explain Japan's security behavior.

The international system that socialized postwar Japan underwent a sea change between 1989 and 1994. Soviet power contracted and then vanished as the USSR disintegrated into its constituent republics. Bipolarity gave way to an era of economic globalization and unchallenged U.S. military predominance. This systemic transformation altered the four subsystemic factors that underlie Japan's strategic evolution.

From Tokyo's perspective, the end of the Cold War actually exacerbated foreign threats. Indeed, the relaxation of East-West tensions contributed to the DPRK's adventurism. The end of the Cold War left North Korea bereft of close allies. Russia (then the USSR) and China normalized relations with South Korea in the early 1990s. As both states expanded economic and political ties with the ROK, North Korea became increasingly isolated. Moreover, the subsidies that Moscow and Beijing had once provided Pyongyang rapidly declined, magnifying the negative economic consequences of the North's *juche* ideology.[5] Deprived of allies and confronted by a collapsing economy, the DPRK resorted to self-help. Building nuclear weapons and medium-range missiles provided the regime with a deterrent; both capabilities also served as leverage to extract aid from the United States, South Korea, and Japan. Even the emergence of the abductions issue stemmed from the DPRK's post–Cold War insecurity. Pyongyang admitted to abducting Japanese nationals in order to receive the economic benefits associated with normalized relations.

Another foreign threat—China's rise as a regional superpower—also reflects the end of a bipolar world order. During much of the Cold War, Soviet power in the Far East preoccupied Chinese military planners. After the breakup of the USSR, the PRC, for the first time since its founding, confronted no immediate threat of invasion. As a result, China could adopt an outward-looking defense strategy that directly influenced areas vital to Japan's national interest—Taiwan, the sea-lanes of East Asia, and the Senkaku islands. In addition, the end of the Cold War provided China with the fiscal resources to develop a modern military. No longer excluded from the global economy, the PRC became the world's largest recipient of foreign direct investment.[6] Torrid economic growth fueled by exports and domestic consumption translated into double-digit increases in military spending. In line with an outward-looking defense strategy, the PRC's new procurements included armaments that induced Japanese anxiety: more sophisticated ballistic missiles, fourth-generation fighter aircraft, and blue-water naval capabilities.[7]

Systemic changes following the end of the Cold War transformed a second variable in Japan's strategic calculus—U.S. expectations. By intensifying regional threats, the new international system increased the utility of the bilateral alliance. As a consequence, Washington's expectations assumed an even greater weight within Tokyo's calculations of national interest. At the same time, the post–Cold War world introduced new, unforeseen priorities into the alliance agenda. During the 1990s, and particularly after September 11, global terrorism and WMD proliferation displaced great power rivals and rogue states as the primary threat to U.S. interests. Thus, U.S. expectations shifted from bilateral cooperation against regional threats—missile defense—to Japanese participation in out-of-area operations like Operation Enduring Freedom and Iraq reconstruction. In effect, systemic changes led to the globalization of the U.S.-Japan alliance.

The interaction between executive leadership, generational change, and the post–Cold War system is less immediate. Koizumi's leadership stemmed from idiosyncratic factors—political courage and popularity. Even so, merely possessing these qualities might not have caused the prime minister to play an intimate role in Japan's strategic transition. The international crises that occurred under a transformed global order provided Koizumi with opportunities to realize his leadership potential. Indeed, in the case of Koizumi, the man made the times, and the times made the man.

Like executive leadership, generational change primarily related to domestic factors. The greater pragmatism of junior lawmakers relative to their senior counterparts reflects divergent historical experiences. Still, realist attitudes among both old and young elites have been catalyzed by the threat environment of the post–Cold War world.

In short, the interaction of systemic changes and subsystemic variables has led Japan to progressively unlearn normative security behavior in favor of realpolitik. The post–Cold War international system is resocializing Japan along realist lines.

A Theory of Strategic Change

Embedding transitional realism within theories of learned behavior resolves many of the weaknesses inherent in other explanations of strategic change. This approach succeeds where both cultural norms and realism fail: it creates a dynamic theory of strategic evolution that possesses some predictive value. First, this approach can explain the origins of a state's current security strategy. A state's contemporary defense policy reflects the socialization that took place after the last reorganization of the international system. Such a rearrangement of the international system is rare. Only three cases of systemic change occurred in the twentieth century: World War I, World War II, and the end of the Cold War.

Second, by applying theories of learned behavior, one can endogenize the mechanism responsible for strategic evolution.

Strategic change occurs through resocialization into a transformed world order. Confronted by a new threat environment, states may abandon previous defense strategies in favor of novel approaches to national security.[8] The reordering of the international system, the event that triggers strategic change, is also made endogenous. Systemic transformations constitute the end product of learned behavior encouraged by the previous world order.

Third, this theory enables limited predictions. Only a massive, systemic change will compel states to learn new forms of security behavior. In the case of transitional realists like Japan, one can predict that the pace of resocialization is proportional to foreign threats. Although a state will ultimately adopt the practices of a realpolitik order, the immediacy of security threats will accelerate the pace of strategic transition.

However, the application of learned behavior to strategic evolution suffers from one failing. This approach cannot predict when and how a systemic change will alter the nature of the international system. For example, in systems based on realpolitik, a world war might merely perpetuate realist behavior. Alternatively, a global conflict might produce a mixed system where particular countries or regions adopt norms-based defense policies. Japan and Western Europe's internal politics following World War II constitute examples of such a system. Consequently, transitional realism cannot provide ex ante insights onto a state's future security strategy. It requires at least the outlines of a new world order to offer predictions. But in this regard, transitional realism is no more flawed than any other theoretical framework.

A learned theory of strategic change is also relevant to contemporary foreign policy making. For example, the European Union's strategic evolution provides a counterpoint to Japan's transitional realism. In effect, the EU has undergone the reverse of transitional realism. Even before the end of the Cold War, the EU had socialized its members' internal behavior along normative lines. Following the collapse of the Soviet Union, norms dictating member interactions expanded to include the EU's external security policy. Learned behavior therefore suggests that because the United States and the EU pursue defense policies premised on different conceptions of the international system—realist versus normative—the transatlantic divide is likely to endure, if not deepen.

Transitional Realism: A Final Word

Like all theories of international relations, transitional realism constitutes an idealized understanding of state behavior. Although a unitary, rational actor would smoothly adapt to a changed international system, an actual state—a messy conglomeration of individuals, interests, and institutions—may not. A norms-based state, if confronted by pressing threats, could overcompensate. An overnight conversion to realism might actually increase insecurity by provoking neighboring countries. Alternatively, institutionalized norms might prove an insurmountable barrier to the ascendance of realpolitik. Trapped in a normative security framework, a state's defense policy could increasingly diverge from strategic reality. Seen in this light, Tokyo's efficient transition from a norms-based to interest-based strategy is nothing short of remarkable. Indeed, Japan's transitional realism has progressed smoothly despite daunting obstacles. Domestic distractions abounded: economic restructuring, pension reform, and political realignment. Institutionalized norms exerted major inertia: Article 9, the Three Nonnuclear Principles, and restrictions on arms exports. And foreign policy shocks occurred at an unprecedented rate: September 11, the North Korean threat, and the Iraq War. Nonetheless, Japan's response to a transformed global order mirrored that of an ideal type state.

Why? The answer lies within the variables that shape Tokyo's strategic trajectory. U.S. policy serves a dual purpose. Washington's expectations catalyze new security initiatives. However, the United States simultaneously restrains the pace of Japan's strategic transition. The existence of the bilateral alliance lessens the impact of foreign threats. By providing a minimum threshold of security, the U.S.-Japan alliance has permitted Tokyo to respond rationally to North Korea's nuclear buildup. At the same time, the confluence of prime ministerial leadership and foreign policy crises has allowed Japan to escape, gradually but inexorably, the straitjacket of institutionalized norms. Last, generational change has stabilized the pace of Japan's transitional realism. The older generation has constituted a source of inertia; yet, the rise of the Young Turks has ensured that this inertia steadily declines.

Thus, while shedding light on the dynamic of strategic evolution, recent Japanese security initiatives yield a host of new questions.

The complex interaction between systemic changes and subsystemic variables represents an exciting, formidable puzzle. In the case of Japan, at least, the result of this interaction is clear: the efficient abandonment of cultural norms in favor of a realpolitik defense strategy.

Notes

[1] In November 2003, an e-mail purportedly written by Abu Mohammed al-Ablaj, a senior Al Qaeda operative, threatened that "if (the Japanese) want to see their economic power destroyed by the military force of Allah, they should send (the SDF) to Iraq . . . ." Quoted in "SDF Stays Put; Tokyo Threatened," *International Herald Tribune*, November 18, 2003.

[2] Marcus Noland, "How Bush Risks Losing Korea," *Financial Times,* January 22, 2004.

[3] *Defense of Japan 2003*, 56–57.

[4] Alexander Wendt, "Anarchy Is What States Make of It: The Social Construction of Power Politics," *International Organization* 46, no. 2 (Spring 1992): 403–407.

[5] On North Korea's ideology of economic autarky, see Don Oberdorfer, *The Two Koreas: A Contemporary History* (New York: Basic Books, 1997), 19–20.

[6] China surpassed the United States as the largest recipient of foreign direct investment in 2003. "FDI Confidence Index," *Global Business Council* 7 (October 2004): 28.

[7] *Defense of Japan 2003*, 64–67; and "East Asia and Australasia," in *The Military Balance, 2002–2003* (London: International Institute for Strategic Studies, 2002).

[8] A changed international system could equally encourage or discourage realist behavior.

8

Epilogue

Since the SDF's initial deployment to Iraq, Tokyo's defense posture has continued to evolve. The establishment of new milestones in Japan's security policy begs the question: Has the transitional model remained a useful mechanism for explaining Japan's strategic evolution? And do the latest developments in Tokyo's defense strategy conform to the theory of transitional realism?

Assessing the most recent milestones in Japan's defense policy—the Araki Report, the National Defense Program Guidelines, and the Security Consultative Committee's February 2005 joint statement—yields an emphatic "yes" to both questions. Since the SDF dispatch to Iraq in January 2004, the impact of foreign threats on Tokyo's security calculus has become even more pronounced; internalized U.S. expectations have continued to influence Japanese defense initiatives profoundly; executive leadership, always highly variable, has been absent from the above policy landmarks; generational change has further declined as a factor underlying Japan's strategic evolution; and public opinion appears poised to become a new, independent variable. Finally, the overall process of transitional realism has endured. Despite a long and sometimes stubborn half-life, normative constraints on Japanese defense behavior have grown progressively weaker.

It is fitting to end by evaluating the impact of constitutional reform on Japan's defense policy. Even if amended, Article 9 will continue to preclude certain SDF roles. "Falluja-like" counterinsurgency operations and out-of-area combat missions—whether under the

UN flag or the framework of the U.S.-Japan alliance—will remain prohibited. So will the provision of logistics to U.S. combatants outside the Far East. However, reinterpretation, revision, or measures short of constitutional reform will likely enable defense activities further removed from combat such as imposing cease-fires, disarming belligerents, policing operations, and escorting humanitarian personnel.

Ultimately, Tokyo's security policy will retain a normative shell despite the triumph of realpolitik. Residual institutionalized norms will serve as pragmatic elements of an interest-based defense strategy.

Evaluating Transitional Realism

The transitional model and overarching theory of transitional realism are derived through case studies spanning a particular time period—September 2001 to January 2004. Japan's defense strategy has remained in flux even after the deployment of SDF personnel to Iraq. In November 2004, the Council on Security and Defense Capabilities, also known as the Araki Commission, released a report articulating a new, integrated security strategy. December 2004 witnessed another landmark development when the GOJ approved new National Defense Program Guidelines. Finally, in mid-February 2005, the U.S.-Japan Security Consultative Committee (SCC) issued a joint statement recognizing shared strategic objectives and the global nature of the bilateral alliance.

These three milestones unarguably differ in myriad ways from the case studies of earlier chapters. No development in the past two years can match the domestic and international publicity that attended SDF deployments to the Indian Ocean and Iraq. Indeed, recent landmarks most resemble the Japanese government's decision to acquire BMD, an internal policy shift that culminated in official papers and pronouncements. Even so, when viewed in totality, events of the last two years demonstrate that the transitional model and transitional realism retain significant explanatory power.

Foreign Threats: Tough World, Tough Neighborhood

Since January 2004, overseas threats constitute an ascendant factor in Japan's security calculus. Three parallel developments manifest the greater primacy of foreign threats. First, the Araki Report and NDPG introduced threat assessments into Japanese defense planning. Until the formulation of both documents, the Basic Defense Force Concept determined SDF roles and capabilities. This concept called for Tokyo to possess the minimum defense capacity required to repel small-scale aggression by a foreign power. In linking SDF capabilities to counterinvasion, the Basic Defense Force Concept represented a Cold War anachronism. After 1991, and especially post-September 11, threats to Japan's security comprised international terrorism, failed states, and regional proliferation of long-range missiles and WMD.

By replacing the Basic Defense Force Concept with an SDF that is "multifunctional, flexible . . . highly ready, mobile, adaptable, and multi-purpose," the Araki Report and NDPG incorporated threat assessments into force structure planning.[1] Both documents explicitly tailored SDF roles and capabilities to security challenges ranging from guerrilla attacks to peacekeeping to missile defense.[2] This matching of capabilities to extant threats emerged during the Japanese government's final deliberations on BMD. In late 2004, the Araki Report and NDPG institutionalized a realist approach to security planning and applied it to the entire gamut of SDF activities.[3]

Second, Tokyo has become sensitive to a wider array of external threats following the SDF's deployment to Iraq. Together, the Araki Report, NDPG, and SCC joint statement signaled a change in Tokyo's conception of security. For the first time, nontraditional threats exercise real weight in Japanese strategic calculations. The first paragraph of the Araki Report articulated this conceptual shift in unequivocal terms: "No security strategy is viable unless it is prepared to deal head-on with threats from non-state actors . . . ."[4] Likewise, the NDPG asserted that "Japan must now deal with new threats and diverse situations . . . ,"[5] and the SCC joint statement noted that "new and emerging threats . . . have surfaced as a common challenge."[6] Moreover, in addition to terrorism and WMD proliferation, global instability writ large—described in the

Araki Report as fragile countries and failed states—is viewed as *directly* jeopardizing Japan's national interest.

This is not to suggest that state-centric threats have undergone a relative decline in Tokyo's security calculus. Far from it. In fact, the third parallel development is that the immediacy of regional threats has increased since the SDF's initial dispatch to Iraq. Predictably, the Araki Report, NDPG, and SCC joint statement identified North Korea as a source of instability within East Asia. More notably, all three documents portrayed China similarly, albeit in a more oblique fashion. The Araki Report mentioned the PRC in relatively benign terms, merely stating that a conflict in the Taiwan Strait would be detrimental to regional and global security.[7] In contrast, the NDPG contained a much stronger assessment of Chinese military activities: "China . . . continues to modernize its nuclear forces and missile capabilities as well as its naval and air forces. China is also expanding its area of operation at sea. We will have to remain attentive to its future actions."[8] Finally, the SCC joint statement specified peaceful resolution of cross-strait tensions and improving the transparency of China's military modernization as common strategic objectives.

Although sometimes distorted in the global media, the inclusion of China in GOJ and bilateral documents testifies to an attitudinal shift occurring at all levels of Japanese society. Since the early 1990s, and particularly after 2003, popular sentiment toward East Asia's rising power has become increasingly cool, if not overtly hostile.[9] The NDPG and SCC joint statement embody this shift in opinion. At the time of the 1995 National Defense Program Outline (NDPO), China's military modernization already engendered anxiety within the JDA. Yet, articulating this concern in the 1995 NDPO would have been impossible because of expected opposition from MOFA, politicians, and the public. Thus, the speed and ease by which the JDA inserted language on China into the NDPG is remarkable. Legislators and Prime Minister Koizumi approved the JDA's language as matter of fact, and the limited Diet debate that did occur actually called for the Japanese government to take a harsher line vis-à-vis the PRC.[10] Additionally, MOFA's China Division, traditionally a bastion of pro-Chinese sentiment, raised no objections.[11]

The SCC joint statement offers a similar picture. Media reports tended to focus on the communiqué's explicit reference to

Taiwan. The inclusion of cross-strait relations in a bilateral document, although unprecedented, meant little in policy terms. Well before February 2005, peaceful resolution of Taiwan's status constituted a shared U.S.-Japan objective. Rather, the communiqué is significant as a manifestation of changed Japanese attitudes toward the PRC. As in the case of the 1995 NDPO, previous joint statements by the Security Consultative Committee could not portray China in an unfavorable light. That the February 2005 SCC did more than call on the PRC to "play a positive and constructive role"[12] reflected an attitudinal shift within MOFA in particular. The China Division, once highly sympathetic toward Beijing, in recent years has viewed the PRC with greater realism.[13] It accepted language on China's military buildup without complaint, and in fact, during the drafting of the joint statement, its members engaged in frank, informal discussion with JDA officials on the whole spectrum of Sino-Japanese relations.[14] Within the GOJ, the China lobby is a shadow of its former self.[15]

Why the rapid hardening of attitudes toward the PRC? Chinese military capabilities—although expanding—do not present a substantially greater threat to Japan now than several years ago. But as postulated in the transitional model, Tokyo assesses external threats via objective measures of military power *and* communicated intentions. Since January 2004, China's conveyed intentions have become more hostile. The incursion of PRC research ships into Japan's exclusive economic zone, the larger issue of conflicting maritime sovereignties, and the discovery of a Chinese nuclear submarine in the waters off Okinawa all communicated unfriendly intent. Hence, capabilities once ignored by elites and the public have assumed a threatening cast. At the popular level, however, growing hostility toward China stems in part from emotional factors. During the 2004 Asian Cup, Japan bashing by PRC fans soured the public's impressions of China.[16] Already low, the PRC's popular standing sank even further in April 2005 following violent anti-Japanese protests in Beijing, Shanghai, and other cities. Occurring several months after the unveiling of the SCC joint statement, these protests have ensured that future defense policies targeting China will enjoy public support.

In many ways, the upsurge of anti-PRC attitudes echoes the emergence of North Korea–phobia. Like North Korea-phobia, anti-Chinese sentiment projects emotion stemming from nonsecurity issues—the Asian Cup and violent street protests—onto military intentions. The political exploitation that characterized North Korea-phobia has recent parallels as well. Aware of diplomatic constraints, some Diet members nonetheless called for the Japanese government to employ even stronger language against China in the NDPG. Such posturing is emblematic of a domestic environment where criticizing the PRC now scores political points among constituents.[17] However, the analogy between North Korea-phobia and the growth of anti-Chinese sentiment should not be pushed too far. Burgeoning economic ties, and thus Japan's national interest, will likely avert the emergence of full-blown "China-phobia." Still, rising antagonism toward the PRC constitutes a striking change in Japanese perceptions of foreign threats.

U.S. Policy: Institutionalizing Expectations

At first glance, U.S. policy appears to have exerted minimal influence over the Araki Report, NDPG, and SCC joint statement. However, from the perspective of internalized expectations, Washington has remained a key driver of Tokyo's strategic evolution. Indeed, the Araki Report and NDPG institutionalized U.S. and global expectations as core components of Japan's defense policy. Specifically, the two documents enshrined the value of international responsibility.[18] Under the Araki Report and NDPG, contributing to the maintenance of global order became a basic principle of Japan's security strategy.

All else being equal, stating the value of Tokyo's "international peace contribution" would not qualify as institutionalizing outside expectations. Concrete policy measures must underpin rhetoric. Both the Araki Report and NDPG did just that. The Araki Report proposed, and the NDPG pledged to "make necessary arrangements to include the promotion of international peace cooperation activities in the Self-Defense Forces mission priorities." In effect, "necessary arrangements" meant amending the SDF law to raise the status of international activities from an "incidental duty" to a co-priority alongside the defense of Japan. Furthermore, by promising to "establish necessary infrastructure to quickly dispatch defense force units overseas . . . ," the NDPG implicitly endorsed the creation of a permanent SDF dispatch law.[19]

Movement toward such a mechanism constitutes a key indicator of Japan's commitment to proactively shape the global security environment. Finally, the force posture called for in the Araki Report and NDPG—rapid response units and more robust logistics capabilities—would undergird an enhanced SDF peacekeeping role.[20]

The institutionalization of outside expectations is largely propelled by changes in Japanese conceptions of security. As terrorism, WMD, and failed states have gained traction within Tokyo's strategic calculus, elites have come to recognize that fulfilling global responsibilities and pursuing Japan's national interest are one and the same. Ex post views of the SDF's deployment to Iraq typify this newfound understanding. In the eyes of national security elites, the benefit of contributing troops has extended beyond the U.S.-Japan alliance. Dispatching the SDF to Iraq has secured Japanese energy interests and helped to reduce conditions that breed terrorism. Moreover, the SDF's presence in Samawah has served as a stimulus for Japanese "soft power" in Iraq and more broadly throughout the Middle East.[21]

The soft power ramification of SDF dispatch to Iraq raises an interesting point. For much of the postwar era, Japan used economic instruments to generate soft power, chiefly Official Development Assistance (ODA). Beginning with the SDF's dispatch to Cambodia in 1992, and particularly since September 11, the benevolent exercise of military power has boosted Japan's global prestige. In a time of fiscal crisis, deploying the SDF to fulfill Japan's international responsibility may increasingly represent a cost-effective basis for soft power.[22]

Executive Leadership: Koizumi Goes MIA?

On the face of it, the most recent shifts in Japan's defense policy suggest a prime minister missing in action. Koizumi's lack of involvement in the Araki Report neither validates nor undermines the transitional model. Given that the Araki Commission served as Koizumi's private advisory panel, to have influenced its deliberations would have been self-defeating. However, the NDPG and SCC joint statement reflected government policy. Yet, by all accounts, Koizumi adopted a hands-off approach toward both documents.[23]

Did the prime minister then go missing in action? Yes, but not without reason. Koizumi's minimal involvement is fully consistent with the transitional model. Although objects of media interest, neither the NDPG nor the SCC joint statement engendered high profile controversy. Each also addressed urgent threats to Japan's security. Consequently, no imperative existed for Koizumi to expend political capital. After the pension scandal, the prime minister had all the more reason to reserve his dwindling popularity for contentious domestic issues like postal reform. For these reasons, Koizumi could, and did, delegate responsibility to bureaucratic actors. Therefore JDA officials, together with the Cabinet Office, served as the principal architects of the NDPG, and the MOFA and JDA drafted the Security Consultative Committee's joint statement.[24]

Generational Change: A Factor in Eclipse

The formulation of policy documents serves as a poor medium for evaluating the relative weight of generational change. Nonetheless, the NDPG offers one anecdote suggesting that the impact of demographics on Japan's security policy continues to decline. When debating modifications to the nonexport principles, Diet members fractured along party rather than generational lines. In this case, the division occurred within the ruling coalition. New Komeito sought to exempt only BMD-related systems from the ban on military exports while the LDP pushed for more far-reaching revisions.[25] The NDPG thus reinforces the lesson of all three case studies—that generational change does not determine the outcome of specific policy debates.

Public Opinion: An Emerging Variable

The decline of generational change as a factor underlying Japan's strategic evolution has coincided with the emergence of a new independent variable—public opinion. Popular sentiment played a major role in earlier case studies. However, before January 2004, public opinion largely functioned as an intervening variable. Specifically, popular sentiment served as a causal mechanism linking foreign threats to new defense initiatives.

In the past two years, public opinion has begun to transcend this role. Once ephemeral and determined by external shocks, popular attitudes toward national security are increasingly long-lived and endogenously generated. Although initially a reaction to the abductions and the DPRK's nuclear weapons program, North Korea-phobia has become more than the sum of Pyongyang's individual provocations. Likewise, rising anti-Chinese sentiment signifies a new public orientation as opposed to a transitory response to particular incidents.

From the perspective of new Japanese defense initiatives, public opinion is today a force to be reckoned with. Across the major parties, constituent views on national security exert increasing influence over the behavior of politicians. For the DPJ, and especially the LDP, this has translated into hard-line posturing vis-à-vis China. Given the increasing centrality of public opinion to Japan's strategic evolution, the transitional model should be modified to include this emerging independent variable.

Transitional Realism: A "Two Steps Forward, One Step Back" Dynamic

The most recent landmarks in Japan's defense policy clearly demonstrate the transitional model's continued relevance, a single modification notwithstanding. Similarly, transitional realism remains a useful predictor of Tokyo's strategic evolution. Both the Araki Report and NDPG exemplify the process by which realpolitik displaces normative conceptions of security. Nevertheless, the discrepancy between the recommendations contained in the Araki Report and the text of the NDPG yields a valuable corollary to transitional realism: institutionalized norms are endowed with a long, stubborn half-life.

In at least three areas, the Araki Report endorsed measures that the NDPG either diluted or omitted entirely. Easing restrictions on arms exports is the first and most publicized measure. The Araki Report called on the Japanese government to exempt alliance BMD cooperation from the ban on military exports. Additionally, by arguing that the GOJ should "explore ways to participate in international joint development project [sic] and role sharing in production," the Araki Report advocated a wholesale reassessment of the Three Principles on Arms Exports.[26] The NDPG exempted missile defense from the nonexport principles. But instead of endorsing more sweeping revisions, the NDPG, or more precisely Chief Cabinet Secretary Hosoda's accompanying statement, favored a case-by-case approach to the overseas transfer of military systems.[27]

The policy debate that produced this case-by-case approach illustrates the "two steps forward, one step back" nature of transitional realism. Enacting comprehensive revisions to the ban on military exports enjoyed significant backing within the JDA, MOFA, and the LDP. Closely attuned to the U.S.-Japan alliance, the JDA and MOFA aggressively pushed for more unimpeded defense-industrial cooperation.[28] For the sake of the bilateral security relationship, and under pressure from domestic arms manufacturers, the LDP similarly favored large-scale changes to Japan's nonexport rules. However, as guarantor of the LDP's legislative majority, New Komeito wielded the political clout to singularly veto changes to the ban on arms exports.[29] Beholden to a pacifist constituency, the party opposed sweeping revisions. So did the Cabinet Office, albeit on the grounds of political risk rather than ideology.[30] Thus, a "two steps forward, one step back" policy compromise—a case-by-case approach to easing arms exports—represented an almost foregone conclusion.

This policy compromise exemplified a unique characteristic of Japan's strategic transition remarked upon in the previous chapter—the efficient abandonment of cultural norms in favor of realpolitik. New Komeito would have torpedoed an all-out attempt to roll back arms export restrictions. Sweeping changes would have also ignited public controversy. Under the adopted case-by-case approach, New Komeito is likely to sanction the export of new, critical military technologies.[31] The only such technology in existence, missile defense, is now exempted from the ban on arms exports. In short, the NDPG fully met Japan's current security needs while smoothly circumventing normative constraints.[32]

The second area where the Araki Report differed from the NDPG is preemption. The Araki Report stopped far short of articulating a preemptive doctrine.[33] Indeed, the document merely sought to foster a national debate on the merits (and demerits) of possessing "offensive capabilities against enemy missile bases . . . ."[34] All the same, reference to offensive strike capabilities in a quasi-official document is of real significance. Before January 2004, preemption existed merely as a loaded term in elite discourse.

The Araki Report advanced two steps forward in advocating a debate on long-range weapons. However, in the NDPG, the Japanese government retreated one step back. Why did the ability to neutralize enemy missile bases go unaddressed in the NDPG? One reason was that only a minority of LDP lawmakers favored long-range strike capabilities. Unless compelled by the LDP, the Cabinet Office—one of the NDPG's main architects—preferred not to initiate a debate on preemption. Strong support for preemptive capabilities was also lacking within the JDA. At a more structural level, although norms opposing preemption have declined, realist calculations actually caution against the acquisition of long-distance weapons. Japanese policymakers are keenly aware of the potential security dilemma inherent in preemptive capabilities.[35] All else being equal, whether the security benefits of long-range weapons would outweigh regional blowback is an open question, the answer to which will dictate Tokyo's final stance on preemptive capabilities.

Beside arms exports and long-range weapons, the Araki Report and NDPG also diverged on the desirable scope of SDF peacekeeping roles. Specifically, the Araki Report proposed that Tokyo consider new peacekeeping missions that might require the use of firearms. Such future SDF roles included "policing operations for maintaining public order" and "monitoring cease-fires and controlling weapons . . . ."[36] In contrast to the Araki Report, the NDPG refrained from elaborating on the scope of future SDF peacekeeping operations. And for good reason, because the missions detailed in the Araki Report would require amending the International Peace Cooperation Law or other legislative measures.

Furthermore, persistent instability in Iraq had rendered popular opinion less receptive to new peacekeeping roles, especially policing. Before the Iraq War, the Japanese public envisioned policing as akin to operations conducted by the UN in East Timor. However, as the Iraqi insurgency mushroomed, the popular image of policing became U.S. tanks and helicopters leveling Falluja, a type of mission seemingly divorced from "international peace cooperation."[37] Unsure of public opinion, the Japanese government opted to prioritize peacekeeping in the NDPG without simultaneously calling for new roles and missions. Once again, the "two steps forward, one step back" approach distinguished the erosion of institutionalized norms.

The Next Frontier: Article 9

In the coming years, Japanese lawmakers, government elites, and the public will likely venture into unknown territory—amending Article 9. Debate on the peace clause has already attracted considerable domestic and international attention. One question is the subject of frequent speculation: How will constitutional change impact Japan's defense policy? The answer depends upon the extent to which Article 9 *actually* constrains Tokyo's security strategy.

One must deconstruct Japan's defense policy to assess real-world restrictions imposed under today's peace clause. The components that together compose Tokyo's defense posture include peacekeeping operations, global security maintenance (nonpeacekeeping), U.S.-Japan tactical cooperation, defense-industrial collaboration, and SDF capabilities. Activities within each grouping can be ordered by *intensity*. In the first three categories, intensity is the degree to which a role or mission approaches combat. Weapons systems, the fourth grouping, can be ranked according to the capacity for inflicting physical damage. In the fifth category, breadth and depth of international engagement differentiate levels of defense-industrial cooperation.

Across the resulting five-column matrix (see table 8.1), what security activities are currently delimited by Article 9? Could measures short of constitutional reform transcend these restrictions? And most important, what SDF roles and missions will the reinterpretation or revision of Article 9 enable?

Peacekeeping Operations

Peacekeeping operations encompass a broad range of security activities. High intensity roles include conducting counterinsurgency, imposing cease-fires, and disarming combatants—in other words,

Table 8.1. Japan's Defense Policy Unpacked

	Peacekeeping	Global Security (non-PKO)	U.S.-Japan Tactical Cooperation	Defense Industrial Cooperation	SDF Capabilities
High Intensity	Counterinsurgency	Combat role in UN multinational coalition	Out-of-area combat operations	Full participation in multinational R&D programs	Nuclear weapons
	Imposing cease-fires	Logistics support for UN combatants	Combat operations in NE Asia	Full participation in U.S. R&D programs	Aircraft carrier
	Disarming combatants		Combat operations in Japanese territory		Long-range weapons (i.e., Tomahawks)
			Out-of-area logistics for U.S. combatants	Selective participation in multinational R&D programs	Long-range fighters, in-flight refueling
	Policing				Blue-water navy
Medium Intensity	NGO escort	MSDF patrols sea-lanes	Out-of-area logistics for U.S. noncombatants	Selective participation in U.S. R&D programs	
	Logistics support for PKO units	MSDF participation in PSI	Logistics for U.S. forces in NE Asia	Participation in multinational BMD programs	Expeditionary units
		Japan Coast Guard participation in PSI	Logistics for U.S. forces in Japanese territory		
	Reconstruction aid	Logistics support for UN noncombatants			
			Intelligence sharing in NE Asia	Participation in U.S. BMD programs	Counter-invasion forces (i.e., tanks, short-range fighters)
Low Intensity	Humanitarian aid	Strategic use of ODA	Intelligence sharing in Japanese territory	Transfer of defense technology blueprints to U.S.	
		Hosting conferences			

peace enforcement. Policing and escort operations—further re-moved from combat—fall along the middle of the intensity spec-trum. Activities unlikely to entail the use of weapons such as logis-tics support, reconstruction aid, and humanitarian work consti-tute low intensity missions. Not surprisingly, normative con-straints and debate surrounding Article 9 pertain to the middle and upper spectrum of peacekeeping.

Peacekeeping and Article 9: An Explanatory Note. Constraints on Japanese peacekeeping are sometimes mistakenly attributed to the prohibition on collective defense.[38] In reality, the SDF's strict rules of engagement stem from the 1992 International Peace Co-operation Law. At the time, the Cabinet Legislation Bureau (CLB) ruled that the use of weapons under a UN mandate could differ from the overseas use of armed force. However, between 1992 and 2005, the GOJ differentiated the two in only a handful of cases: while serving abroad, Japanese troops could discharge firearms (1) in self-defense, (2) to protect SDF war matériel, and (3) to safe-guard unarmed foreigners who fulfill carefully defined condi-tions.[39] In all other settings, SDF peacekeepers employ weapons without constitutional sanction.

National security elites—defense-savvy politicians and bu-reaucrats alike—are increasingly dissatisfied with the CLB's ap-proach to peacekeeping. Various objections exist, but all are essen-tially premised on one fundamental argument: the use of armed force that Article 9 proscribes and that employed by members of a UN peacekeeping mission differ categorically.[40] This argument may well serve as the basis for reinterpretation or revision of the peace clause.

Constitutional Reform: Ex Ante Missions. What peacekeep-ing roles does Article 9 circumscribe? Could new missions be en-abled through nonconstitutional means? To begin with, the SDF's rules of engagement are clearly inadequate for counterinsurgency. Neither a permanent dispatch mechanism nor legislation easing the use of weapons could alone provide legal authorization.[41] In-stead, the Diet must overturn the CLB's prior interpretation by unequivocally distinguishing the sovereign exercise of military power from the use of armed force during peacekeeping. Even then, counterinsurgency would require capabilities and training the SDF currently lacks.[42]

   Like counterinsurgency, imposing cease-fires and disarming combatants would necessitate more lenient rules of engagement. However, whether these roles could be enabled without the reinterpretation or revision of Article 9 is more ambiguous. Imposing unwanted cease-fires and compelling parties to disarm would entail the use of armed force. However, an expanded use of weapons might suffice in cases where belligerents wholeheartedly welcomed the end of hostilities. Yet, such postwar scenarios are rare. In the anarchic conditions that typically bracket internal conflicts, the use of weapons would blur into that of armed force. Thus, as long as the CLB's interpretation endures, normative constraints will prevent the SDF from participating in peace enforcement missions altogether.[43]

   Japanese troops could potentially conduct policing and escort operations in the immediate future. In both cases, legal barriers are surmountable short of constitutional change. Revising the International Peace Cooperation Law, broadening the use of weapons via new legislation, establishing a permanent dispatch law, or a permutation of the three could permit the SDF to undertake policing operations.[44] To escort staff belonging to nongovernmental organizations (NGOs), the use of weapons would need to be enlarged, though to a lesser degree than that of policing. Moreover, a precedent exists for shielding NGO personnel: SDF peacekeepers already offer protection to visiting dignitaries.[45]

   Constitutional Reform: Ex Post Missions. What peacekeeping activities will reinterpretation or revision enable? The LDP's current approach to amending Article 9 would allow for the entire intensity spectrum. Authorizing the use of armed force on behalf of international organizations, either in the text of Article 9 or concurrent security legislation, would remove the chief obstacle to a larger Japanese peacekeeping role. If revisions to Article 9 fully reflect the LDP's proposals, constraints on peacekeeping will shift from institutionalized norms to public opinion and the SDF's capabilities. Both will limit or entirely preclude counterinsurgency missions, even if conducted under the aegis of the UN.[46]

   The DPJ has struggled to frame a unified position on Article 9. As of mid-2005, the party appears to be moving toward endorsing an international peace cooperation corps (IPCC) as an interim step for expanding Japan's global contribution. According to its advocates, the IPCC would use armed force under a UN mandate because such missions are "on a different plane than Article 9."[47] If the DPJ proposes the creation of an IPCC, the party will thus call for sweeping constitutional reinterpretation. Proponents of the IPCC favor the unlimited use of armed force. However, objections from the party's left wing may ensure that "Falluja-like" counterinsurgency operations remain absent from any final proposal.

From a peacekeeping perspective, the IPCC would render the DPJ's ambitions to amend Article 9 wholly irrelevant. Constitutional revision would simply establish a clearer basis for the IPCC's roles and missions.[48] In the event that the IPCC fails to move beyond intra-party discussion, it heralds the DPJ's overall approach to Article 9: enabling Japan to "actively participate in the UN collective security mechanism" through nearly the entire spectrum of peacekeeping.[49]

New Komeito's flexibility or lack thereof might be deemed a key "known unknown" of constitutional reform. Accountable to a constituency that considers the text of Article 9 untouchable, the party opposes the overseas use of armed force irrespective of a UN mandate. Instead, the more moderate elements within New Komeito are inclined to leverage non-constitutional means— broadening the use of weapons—to expand Japan's peacekeeping role. Even so, only escorting NGO personnel is likely to enjoy widespread support among party lawmakers. Policing operations, if conducted on a case-by-case basis, are favored by a minority inside the party.[50] Thus, New Komeito's vision of Japanese peacekeeping appears strongly at odds with that of its coalition partner, the LDP. Yet at the same time, New Komeito lawmakers are keen to avoid the fate of Japan's old Left—irrelevance brought about by increasingly sclerotic pacifist principles. In the long term, blanket opposition to the use of armed force during peacekeeping may be politically untenable.

Global Security Maintenance

More so than peacekeeping, global security operations span an array of disparate activities. At the top of the intensity spectrum is unqualified Japanese participation in a UN-authorized coalition resembling that of the Gulf War. A notch lower on the intensity scale lies SDF logistics for combatants belonging to a UN multinational force. Mid-level operations include providing rear-area support to members of a UN coalition, patrolling sea lines of communication, and inspecting foreign vessels as part of the Proliferation Security Initiative. Activities at the lower end of the intensity spectrum are conducted by civilians: the strategic disbursement of ODA, and hosting multinational, security-related conferences.

Constitutional Reform: Ex Ante Operations. Japan's inability to use armed force overseas precludes global security activities at the upper tier of the intensity spectrum. Fighting alongside other members of a UN coalition would contravene the CLB's interpretation of Article 9. The link between logistics and the overseas use of armed force is more subtle. Prima facie, supplying ammunition and transporting friendly military personnel are constitutional. However, when the SDF provides such support to UN combatants, logistics support becomes inextricably linked to the use of armed force.[51] For example, by delivering ammunition to UN soldiers on a front line, the SDF would engage in battle, at least in spirit if not in fact.

Short of sweeping reinterpretation or amendment of Article 9, no viable avenue exists for enabling the SDF to fight under the UN flag. But logistics support is a different matter. The Japanese government could employ nonconstitutional means—narrowing the definition of combatants—to offer logistics support to a wider range of UN troops. Indeed, the GOJ's arbitrary definition of U.S. noncombatants serves as a model in this respect.

Constraints on Japanese maritime security operations exist separately from Article 9. The authorities derived from the SDF Law are inadequate for certain MSDF missions such as patrolling sea-lanes and inspecting ships on the high seas for WMD.[52] Moreover, the legacy of World War II has rendered Tokyo hesitant to dispatch the MSDF to East Asian waters for more than disaster relief. As a consequence, the Japan Coast Guard has played a dominant role in the Proliferation Security Initiative.[53] Because restrictions on maritime security operations stem from legal authorities and regional concerns, the reinterpretation or revision of Article 9 will have no bearing on the MSDF's ability to shape the international security environment.

Constitutional Reform: Ex Post Operations. Aside from peacekeeping, will constitutional reform unlock new global security operations? Not under the current political alignment. New

Komeito's influence will ensure that LDP-initiated revisions reinforce the status quo. Short of a sea change in the party's orientation, New Komeito will oppose a UN combat role for Japanese troops. The party would also reject any form of logistics that blurs into the overseas use of armed force.[54]

As for the DPJ, proponents of the international peace cooperation corps claim that it could potentially engage in combat as part of a UN coalition. However, the party's left wing insists that the IPCC should be limited to rear-area support.[55] To achieve an intra-party consensus, advocates of the IPCC will likely concede a front-line combat role in return for expanded logistics operations. A similar compromise will probably characterize the DPJ's approach toward global security activities under a revised Article 9.

U.S.-Japan Tactical Cooperation

Whereas resemblance to combat determines whether peacekeeping and other global security activities are constrained by Article 9, geography, even more than intensity, differentiates U.S.-Japan tactical cooperation. Out-of-area missions, the first geographic tier, include alliance combat operations, logistics support for U.S. war fighters, and provisioning U.S. noncombatants. The second and third tiers—respectively the ill-defined area surrounding Japan and Tokyo's land and maritime sovereignties— each encompass bilateral combat operations, logistics support, and intelligence sharing.

The overall nature of restrictions on U.S.-Japan tactical cooperation is straightforward: the ban on collective defense poses the primary obstacle to new bilateral missions. As of mid-2005, the Japanese government's working definition of collective defense could be summarized by two criteria: (1) a bilateral mission that is not aimed at defending Japan and (2) a mission where the SDF participates in combat or directly facilitates the use of armed force by U.S. troops. However, in practice, this classification leaves space for considerable ambiguity. What operations qualify as Japan's self-defense? And when does logistics support become abetting combat? Consequently, several forms of tactical cooperation exist in a constitutional gray zone. Others have become enabled as the GOJ's definition of collective defense evolved following September 11.

Constitutional Reform: Ex Ante Cooperation. Bilateral combat operations outside the Far East clearly fall under the Japanese government's working definition of collective defense. One would be hard-pressed to classify the stability of Iraq or Afghanistan as central to the defense of Japan. Needless to say, SDF personnel fighting alongside U.S. troops would fulfill the second criterion for collective defense—engaging in combat. The Koizumi administration has demonstrated great skill in quietly redefining collective defense to expand the scope of U.S.-Japan security cooperation. However, interpretational salami tactics will not suffice to enable bilateral combat missions in the Middle East and other global hot spots.[56] Such missions would constitute a quantum leap from Tokyo's current defense posture rather than an incremental change. Ignoring domestic politics, the only avenue for realizing out-of-area bilateral combat operations is to openly reinterpret or revise Article 9.

The GOJ's definition of collective defense also embraces provisioning out-of-area U.S. combatants. To begin with, this form of support is disconnected from Japan's self-defense. Furthermore, aiding front-line U.S. troops might be inextricably linked to their subsequent use of armed force. Yet, postmodern warfare has blurred the distinction between combatants and noncombatants. This shadowy divide is exemplified by Japanese logistics operations in the Indian Ocean and Iraq. In the case of the former mission, the MSDF can refuel any type of U.S. vessel.[57] Although the launching point for offensive operations, an aircraft carrier qualifies as a noncombatant.[58] In the case of the latter mission, the ASDF may airlift coalition soldiers. Given the frontless nature of the Iraqi insurgency, these troops could use armed force shortly after disembarkation. The ambiguous, indeed arbitrary distinction between combatants and noncombatants is conducive to interpretational salami tactics. For example, the GOJ could deem the transport of weapons and ammunition in Iraq—currently unconstitutional—as consistent with the ban on collective defense when conducted between "safe areas." Japanese logistics support for out-of-area U.S. combatants or, more precisely, newly defined noncombatants could therefore increase in the absence of constitutional reform.

Legal ambiguity similarly characterizes bilateral combat operations in Japan's periphery. During a regional contingency, the

SDF may provide U.S. forces with logistics support and intelligence. To do more would violate the prohibition on collective defense. Armed intervention would exceed the minimum use of force necessary for the defense of Japan and obviously entail the SDF's participation in combat. However, the elastic definition of self-defense offers a constitutional loophole. The GOJ may invoke the right of self-defense when responding to the commencement of an attack on Japan. The criteria for defining an impending act of aggression are relatively flexible.[59] As a result, determining whether a conflict in Northeast Asia prefigures an attack on Japan would largely be a matter of political will. Should the Japanese government desire to intervene militarily in a China-Taiwan conflict or a clash on the Korean peninsula, it could do so under today's Article 9.

Intelligence sharing in Japan's periphery once typified the intra-alliance stovepipes raised by the ban on collective defense. To cite only one example, in mid-2002 Japanese Aegis destroyers were unable to exchange battle-theater imagery with their U.S. counterparts.[60] Since then the GOJ has deepened intelligence sharing by altering the definition of collective defense. As of mid-2005, only the provision of targeting data to U.S. forces in Japan's periphery remains outside the interpreted scope of Article 9.[61] Still, though freed of normative constraints, many forms of intelligence sharing have yet to be realized: the United States and Japan lack an integrated air defense network and, more broadly, an alliance-wide mechanism for the real-time exchange of intelligence. However, the obstacle is bureaucratic rather than constitutional. From Washington's perspective, more urgent priorities such as the SDF's presence in postwar Iraq have dominated the alliance agenda. On the Japanese side, heightened intelligence sharing lacks uniform support, even among national security elites. The intra-alliance exchange of intelligence thus demonstrates that the rollback of institutionalized norms does not automatically promote new forms of U.S.-Japan tactical cooperation.

Constitutional Reform: Ex Post Cooperation. With the possible exception of alliance combat operations in Japan's periphery, the scope of bilateral cooperation will undergo minimal change following the reinterpretation or revision of Article 9. Among the three major parties, the LDP most favors an unlimited right of collective defense. Nonetheless, the LDP is unlikely to endorse constitutional reforms that enable Japanese troops to fight alongside U.S. forces across the globe. Indeed, advocating such operations would render a cross-party consensus on collective defense even more untenable. As a result, the LDP's constitutional platform will not undergird bilateral combat missions outside the Far East or, for that matter, out-of-area logistics for U.S. combatants.

However, the party will probably move to enable the exercise of collective defense in Japan's periphery, either through revisions to Article 9 or accompanying basic security legislation. The LDP's ambitions regarding collective defense would translate into a constitutional foundation for alliance combat operations in Northeast Asia—a development of real significance. Utilizing a constitutional loophole to enable the SDF's armed intervention in near-area conflicts represents a stopgap measure. Although elastic, the criteria for identifying the commencement of an armed attack on Japan are not infinitely flexible.[62] If able to exercise the right of collective defense regionally, Tokyo could participate in U.S. combat operations at any stage of a Northeast Asian contingency. Equally important, the ban on collective defense would no longer obstruct bilateral mission planning. Liberated from norms-induced uncertainty, alliance managers in Washington and Tokyo could work toward a more seamless response to future crises in Japan's periphery.

Exercising the right of collective defense continues to engender controversy within the DPJ. The party opposes Japan's military participation in cases "like Iraq where the right of self-defense is not invoked . . . conducted by coalitions of the willing that operate outside of the UN framework."[63] Thus, DPJ-proposed reinterpretation or revision will not support the expansion of alliance security activities outside the Far East. As for exercising the right of collective defense in Japan's periphery, the party's final position is still unreadable. The only identifiable trend is that an increasing number of DPJ lawmakers favor enlarging the definition of self-defense to facilitate bilateral combat operations during a regional contingency.[64]

Like the DPJ, New Komeito would contest any effort to establish a legal foundation underpinning bilateral combat operations beyond Northeast Asia. Employing the right of collective defense to offer logistics to out-of-area U.S. war fighters would also provoke opposition from party lawmakers.[65] However, New

Komeito's stance on alliance combat missions in Japan's periphery is less monolithic; party politicians are split over the exercise of collective defense within the Far East.[66] As a result, constitutional reform could potentially pave the way for a more muscular bilateral response to regional crises.

Defense-Industrial Cooperation

Of the five components that together compose Japan's security policy, defense-industrial cooperation is the most constrained by institutionalized norms. Tokyo may transfer military technology blueprints to U.S. firms. In the case of BMD, Japan may also engage in joint development and production with the United States. Participation in a wider array of U.S. military projects and membership in multinational defense-industrial consortia remain off limits. The Three Principles on Arms Exports are a set of policy guidelines. As such, reinterpreting or revising Article 9 will not enable Japan to embark on new forms of defense-industrial collaboration.

SDF Capabilities

The second clause of Article 9 states that "land, sea, and air forces, as well as other war potential, will never be maintained."[67] Yet, only one SDF capability—an aircraft carrier—is still clearly forbidden by the peace clause. Under the GOJ's current interpretation of Article 9, Japan may possess armaments at the upper tier of the intensity spectrum—nuclear weapons, preemptive capabilities; the middle tier—long-range fighters, a blue-water navy; and the lower tier—expeditionary units and counterinvasion forces.

Constitutional Reform: Ex Ante Capabilities. Although designated a Self-Defense Force, Japan's de facto military deploys formidable capabilities. Indeed, since the SDF's very inception, the Japanese government has progressively narrowed the definition of banned "war potential." Fifty years of creeping reinterpretation have, from a constitutional perspective, enabled virtually the entire intensity spectrum. Even nuclear weapons and long-range missiles—currently absent from the SDF's inventory—are partly exempted from the peace clause.[68] Thus, as of mid-2005, an aircraft carrier represents the only military hardware unequivocally disallowed under Article 9.

Constitutional Reform: Ex Post Capabilities. All of the three mainstream parties view stipulating the SDF's existence as an element of constitutional reform. The LDP in particular plans to reestablish the SDF as a Self-Defense Military. Such changes will be wholly symbolic given that the Japanese government has already delinked most armaments from Article 9. Enshrining Japan's armed forces in the constitution will occur years, if not decades too late to broaden the legal scope of SDF capabilities.

Patterns and Projections

Whither Japan? At a strategic level, two simultaneous patterns have emerged in the period following September 11. The first pertains to Japan's transition from a norms-based to interest-based defense policy. Although Tokyo's current strategic trajectory points toward "normalcy," the projected end state is partly a mirage. Even after the revision of Article 9, Japan's defense policy will remain subject to normative constraints, albeit in weakened form.

To dwell overmuch on the peace clause risks overlooking a more fundamental barrier to "normalcy"—national interest. Discarding normative restrictions en masse would be detrimental to Japan. Institutionalized norms constitute a buffer against ever-rising U.S. expectations. More important, certain normative structures may serve as effective tools of a realpolitik defense strategy. Regardless of a UN mandate, Tokyo may derive few benefits from the SDF's armed intervention in conflicts beyond East Asia. At the same time, out-of-area combat operations would irrevocably damage a key source of soft power—Japan's image as a peace-loving state—an image that is not incompatible with likely changes to Article 9. Consequently, even over a longer time horizon, limiting the overseas use of armed force and the exercise of collective defense will represent an optimal trade-off between hard and soft power.

By the same logic, Tokyo will choose to retain the nonnuclear principles indefinitely. Realist calculations favor eschewing nuclear weapons. Compared to an implicit policy, the Three Nonnuclear Principles offer a more potent reassurance to neighboring states. In short, institutionalized norms—stripped of symbolic meaning and harnessed to a realist defense policy—will endure. Yet, beneath this normative shell, Japan's security outlook will be wholly realpolitik.

The second pattern relates to Tokyo's orientation. The post–Cold War world presented Japan's leadership with three strategic options: becoming a "Britain of the East," emphasizing regionalism, and pursuing autarky. From the mid-1990s onward, Japan chose incremental movement toward the UK model. Since September 11, measured steps have given way to major leaps as Tokyo embraced the bilateral alliance as the only viable guarantor of its security.

And yet, an enlargement of indigenous capabilities has accompanied the latest consolidation of the U.S.-Japan alliance. In many cases, new Japanese systems are a byproduct of closer bilateral cooperation. However, some new capabilities also signify a hedge against an unpredictable future. By deploying its own missile defense system, Tokyo is less dependent upon the United States for extended deterrence vis-à-vis Pyongyang. Accumulating the subcomponents for a preemptive capability—in-flight refueling and precision-guided munitions—will achieve the same end.

That Tokyo is hedging against intra-alliance uncertainty should come as little surprise. No state guided by realpolitik would rely on a single ally for security without at least establishing the kernel of a new strategic option—in Japan's case, autarky-lite. This bet-hedging behavior poses no threat to the bilateral relationship. Indeed, so long as Washington remains a committed ally, Tokyo's bid for greater self-reliance will enhance the scope of U.S.-Japan security cooperation.

Notes

[1] Japan Defense Agency, "National Defense Program Guidelines, FY 2005–," 5.

[2] Araki Commission, Araki Report, 6, 24–27.

[3] Author's interview with Cabinet Office official, Tokyo, November 2004.

[4] Araki Report, 3.

[5] Japan Defense Agency, "National Defense Program Guidelines," 3.

[6] U.S. Department of State, "Joint Statement of the U.S.-Japan Security Consultative Committee," February 19, 2005, http://www.state.gov/r/pa/prs/ps/2005/42490.htm.

[7] Araki Report, 3, 10.

[8] Japan Defense Agency, "National Defense Program Guidelines," 10–11.

[9] Between 2003 and 2004, the proportion of Japanese expressing "no sense of closeness" with China jumped from 48 percent to 58 percent. Cabinet Office, "Gaikou ni kan suru seronchousa," 2004.

[10] Author's interviews with Cabinet Office official and JDA official, Tokyo, March 2005.

[11] Author's interview with GOJ official, Tokyo, April 2005.

[12] U.S. Department of State, "Joint Statement of the U.S.-Japan Security Consultative Committee."

[13] Author's interviews with JDA officials, Tokyo, March 2005; and author's interview with GOJ official, Tokyo, April 2005.

[14] Author's interview with JDA officials, Tokyo, March 2005.

[15] The decline of the Hashimoto faction has also dealt a blow to China sympathizers within the Japanese government.

[16] According to an *Asahi Shimbun* poll conducted after the Asian Cup, 61 percent of respondents reported that their image of China had worsened. James J. Pryzstup, "A Volatile Mix: Natural Gas, a Submarine, a Shrine, and a Visa," *Comparative Connections* 6, no. 4 (October–December 2004): 119–133.

[17] Interview with LDP Upper House member, Tokyo, April 2005.

[18] In the case of alliance responsibility, institutionalization in the form of the U.S.-Japan Security Treaty, the original Defense Guidelines, and the revised Defense Guidelines predated, or coincided with Japan's internalization of U.S. expectations.

[19] Japan Defense Agency, "National Defense Program Guidelines," 3, 9.

[20] Araki Report, 5, 26.

[21] Interview with Yoshinori Ohno, Tokyo, March 10, 2005.

[22] Compared to Japan's $13 billion financial contribution following the Gulf War, SDF dispatch to Iraq has occurred on the cheap: the SDF's activities in Samawah cost approximately $120 million per year. Samawah calculation based on yen figure in untranslated edition of Japan Defense Agency (JDA), *Defense of Japan 2004* (Tokyo: JDA, July 2004), 370.

[23] Author's interview with Shunji Yanai, Tokyo, April 19, 2005; and author's interviews with Japanese security specialists, JDA official, Cabinet Office official, and GOJ official, Tokyo, March/April 2005.

[24] Author's interview with Cabinet Office official, Tokyo, November 2004; and author's interviews with JDA official and GOJ official, Tokyo, March/April 2005.

[25] David Fouse, "Japan's FY 2005 National Defense Program Outline: New Concepts, Old Compromises," *Asia-Pacific Security Studies* 4, no. 3 (March 2005): 3.

[26] Araki Report, 22.

[27] Cabinet Office, "Statement by the Chief Cabinet Secretary," December 10, 2004, http://www.kantei.go.jp/foreign/tyokan/2004/1210statement_e.html.

[28] Author's interview with Cabinet Office official, Tokyo, March 2005.

[29] Author's interview with Yoshinori Ohno, Tokyo, March 2005.

[30] From the start, then chief cabinet secretary Fukuda favored a step-by-step approach to easing the ban on arms exports. Author's interview with Cabinet Office official, Tokyo, March 2005.

[31] Author's interview with Masao Akamatsu, Tokyo, June 29, 2005.

[32] Author's interview with Yoshinori Ohno, Tokyo, March 10, 2005; and author's interview with Cabinet Office official, Tokyo, March 2005.

[33] The Araki Commission's internal debate on long-range capabilities mirrored the language of the final report. Author's interview with Shunji Yanai, Tokyo, April 19, 2005; and author's interviews with Japanese security specialists, Tokyo, April 2005.

[34] Araki Report, 29.

[35] Author's interviews with Cabinet Office official, Tokyo, March and April 2005.

[36] Araki Report, 20, 26.

[37] Author's interview with Cabinet Office official, Tokyo, March 2005.

[38] Many lawmakers and members of the Japanese media subscribe to this mistaken view. Author's interview with JDA official, Tokyo, March 2005; and author's interview with Shigeru Ishiba, Tokyo, April 18, 2005.

[39] "Buki no shiyou to buryoku no koushi no kankei nitsuite" (Relationship between the use of weapons and the use of armed force) in Japan Defense Agency, *Hand Book for Defense 2005* (Tokyo: Asagumo News Editorial Office, 2005), 668; Excerpt of "GOJ official statement on the use of weapons prescribed by Article 95 of the SDF Law." English translation provided by JDA official, Tokyo, June 2005; and Katsumi Ishizuka, "The Evolution of Japan's Policy towards UN Peacekeeping Operations" (paper presented at the Fifteenth Annual Meeting of the Academic Council on the United Nations System, Cascais, Portugal, June 21–23, 2002), 25.

[40] Author's interview with Shigeru Ishiba, Tokyo, April 18, 2005; and author's interviews with JDA official, Cabinet Office official, and Japanese security specialists, Tokyo, April 2005.

[41] Author's interviews with Cabinet Office official and GOJ official, Tokyo, April 2005.

[42] Author's interview with LDP Upper House member, Tokyo, April 2005; and author's interview with Shigeru Ishiba, Tokyo, April 18, 2005.

[43] Author's interviews with LDP Upper House member and GOJ official, Tokyo, April 2005.

[44] Author's interview with Shigeru Ishiba, Tokyo, April 18, 2005; and author's interviews with LDP Upper House member and Cabinet Office official, Tokyo, April 2005.

[45] Author's interview with JDA official, Tokyo, April 2005.

[46] In an interview, Shigeru Ishiba remarked only upon the SDF's capabilities as a limiting factor. He was relatively sanguine about public opinion, provided that the GOJ could link counterinsurgency to Japan's national interest and global stability. Author's interview, Tokyo, April 18, 2005; and author's interviews with Cabinet Office official and Japanese security specialist, Tokyo, April 2005.

[47] "DPJ Nods to Japan's Military Role for International Contributions," *Asahi Shimbun*, July 22, 2005.

[48] Author's interview with DPJ staffer, Kyoto, July 24, 2005.

[49] Author's translation. Internal DPJ memorandum titled "Constitution and Security: Draft of Main Points," April 20, 2005.

[50] Author's interview with Cabinet Office official, Tokyo, April 2005; author's interview with Masao Akamatsu, Tokyo, June 29, 2005; and author's interview with Otohiko Endo, July 1, 2005.

[51] The Japanese term for this linkage is *itaika*, literally translated as "unification." Author's interview with JDA official, Tokyo, April 2005.

[52] The MSDF can only patrol sea-lanes under the following three conditions: (1) the Japan Coast Guard lacks the capability to conduct the mission; (2) the mission is limited to the high seas; and (3) the JDA has received the prime minister's authorization. Given that the Malacca Strait and many other critical maritime areas lie within national waters, the MSDF cannot undertake useful sea-lane patrols. In the case of the Proliferation Security Initiative, the current SDF Law does not enable the MSDF to interdict and inspect ships during peacetime. Author's interview with Shigeru Ishiba, Tokyo, April 18, 2005.

[53] In October 2004, the MSDF set a new precedent by participating in a PSI exercise as more than an observer.

[54] Author's interview with Masao Akamatsu, Tokyo, June 29, 2005.

[55] Author's interview with DPJ staffer, Kyoto, July 24, 2005.

[56] Author's interview with Japanese security specialist, Tokyo, April 2005.

[57] Author's interview with JDA official, Tokyo, April 2005.

[58] In January 2003, the Cabinet Legislation Bureau ruled that refueling an aircraft carrier (the USS *Kitty Hawk*) that subsequently launched attacks against Iraq would not violate the ban on collective defense. Richard J. Samuels, "Politics, Security Policy, and Japan's Cabinet Legislation Bureau: Who Elected These Guys, Anyway?" *Japan Policy Research Institute Working Paper*, no. 99 (March 2004), http://www.jpri.org/publications/workingpapers/wp99.html.

[59] Such criteria include the departure of an invasion fleet, the erection of missiles by a hostile state, and the positioning of ships to attack Japan's merchant fleet. Author's interview with JDA official, Tokyo, April 2005.

[60] Yukio Okamoto, "Japan and the United States: The Essential Alliance," *Washington Quarterly* 25, no. 2 (Spring 2002): 66.

[61] The SDF may not provide U.S. forces with targeting data until the commencement of an attack on Japan, where exchanging such information qualifies as self-defense. Author's interview with JDA official, Tokyo, April 2005.

[62] For example, unless attacked, the MSDF could not intervene in a high seas battle between the U.S. Navy and a DPRK ship. Author's interview with Shunji Yanai, Tokyo, April 19, 2005.

[63] Internal DPJ memorandum, April 20, 2005.

[64] Author's interview with DPJ staffer, Kyoto, July 24, 2005.

[65] Author's interviews with Cabinet Office official and GOJ official, Tokyo, April 2005.

[66] Author's interview with Masao Akamatsu, Tokyo, June 29, 2005.

[67] Text of Article 9 quoted in Rust Deming, "Japan's Constitution and Defense Policy: Entering a New Era," *INSS Strategic Forum* no. 213 (November 2004): 1.

[68] In the early 1950s, the Cabinet Legislation Bureau ruled that if no other recourse existed, Japan could possess defensive nuclear weapons and preempt an imminent act of aggression. Author's interview with senior SDF officer, Tokyo, March 2005; also see Samuels, "Politics, Security Policy, and Japan's Cabinet Legislation Bureau."

Select Bibliography

Armacost, Michael H. *Friends or Rivals? The Insider's Account of U.S.-Japan Relations.* New York: Columbia University Press, 1996.

Armitage, Richard L., and Joseph S. Nye et al. "The United States and Japan: Advancing toward a Mature Partnership." *INSS Special Report*, October 11, 2000.

Center for Strategic and International Studies (CSIS), *Generational Change in Japan: Its Implications for U.S.-Japan Relations.* Washington, D.C.: CSIS, August 2002.

Cha, Victor D. *Alignment despite Antagonism: The United States–Korea–Japan Security Triangle.* Stanford, Calif.: Stanford University Press, 1999.

Cossa, Ralph A., ed. *Restructuring the U.S.-Japan Alliance: Toward a More Equal Partnership.* Washington, D.C.: The CSIS Press, 1997.

Cronin, Richard P. "Japan-U.S. Cooperation on Ballistic Missile Defense: Issues and Prospects." CRS Report for Congress RL31337, Washington, D.C., March 19, 2002.

Deming, Rust. "Japan's Constitution and Defense Policy: Entering a New Era." *INSS Strategic Forum*, no. 213 (November 2004).

Friedberg, Aaron L. "Ripe for Rivalry: Prospects for Peace in a Multipolar Asia." *International Security* 18, no. 3 (Winter 1993/1994).

Gilpin, Robert. *The Political Economy of International Relations.* Princeton, N.J.: Princeton University Press, 1987.

Glosserman, Brad, et al., eds. *United States–Japan Strategic Dialogue: Beyond the Defense Guidelines.* Honolulu: Pacific Forum CSIS, 2001.

Green, Michael J. *Japan's Reluctant Realism: Foreign Policy Challenges in an Era of Uncertain Power.* New York: Palgrave, 2001.

———. "State of the Field Report: Research on Japanese Security Policy," *AccessAsia Review* 2, no. 1 (1998).

Heginbotham, Eric, and Richard J. Samuels. "Japan." In *Asian Aftershocks: Strategic Asia 2002–2003*, ed. Richard J. Ellings and Aaron L. Friedberg. Seattle: National Bureau of Asian Research, 2003.

Hosoya, Chihiro, and Tomohito Shinoda, eds. *Redefining the Partnership: The United States and Japan in East Asia*. Lanham, Md.: University Press of America, Inc., 1998.

Hughes, Christopher. *Japan's Reemergence as a "Normal" Military Power?* Oxford: Oxford University Press, 2004.

———. "Japan's Security Policy and the War on Terror: Steady Incrementalism or Radical Leap?" Working paper published by the Centre for the Study of Globalisation and Regionalisation, University of Warwick, United Kingdom, August 2002.

Ikenberry, G. John, and Takashi Inoguchi, eds. *Reinventing the Alliance: U.S.-Japan Security Partnership in an Era of Change*. New York: Palgrave Macmillan, 2003.

Ishizuka, Katsumi. "The Evolution of Japan's Policy towards UN Peacekeeping Operations." Paper presented at the Fifteenth Annual Meeting of the Academic Council on the United Nations System, Cascais, Portugal, June 21–23, 2002.

Katzenstein, Peter J. *Cultural Norms and National Security: Police and Military in Postwar Japan*. Ithaca: Cornell University Press, 1996.

Keohane, Robert O. *After Hegemony: Cooperation and Discord in the World Political Economy*. Princeton, N.J.: Princeton University Press, 1984.

Keohane, Robert O., and Joseph S. Nye. *Power and Interdependence*. 3rd edition. New York: Longman, 2001.

Manyin, Mark E. "Japan–North Korea Relations: Selected Issues." CRS Report for Congress RL32161. Washington, D.C., November 26, 2003.

Matthews, Eugene A. "Japan's New Nationalism." *Foreign Affairs* 82, no. 6 (November/December 2003).

Mearsheimer, John J. *The Tragedy of Great Power Politics*. New York: W.W. Norton and Company, 2001.

Oberdorfer, Don. *The Two Koreas: A Contemporary History*. New York: Basic Books, 1997.

Okimoto, Daniel I. "The Japan-America Security Alliance: Prospects for the Twenty-First Century." Occasional paper published by the Asia-Pacific Research Center, Stanford University, California, 1998.

Samuels, Richard J. "Politics, Security Policy, and Japan's Cabinet Legislation Bureau: Who Elected These Guys, Anyway?" *Japan Policy Research*

Institute Working Paper, no. 99 (March 2004), http://www.jpri.org/publi-cations/workingpapers/wp99.html.

———. *"Rich Nation, Strong Army": National Security and the Technological Transformation of Japan*. Ithaca, N.Y.: Cornell University Press, 1994.

Schoppa, Leonard. "Two-Level Games and Bargaining Outcomes: Why *Gaiatsu* Succeeds in Some Cases but Not Others." *International Organization* 47, no. 3 (Summer 1993).

Self, Benjamin L., and Jeffrey W. Thompson, eds. *Japan's Nuclear Option: Security, Politics, and Policy in the 21st Century*. Washington, D.C.: Henry L. Stimson Center, December 2003.

Snyder, Glenn. "The Security Dilemma in Alliance Politics," *World Politics* 36, no. 4 (1984).

Swaine, Michael, Rachel Swanger, and Takashi Kawakami. *Japan and Ballistic Missile Defense*. Santa Monica, Calif.: RAND Corporation, 2001.

Vogel, Steven K., ed. *U.S.-Japan Relations in a Changing World*. Washington, D.C.: The Brookings Institution, 2002.

Waltz, Kenneth N. "Anarchic Orders and Balances of Power." In *Neorealism and Its Critics*, ed. Robert O. Keohane. New York: Columbia University Press, 1986.

Wendt, Alexander. "Anarchy Is What States Make of It: The Social Construction of Power Politics," *International Organizations* 46, no. 2 (Spring 1992).

Index

Page numbers followed by the letters n and t refer to notes and tables, respectively.

About the Author

Daniel M. Kliman received his B.A. from Stanford University in California, was a Fulbright Fellow at Kyoto University in Japan, and is now pursuing a Ph.D. at Princeton University in New Jersey. He has been affiliated with the Institute for Defense Analyses in Washington, D.C., the Center for International Security and Cooperation at Stanford, and the Institute for International Policy Studies in Tokyo. In Washington, D.C., he has served in the Office of the Under Secretary of Defense for Policy and the Senate Committee on Foreign Relations. He has also worked in the Political Section at the U.S. Embassy in Tokyo.